MATTHEW LEVERING (PhD, Boston College) is associate professor of theology at Ave Maria University in Naples, Florida. He is coauthor of *Holy People, Holy Land* and *Knowing the Love of Christ*.

General Editor
R. R. Reno (PhD, Yale University) is associate professor of theology at Creighton University. He is the coauthor of *Heroism and the Christian Life* and has published essays in *First Things* and *Pro Ecclesia*.

EZRA &
NEHEMIAH

Brazos Theological Commentary on the Bible

Series Editors

R. R. Reno, General Editor
Creighton University
Omaha, Nebraska

Robert W. Jenson
Center of Theological Inquiry
Princeton, New Jersey

Robert Louis Wilken
University of Virginia
Charlottesville, Virginia

Ephraim Radner
Wycliffe College
Toronto, Ontario

Michael Root
Lutheran Theological Southern Seminary
Columbia, South Carolina

George Sumner
Wycliffe College
Toronto, Ontario

EZRA & NEHEMIAH

MATTHEW LEVERING

BrazosPress
Grand Rapids, Michigan

Published by Brazos Press
a division of Baker Publishing Group
P.O. Box 6287, Grand Rapids, MI 49516-6287
www.brazospress.com

Printed in the United States of America

Library of Congress Cataloging-in-Publication Data

Levering, Matthew, 1971–
    Ezra & Nehemiah / Matthew Levering.
        p.   cm. — (Brazos theological commentary on the Bible)
    Includes bibliographical references and indexes.
    ISBN 10: 1-58743-161-0 (cloth)
    ISBN 978-1-58743-161-6 (cloth)
    1. Bible. O.T. Ezra—Commentaries. 2. Bible. O.T. Nehemiah—Commentaries.
I. Title. II. Title: Ezra and Nehemiah. III. Series.
BS1355.53.L48 2007
222'.707—dc22   2007028245

Dedicated to
Ralph and Patty Levering

CONTENTS

SERIES PREFACE

Near the beginning of his treatise against Gnostic interpretations of the Bible, *Against the Heresies*, Irenaeus observes that Scripture is like a great mosaic depicting a handsome king. It is as if we were owners of a villa in Gaul who had ordered a mosaic from Rome. It arrives, and the beautifully colored tiles need to be taken out of their packaging and put into proper order according to the plan of the artist. The difficulty, of course, is that Scripture provides us with the individual pieces, but the order and sequence of various elements are not obvious. The Bible does not come with instructions that would allow interpreters to simply place verses, episodes, images, and parables in order as a worker might follow a schematic drawing in assembling the pieces to depict the handsome king. The mosaic must be puzzled out. This is precisely the work of scriptural interpretation.

Origen has his own image to express the difficulty of working out the proper approach to reading the Bible. When preparing to offer a commentary on the Psalms he tells of a tradition handed down to him by his Hebrew teacher:

> The Hebrew said that the whole divinely inspired Scripture may be likened, because of its obscurity, to many locked rooms in our house. By each room is placed a key, but not the one that corresponds to it, so that the keys are scattered about beside the rooms, none of them matching the room by which it is placed. It is a difficult task to find the keys and match them to the rooms that they can open. We therefore know the Scriptures that are obscure only by taking the points of departure for understanding them from another place because they have their interpretive principle scattered among them.[1]

As is the case for Irenaeus, scriptural interpretation is not purely local. The key in Genesis may best fit the door of Isaiah, which in turn opens up the

---

1. Fragment from the preface to *Commentary on Psalms 1–25*, preserved in the *Philokalia* (trans. Joseph W. Trigg; London: Routledge, 1998), 70–71.

meaning of Matthew. The mosaic must be put together with an eye toward the overall plan.

Irenaeus, Origen, and the great cloud of premodern biblical interpreters assumed that puzzling out the mosaic of Scripture must be a communal project. The Bible is vast, heterogeneous, full of confusing passages and obscure words, and difficult to understand. Only a fool would imagine that he or she could work out solutions alone. The way forward must rely upon a tradition of reading that Irenaeus reports has been passed on as the rule or canon of truth that functions as a confession of faith. "Anyone," he says, "who keeps unchangeable in himself the rule of truth received through baptism will recognize the names and sayings and parables of the scriptures."[2] Modern scholars debate the content of the rule on which Irenaeus relies and commends, not the least because the terms and formulations Irenaeus himself uses shift and slide. Nonetheless, Irenaeus assumes that there is a body of apostolic doctrine sustained by a tradition of teaching in the church. This doctrine provides the clarifying principles that guide exegetical judgment toward a coherent overall reading of Scripture as a unified witness. Doctrine, then, is the schematic drawing that will allow the reader to organize the vast heterogeneity of the words, images, and stories of the Bible into a readable, coherent whole. It is the rule that guides us toward the proper matching of keys to doors.

If self-consciousness about the role of history in shaping human consciousness makes modern historical-critical study critical, then what makes modern study of the Bible modern is the consensus that classical Christian doctrine distorts interpretive understanding. Benjamin Jowett, the influential nineteenth-century English classical scholar, is representative. In his programmatic essay "On the Interpretation of Scripture," he exhorts the biblical reader to disengage from doctrine and break its hold over the interpretive imagination. "The simple words of that book," writes Jowett of the modern reader, "he tries to preserve absolutely pure from the refinements or distinctions of later times." The modern interpreter wishes to "clear away the remains of dogmas, systems, controversies, which are encrusted upon" the words of Scripture. The disciplines of close philological analysis "would enable us to separate the elements of doctrine and tradition with which the meaning of Scripture is encumbered in our own day."[3] The lens of understanding must be wiped clear of the hazy and distorting film of doctrine.

Postmodernity, in turn, has encouraged us to criticize the critics. Jowett imagined that when he wiped away doctrine he would encounter the biblical text in its purity and uncover what he called "the original spirit and intention of the authors."[4] We are not now so sanguine, and the postmodern mind thinks interpretive frameworks inevitable. Nonetheless, we tend to remain modern

2. *Against the Heretics* 9.4.
3. Benjamin Jowett, "On the Interpretation of Scripture," in *Essays and Reviews* (London: Parker, 1860), 338–39.
4. Ibid., 340.

in at least one sense. We read Athanasius and think him stage-managing the diversity of Scripture to support his positions against the Arians. We read Bernard of Clairvaux and assume that his monastic ideals structure his reading of the Song of Songs. In the wake of the Reformation, we can see how the doctrinal divisions of the time shaped biblical interpretation. Luther famously described the Epistle of James as a "strawy letter," for, as he said, "it has nothing of the nature of the Gospel about it."[5] In these and many other instances, often written in the heat of ecclesiastical controversy or out of the passion of ascetic commitment, we tend to think Jowett correct: doctrine is a distorting film on the lens of understanding.

However, is what we commonly think actually the case? Are readers naturally perceptive? Do we have an unblemished, reliable aptitude for the divine? Have we no need for disciplines of vision? Do our attention and judgment need to be trained, especially as we seek to read Scripture as the living word of God? According to Augustine, we all struggle to journey toward God, who is our rest and peace. Yet our vision is darkened and the fetters of worldly habit corrupt our judgment. We need training and instruction in order to cleanse our minds so that we might find our way toward God.[6] To this end, "the whole temporal dispensation was made by divine Providence for our salvation."[7] The covenant with Israel, the coming of Christ, the gathering of the nations into the church—all these things are gathered up into the rule of faith, and they guide the vision and form of the soul toward the end of fellowship with God. In Augustine's view, the reading of Scripture both contributes to and benefits from this divine pedagogy. With countless variations in both exegetical conclusions and theological frameworks, the same pedagogy of a doctrinally ruled reading of Scripture characterizes the broad sweep of the Christian tradition from Gregory the Great through Bernard and Bonaventure, continuing across Reformation differences in both John Calvin and Cornelius Lapide, Patrick Henry and Bishop Bossuet, and on to more recent figures such as Karl Barth and Hans Urs von Balthasar.

Is doctrine, then, not a moldering scrim of antique prejudice obscuring the Bible, but instead a clarifying agent, an enduring tradition of theological judgments that amplifies the living voice of Scripture? And what of the scholarly dispassion advocated by Jowett? Is a noncommitted reading, an interpretation unprejudiced, the way toward objectivity, or does it simply invite the languid intellectual apathy that stands aside to make room for the false truism and easy answers of the age?

This series of biblical commentaries was born out of the conviction that dogma clarifies rather than obscures. The Brazos Theological Commentary on

5. *Luther's Works*, vol. 35 (ed. E. Theodore Bachmann; Philadelphia: Fortress, 1959), 362.
6. *On Christian Doctrine* 1.10.
7. *On Christian Doctrine* 1.35.

the Bible advances upon the assumption that the Nicene tradition, in all its diversity and controversy, provides the proper basis for the interpretation of the Bible as Christian Scripture. God the Father Almighty, who sends his only begotten Son to die for us and for our salvation and who raises the crucified Son in the power of the Holy Spirit so that the baptized may be joined in one body—faith in *this* God with *this* vocation of love for the world is the lens through which to view the heterogeneity and particularity of the biblical texts. Doctrine, then, is not a moldering scrim of antique prejudice obscuring the meaning of the Bible. It is a crucial aspect of the divine pedagogy, a clarifying agent for our minds fogged by self-deceptions, a challenge to our languid intellectual apathy that will too often rest in false truisms and the easy spiritual nostrums of the present age rather than search more deeply and widely for the dispersed keys to the many doors of Scripture.

For this reason, the commentators in this series have not been chosen because of their historical or philological expertise. In the main, they are not biblical scholars in the conventional, modern sense of the term. Instead, the commentators were chosen because of their knowledge of and expertise in using the Christian doctrinal tradition. They are qualified by virtue of the doctrinal formation of their mental habits, for it is the conceit of this series of biblical commentaries that theological training in the Nicene tradition prepares one for biblical interpretation, and thus it is to theologians and not biblical scholars that we have turned. "War is too important," it has been said, "to leave to the generals."

We do hope, however, that readers do not draw the wrong impression. The Nicene tradition does not provide a set formula for the solution of exegetical problems. The great tradition of Christian doctrine was not transcribed, bound in folio, and issued in an official, critical edition. We have the Niceno-Constantinopolitan Creed, used for centuries in many traditions of Christian worship. We have ancient baptismal affirmations of faith. The Chalcedonian definition and the creeds and canons of other church councils have their places in official church documents. Yet the rule of faith cannot be limited to a specific set of words, sentences, and creeds. It is instead a pervasive habit of thought, the animating culture of the church in its intellectual aspect. As Augustine observed, commenting on Jeremiah 31:33, "The creed is learned by listening; it is written, not on stone tablets nor on any material, but on the heart."[8] This is why Irenaeus is able to appeal to the rule of faith more than a century before the first ecumenical council, and this is why we need not itemize the contents of the Nicene tradition in order to appeal to its potency and role in the work of interpretation.

Because doctrine is intrinsically fluid on the margins and most powerful as a habit of mind rather than a list of propositions, this commentary series

---

8. *Sermon* 212.2.

cannot settle difficult questions of method and content at the outset. The editors of the series impose no particular method of doctrinal interpretation. We cannot say in advance how doctrine helps the Christian reader assemble the mosaic of Scripture. We have no clear answer to the question of whether exegesis guided by doctrine is antithetical to or compatible with the now-old modern methods of historical-critical inquiry. Truth—historical, mathematical, or doctrinal—knows no contradiction. But method is a discipline of vision and judgment, and we cannot know in advance what aspects of historical-critical inquiry are functions of modernism that shape the soul to be at odds with Christian discipline. Still further, the editors do not hold the commentators to any particular hermeneutical theory that specifies how to define the plain sense of Scripture—or the role this plain sense should play in interpretation. Here the commentary series is tentative and exploratory.

Can we proceed in any other way? European and North American intellectual culture has been de-Christianized. The effect has not been a cessation of Christian activity. Theological work continues. Sermons are preached. Biblical scholars turn out monographs. Church leaders have meetings. But each dimension of a formerly unified Christian practice now tends to function independently. It is as if a weakened army had been fragmented, and various corps had retreated to isolated fortresses in order to survive. Theology has lost its competence in exegesis. Scripture scholars function with minimal theological training. Each decade finds new theories of preaching to cover the nakedness of seminary training that provides theology without exegesis and exegesis without theology.

Not the least of the causes of the fragmentation of Christian intellectual practice has been the divisions of the church. Since the Reformation, the role of the rule of faith in interpretation has been obscured by polemics and counterpolemics about *sola scriptura* and the necessity of a magisterial teaching authority. The Brazos Theological Commentary on the Bible series is deliberately ecumenical in scope, because the editors are convinced that early church fathers were correct: church doctrine does not compete with Scripture in a limited economy of epistemic authority. We wish to encourage unashamedly dogmatic interpretation of Scripture, confident that the concrete consequences of such a reading will cast far more light on the great divisive questions of the Reformation than either reengaging in old theological polemics or chasing the fantasy of a pure exegesis that will somehow adjudicate between competing theological positions. You shall know the truth of doctrine by its interpretive fruits, and therefore in hopes of contributing to the unity of the church, we have deliberately chosen a wide range of theologians whose commitment to doctrine will allow readers to see real interpretive consequences rather than the shadowboxing of theological concepts.

Brazos Theological Commentary on the Bible has no dog in the current translation fights, and we endorse a textual ecumenism that parallels our diversity of ecclesial backgrounds. We do not impose the thankfully modest inclusive-language agenda of the New Revised Standard Version, nor do we insist upon the glories of the Authorized Version, nor do we require our commentators to create a new translation. In our communal worship, in our private devotions, in our theological scholarship, we use a range of scriptural translations. Precisely as Scripture—a living, functioning text in the present life of faith—the Bible is not semantically fixed. Only a modernist, literalist hermeneutic could imagine that this modest fluidity is a liability. Philological precision and stability is a consequence of, not a basis for, exegesis. Judgments about the meaning of a text fix its literal sense, not the other way around. As a result, readers should expect an eclectic use of biblical translations, both across the different volumes of the series and within individual commentaries.

We cannot speak for contemporary biblical scholars, but as theologians we know that we have long been trained to defend our fortresses of theological concepts and formulations. And we have forgotten the skills of interpretation. Like stroke victims, we must rehabilitate our exegetical imaginations, and there are likely to be different strategies of recovery. Readers should expect this reconstructive—not reactionary—series to provide them with experiments in postcritical doctrinal interpretation, not commentaries written according to the settled principles of a well-functioning tradition. Some commentators will follow classical typological and allegorical readings from the premodern tradition; others will draw on contemporary historical study. Some will comment verse by verse; others will highlight passages, even single words that trigger theological analysis of Scripture. No reading strategies are proscribed, no interpretive methods foresworn. The central premise in this commentary series is that doctrine provides structure and cogency to scriptural interpretation. We trust in this premise with the hope that the Nicene tradition can guide us, however imperfectly, diversely, and haltingly, toward a reading of Scripture in which the right keys open the right doors.

R. R. Reno

PREFACE

The Holy Spirit inspired the biblical authors and all the men and women who strove after the Babylonian exile to be faithful to the covenantal plan of salvation that God has "prepared in the presence of all peoples, a light for revelation to the Gentiles, and for glory to thy people Israel" (Luke 2:31–32). The aim of this commentary is to understand this "glory" more deeply. If this aim has been even partially achieved, Rusty Reno deserves much of the credit. Not only did Rusty graciously allow me to write this commentary for his series, but also he offered superb criticisms on two drafts of the manuscript that greatly improved the final version. In addition to Rusty, I should thank David Solomon and his Center for Ethics and Culture at the University of Notre Dame. David's invitation to serve as the Myser Fellow at the Center for Ethics and Culture during the 2006–2007 academic year enabled me to write the commentary. Let me also acknowledge Rodney Clapp for his vision for Brazos Press and the privilege of working with him.

This commentary, which chronicles the labors of Ezra and Nehemiah to renew and reform Israel, is in its way a tribute to the renewal that Rusty, David, and Rodney are accomplishing for the church in the difficult context of the contemporary academy. This work of renewal is also being carried on by my friends and colleagues at Ave Maria University. Of the many who should be mentioned I make special note of Michael Dauphinais and Fr. Matthew Lamb, whose encouragement and support stand at the heart of my work.

The books of Ezra and Nehemiah are marked by a number of lengthy journeys. In this context I rejoice to be married to such a wonderful wife as Joy, who made possible our journey from Naples, Florida, to South Bend, and who enabled our family to settle into a new home for the year. To Joy "I give thanks to God always for you because of the grace of God which was given you in Christ Jesus" (1 Cor. 1:4). May God bless our lives together unto eternal life.

My children, David, Andrew, Irene, John, and Daniel, each in their unique way, manifest the great generosity and love of God.

My parents, Ralph and Patty Levering, not only gave me life and raised me, but also inspired my love for the Old Testament. To them I dedicate this commentary.

ABBREVIATIONS

Acts	Acts	Judg.	Judges
Amos	Amos	1 Kgs.	1 Kings
1 Chr.	1 Chronicles	2 Kgs.	2 Kings
2 Chr.	2 Chronicles	Lam.	Lamentations
Col.	Colossians	Lev.	Leviticus
1 Cor.	1 Corinthians	Luke	Luke
2 Cor.	2 Corinthians	Mal.	Malachi
Dan.	Daniel	Mark	Mark
Deut.	Deuteronomy	Matt.	Matthew
Eccl.	Ecclesiastes	Mic.	Micah
Eph.	Ephesians	Nah.	Nahum
Esth.	Esther	Neh.	Nehemiah
Exod.	Exodus	Num.	Numbers
Ezek.	Ezekiel	Obad.	Obadiah
Ezra	Ezra	1 Pet.	1 Peter
Gal.	Galatians	2 Pet.	2 Peter
Gen.	Genesis	Phil.	Philippians
Hab.	Habakkuk	Phlm.	Philemon
Hag.	Haggai	Prov.	Proverbs
Heb.	Hebrews	Ps.	Psalms
Hos.	Hosea	Rev.	Revelation
Isa.	Isaiah	Rom.	Romans
Jas.	James	Ruth	Ruth
Jer.	Jeremiah	1 Sam.	1 Samuel
Job	Job	2 Sam.	2 Samuel
Joel	Joel	Song	Song of Songs
John	John	1 Thess.	1 Thessalonians
1 John	1 John	2 Thess.	2 Thessalonians
2 John	2 John	1 Tim.	1 Timothy
3 John	3 John	2 Tim.	2 Timothy
Jonah	Jonah	Titus	Titus
Josh.	Joshua	Zech.	Zechariah
Jude	Jude	Zeph.	Zephaniah

INTRODUCTION

The Approach of the Present Commentary

Can and should the Bible be read as a unified story of the triune God's creative and redemptive work? Answering in the negative, Catholic biblical scholar John Collins states: "The internal pluralism of the Bible, both theological and ethical, has been established beyond dispute" (2005, 160–61). Any unity of the Bible, for Collins, must be imposed from outside. Although to show that the Bible's "internal pluralism" in fact manifests a deeper unity is beyond the ability of any one commentary, the goal of this theological commentary on the books of Ezra and Nehemiah is to illumine how these two books fit into the unity of the Bible. Through the commentary genre, I seek to explore how the books of Ezra and Nehemiah belong to the unified biblical revelation of God's covenantal gift of holiness.

Three aspects in particular, therefore, distinguish the approach taken by the present commentary. First, the commentary employs the template of "holy people and holy land" that Michael Dauphinais and I put forward as a way of understanding the unity within diversity of the biblical story from Genesis to Revelation (Dauphinais and Levering 2005). This template (for lack of a better word) is simply another way of agreeing with St. Augustine that the entire Bible is about *caritas*, self-giving love. The holiness of the people means their being constituted as a people of justice in relation to God and fellow human beings. How does God make his people holy? Through covenants, he begins to set this holiness in place by means of a law and then a king whose task it is to establish justice and to instill the law in his people. Jesus Christ fulfills this law for the entire people as the true king. The holiness of the land means God's indwelling, at first through the tabernacle and the ark of the covenant in the wilderness, then more closely in the temple and its sacrificial worship. The fulfillment of God's indwelling is likewise accomplished by Jesus as the incarnate Son of God.[1]

Jesus could not have fulfilled this divine plan had there been no Ezra and Nehemiah, for without them—and the other central figures described in the books of Ezra and Nehemiah—there would have been no return to the land after the Babylonian exile, no rebuilding of the temple, and no restoration of the law. The time of Ezra and Nehemiah was one of intense striving toward the promised covenantal fulfillment of holy people and holy land. When this fulfillment comes in Jesus, it is not a negation or displacement of the striving recorded in these two books. Jesus could not have symbolically acted out the fulfillment of Israel had there no longer been the Torah to read or the temple in which to celebrate the festivals. To use an analogy, the consummation of a marriage does not do away with, but rather completes from within, the promises of the courtship.

My commentary emphasizes that Ezra and Nehemiah are faithful continuers of the covenantal tradition of Abraham, striving toward the full consummation of holy people and holy land, but without attaining such consummation.[2] This reading of Ezra and Nehemiah constitutes an effort to appreciate the theological heart of the struggle to rebuild the temple and to hand on the Torah after the exile, and it also accords with a widespread scholarly view that Ezra the Scribe played an important role in receiving, editing, and handing on the Torah.

1. For a theological account of Israel's law and temple, see Levering 2002.
2. Cf. Bryan 2002 regarding the concept of the "restoration" of Israel, a concept whose importance has been recognized especially by N. T. Wright. Drawing on McGonville 1986, Bryan notes that "the failure of the promises of restoration to materialize after the return of the exiles from Babylon produced a monumental theological difficulty, which could not be and was not explained as simply a continuation of the exile. The complex history which followed the return from Babylon was matched by a similarly complex theological response. One response is seen in texts, frequently cited by Wright, which stem from the period immediately following the return of the captives from Babylon and lament the fact that, despite the return from exile, the people remain slaves in their own land (Ezra 9.8–9; Neh. 9.36). But recent scholarship on Ezra-Nehemiah has brought into focus the importance of seeing the way a partially realized eschatology is at work in the books. J. G. McConville, building on the work of K. Koch, has highlighted a number of echoes in Ezra and Nehemiah of prophetic restoration texts; such echoes reveal that *the return was viewed as part of the restoration* and regarded as the awaited new Exodus from Babylon. However, the restoration is viewed not as a once-and-for-all act of God but as an ongoing process in which the repentance and covenant faithfulness of the people play a part. In other words, the problem of Ezra-Nehemiah is not so much one of continuing exile but of incomplete restoration; for the author(s) of Ezra-Nehemiah, to equate the two, as Wright does, would have been to deny a key moment in the outworking of God's eschatological purposes" (2002, 16 [emphasis original]). Without denying that the books of Ezra and Nehemiah envision a "partially realized eschatology," I think that by Jesus's time (and even in Ezra's and Nehemiah's times) the inadequacy of the "partial realization" was sufficiently apparent as to justify Wright in his claim regarding "continuing exile."

Second, the commentary suggests that the books of Ezra and Nehemiah are best appropriated and understood in light of other biblical texts. Since the task of discovering and entering into the meaning of biblical revelation is the reason for reading the books of Ezra and Nehemiah, their status as canonical scripture is the most important thing about them. To understand how they belong to scripture requires reflecting upon their words in light of the entire scriptures. "Commentary" in this sense is a contemplative exercise, seeking to understand how the books of Ezra and Nehemiah embody and develop God's teaching (*sacra doctrina*)—whose center is the living God revealed most fully in Christ Jesus—as that teaching draws us into its wise understanding of reality at whose heart is *caritas*. At times, as is also the case with the patristic and medieval exegesis that I enjoy,[3] this gives the commentary the flavor of a pastiche of biblical quotations: in such cases the commentary attempts both to inform and to form.

The present commentary makes no claim to be a historical or literary study of the books of Ezra and Nehemiah, although I do intend to give a sense of the narrative flow of the books. Where it seems needed, I have included some historical-critical footnotes. On the basis of archeological findings, including Egyptian and Persian texts from the same time period, historical-critical scholarship generally affirms that most of the events, persons, and problems depicted in the books of Ezra and Nehemiah are historical, although the presentation of these events, persons, and problems is colored by the perspectives and limited knowledge of the authors and/or editors of the material.[4]

In accord with the freedom that the Brazos Theological Commentary on the Bible offers for experimental and exploratory approaches, I have not attempted to include much of the information that I have found in the standard commentaries. This decision implies no negative judgment on these commentaries, but instead simply indicates the impossibility of an exhaustive commentary

3. See, for example, Weinandy's remarks about Thomas Aquinas's *Commentary on the Letter to the Hebrews*: "Here at the very outset of his *Commentary*, we find the first of numerous examples of Aquinas creatively drawing upon passages from the whole Bible to illustrate more fully, to develop more broadly, or to sanction more convincingly truths contained within Hebrews itself. For Aquinas, the various biblical books, with their distinctive revelational content, help to clarify and to complement one another and so this interplay advances one's understanding of the individual books themselves. Thus, the variety and the scope of the scripture passages Aquinas weaves within his *Commentary* on Hebrews is staggering in number and impressive in content. This is important for, while he obviously recognizes that each book of the Bible possesses its own genre and its own unique revelational and theological focus, it clearly demonstrates that Aquinas perceives the whole biblical narrative, Old and New Testaments together, as proclaiming the one complete gospel, and thus it is only in the interrelationship, and so the interweaving, of the whole biblical content that one is able to come to a full understanding of that gospel" (2005, 223–24).

4. For a historical-critical commentary, see Blenkinsopp 1988; for a literary commentary, see Throntveit 1992.

that achieves every desirable end.[5] If as Hans Urs von Balthasar observes "truth is symphonic," then so too are commentaries.[6]

Third, my commentary is distinguished by how it approaches the meaning of history itself. As commonly understood, history is the study of the linear progression of time. History therefore seeks by means of archeological, philological, and other tools to understand how the biblical writings correspond to the linear historical timeline reconstructed from biblical and nonbiblical sources. From this historical perspective, the two central questions regarding the books of Ezra and Nehemiah have generally been who wrote them and to what degree the books' contents correspond to the events that occurred during the time period that the books purport to describe. Theological commentary on scripture, however, recognizes a second and deeper dimension of human history, one that completes and enriches the first (linear) dimension of history—namely, from eternity the Creator God, the Trinity, brings forth time with its fulfillment already in view, and so in God's knowledge earlier persons and events relate to later ones in ways that escape the historian's tools. Likewise, later persons and events have connections to earlier ones that would appear anachronistic from a strictly linear or horizontal historical perspective that is unaware of the inner relationality of history. These connections and relationships are the ways in which human beings (whether figures from the biblical narrative or unknown biblical authors and editors who lived well after the time that they wrote about) participate, consciously or not, in God's creative and redemptive purposes. Put another way, history's patterns are not merely, or strictly, chronological; patterns of participation in the history of creation and salvation draw past, present, and future into a complex unity, grounded in the unity of all things coming forth and returning to the triune Creator and Redeemer (see Levering forthcoming).

---

5. In his editorial preface to this series, R. R. Reno states: "Because doctrine is intrinsically fluid on the margins and most powerful as a habit of mind rather than a list of propositions, this commentary series cannot settle difficult questions of method and content at the outset. The editors of the series impose no particular method of doctrinal interpretation. We cannot say in advance how doctrine helps the Christian reader assemble the mosaic of Scripture." The very boldness of the project to reclaim the practice of exegetical commentaries by theologians, rather than by scholars who possess an expertise in the biblical book under discussion, requires modest claims regarding each individual effort. For initial concerns about the project, see the symposium on Jaroslav Pelikan's *Acts* (2005)—the first volume in the Brazos Theological Commentary on the Bible—in *Pro Ecclesia* 16 (2007): Behr 2007; Daley 2007; and Rowe and Hays 2007.

6. Discussing biblical exegesis, von Balthasar remarks: "We cannot wrench Christ loose from the Church, nor can we dismantle the Church to get to Christ. If we really want to hear something intelligible, we are obliged to listen to the entire polyphony of revelation" (1987, 11). I have tried to attend to this insight in this commentary. Von Balthasar adds that "it is utter folly to try to 'grasp' Christ: he always slipped through the hands of those who wanted to seize him" (1987, 11). The same could even be said of the books of Ezra and Nehemiah.

For example, the letter to the Hebrews affirms that Moses possesses the same faith that first-century believers on Jesus possess. Such a claim would appear anachronistic to the historian, but not to the theologian. The doctrines of creation and redemption instruct the theologian in a deeper dimension of history, namely, the participation in the living God that, by creation and by grace, human beings from very different times and places enjoy in common. What appears to be an anachronism is in fact a fundamental truth about the nonchronological interrelationships that belong to persons who live in widely variant times and places, due to the active presence of the triune God's work in human history.

Through these three elements—(1) God's gift of covenantal holiness, (2) contemplation of biblical texts through other biblical texts, and (3) the non-chronological relationships through which past, present, and future human beings share in different ways in the same realities—the story of Ezra and Nehemiah becomes our story even while remaining their story.

A Dearth of Commentaries

Neither the fathers of the church nor most theologians since have paid much attention to the books of Ezra and Nehemiah. Although theologians rightly have studied the Torah and temple of Israel, this interest has generally not extended to study of the history of the restoration of the Torah and temple as narrated canonically in the books of Ezra and Nehemiah. In the Jewish rabbinic tradition Ezra becomes an exalted figure for his restoration of the Torah. But the great Jewish commentators focused their labors on the Torah, not on such books as Ezra and Nehemiah.

The Venerable Bede in the eighth century was the first Christian theologian to write a commentary on the books of Ezra and Nehemiah, part of a trilogy that also included commentaries on the tabernacle and on the temple. His theological interest in the tabernacle and the temple led him to investigate, largely by means of the spiritual sense, the books of Ezra and Nehemiah. Bede's commentary draws on some brief historical comments made by the Jewish historian Josephus and by Jerome in his translation of this section of the Bible. Bede's work, however, did not inspire further attempts; his commentary is "the first and only complete exegesis of Ezra-Nehemiah produced in the Middle Ages" (Scott DeGregorio, in Bede 2006, xv), which means that for hundreds of years after Bede finished his work, nothing further was done. The medieval *Glossa ordinaria* on scripture relies entirely upon Bede for its remarks on the books of Ezra and Nehemiah (Bede 2006, xiii n2).

Comparatively speaking, recent historical-critical scholars and theologians have devoted a bit more energy to Ezra and Nehemiah. A glimpse at the scholarship suggests that it is highly divided, with some scholars evaluating the historical and/or theological value of the books of Ezra and Nehemiah quite positively and others quite negatively. A few examples of such scholarship will set in contemporary context the approach taken by this commentary and will help to answer the question of why and how the contemporary church might find theologically helpful another commentary on Ezra and Nehemiah.

Recent Historical and Theological Evaluations

Among those who appraise the books negatively, Lester Grabbe, in his recent historical-critical commentary on the books of Ezra and Nehemiah, observes that "it is very possible that there was a historical Ezra" (1998, 153). Grabbe finds, however, that while "most of the individual episodes within the Ezra story could conceivably have a historical basis . . . they could equally have been invented" (1998, 153). He concludes that historical-critical research cannot affirm anything about Ezra: "To decide that one [episode] is historical and another not appears to be arbitrary in light of present knowledge. For example, it is tempting to say that whatever the problems with the Ezra tradition, at least the story that he had something to do with the law is credible. However, this is to favour the later development of the tradition over the earlier" (1998, 153). He accepts that the book of Nehemiah seems more likely to be based upon material that goes back to Nehemiah himself, although for this conclusion "probably the main argument is the very subjective and personal one that the NM [Nehemiah Memoir] strikes the reader as a real outpouring of an individual at a particular time" (1998, 155).

Yet Grabbe finds Nehemiah to be a rather unsavory character. Nehemiah "evidently had the knack of antagonizing those around him" and "those who found him a pain were not just a few local dignitaries; rather, they included priests, prophets, nobles, and even people who evidently did their best to get along with Nehemiah while still disagreeing with some of his measures" (1998, 161, 163). Nehemiah appears to exaggerate greatly the perfidy of his enemies, while completely failing to notice his own "relentless and unyielding nature" for which "compromise and conciliation were anathema" (1998, 180). Grabbe observes: "No wonder that when he left the province to return to Babylon for a period of time, people were quick to abandon the more extreme of his reforms" (1998, 167). Furthermore, Nehemiah is no friend of the poor, despite "simplistic and misleading" attempts to portray him as such (1998, 173). Ultimately Nehemiah's legacy depends, Grabbe suggests, upon whether one approves of the "bigoted" views that lead him to be "the champion of those who argue for an exclusivistic religion," what Grabbe calls "conservative Judaism—the Judaism of the *stetl* and the ghetto" (1998, 180, 182).

Grabbe's conclusions, with which I have no sympathy, are based upon his historical-critical reading of the texts, but criticism of the project of Ezra and

Nehemiah can just as easily flow from theological readings. Hans Urs von Balthasar, for instance, finds the significance of Ezra and Nehemiah to consist in their unconscious witness to the end of sacred history: "The fact that 'sacred history' ceases in the post-exilic period is one of the most terrible things in the biblical revelation. At first, the attempt is made to interpret the poor fare of the events after the return from exile as a continuation of sacred history: we find this in Nehemiah and Ezra. This is like a brook in the process of drying up" (1991, 370).[7] For von Balthasar, their emptiness exposes the need for God to draw together the covenantal realities by means of a "form" that cannot be deduced from within the old covenant (as Ezra and Nehemiah mistakenly, von Balthasar thinks, tried to do).[8] At a deeper level, von Balthasar considers that their emptiness witnesses to the abandonment of Israel, already lived out by the prophet Jeremiah, that prefigures Christ's kenotic abandonment by the Father on the cross. But because their emptiness is entirely unintentional—Ezra and Nehemiah thought that they were accomplishing something worthwhile however small—the books of Ezra and Nehemiah make for awkward reading.

Still more negatively, in his essay entitled "On Not Being in Charge" John Howard Yoder argues that Ezra and Nehemiah constitute a terrible departure from the "common Jewish legacy" of Jews and Christians "from Jeremiah into the Middle Ages," a legacy that Yoder terms "the 'not in charge' stance of Jewry" (2003, 170). This "not in charge" position—by which phrase Yoder seeks to capture what christological pacifism means—was opposed by two groups of Jews: those who set themselves in armed opposition to the empires of the time and those who sought support from the empires. The former includes the

---

7. Ezra and Nehemiah fare somewhat better in this brief survey than do other late writings. Von Balthasar goes on to say: "The Books of Chronicles merely adapt past sacred history to the ideology of Judaism and of the Levitical service in the temple. The Books of Maccabees do not succeed in portraying anything other than the secular history of a religious war carried out with pious enthusiasm and heroic idealism. Despite this, all of these books can certainly be inspired, and belong to the canon of the 'sacred books,' just like the 'midrashim' of Esther, Judith and Tobit; but, at least from the perspective of salvation history, they lie a whole level lower down. Sacred history in the ancient sense begins again only with John the Baptist. This is the difficulty that for Judaism cannot be resolved: how could the period which was empty of significance for salvation history be filled and shaped, if it was no longer given a structure by the salvific acts of God in history or dented by his eternity?" (1991, 370). Von Balthasar sees Ezra and Nehemiah as initiating "the beginning of Judaism" (1991, 376; cf. 387).

8. "The outward defeat of God's enemies, which for a very long time ancient Israel also counted on, was seen to accomplish nothing where the most interior spiritual oppositions are concerned. No glory of the gods has as its opposite what is called 'sin' in the biblical sense; and only the glory of the living God, which lacks all analogies, can, by its 'wildly strange and astounding works' (Is 28.21), put an end to that darkness which at first appeared to set a limit to the extent of the lordship of God's glory. And it is above all in the time of classical prophecy and in the melting pot of the Exile, that Israel will, through its experience of suffering, become aware of this interior and hidden drama, so deeply aware of it, in fact, that it already reaches the threshold of the New Covenant with regard to the content of its faith" (von Balthasar 1991, 16–17).

Maccabees in the second century BC and the Zealots in the first and second centuries AD; despite some military successes, this position was eventually crushed, leading to the final destruction of the temple and to the remaking of Jerusalem as a Gentile city. The latter was the position taken by Ezra, Nehemiah, and similar movements up to the Sadducees in the time of Christ. Yoder says of this position: "Ultimately it failed" (2003, 170).[9]

By accepting the use of military force and trying to claim authority to "be in charge," Ezra and Nehemiah take steps not only to reestablish the Torah and temple, but also to reclaim a military kingship in Israel. In contrast, "the 'Judaism' which survived after the last Zealot defeat in 135 assumed the same stance which Jewry everywhere else but in Palestine had already been taking since Jeremiah, namely 'seeking the peace of the city where they had been sent' (Jer. 29:4–7)" (Yoder 2003, 170–71). Ezra and Nehemiah, on Yoder's reading, thus mark an ultimately disastrous decision to go against Jeremiah's prophetic witness and the understanding of Judaism that emerged during and after the Babylonian exile.

This understanding or "ethos of Jewry"—centered upon the synagogue, the Torah, and the rabbinate ("a non-sacerdotal, non-hierarchical, non-violent leadership elite whose power is not civil but intellectual")—belongs, Yoder thinks, also to the ethics of early Christianity. Seeking to place Christian ethics in its Jewish context, Yoder states: "It is rather the case that Jesus' impact in the first century added more and deeper authentically Jewish reasons, or reinforced and further validated the already expressed Jewish reasons, for the already established ethos of not being in charge and not considering any local state structure to be the primary bearer of the movement of history" (2003, 171). The "ethos of not being in charge" does not result in a quietistic or separatist movement unable to contribute to human civilization. On the contrary, renouncing violence and military prestige after Jeremiah aided the Jews: "Not being in charge of the civil order is sometimes a more strategic way to be important for its survival or its flourishing than to fight over or for the throne" (2003, 172).

Yoder is not naïve; he is well aware that such Jewish communities, like the early Christian communities that shared their ethos, produced a mixed reaction that at times involved serious and sustained persecution. For Yoder, however, "both the phenomenon of occasional persecution and the event of its ultimately ending bear witness to the cultural and even political power of a morally committed minority" (2003, 172). Their nonconformity, which put their lives at risk as a sign of their "resistance for the sake of justice and the honour of God" (2003, 172), also made them particularly valuable to the broader communi-

9. For a somewhat similar position with regard to the New Testament Jewish context, see Hays 1999, who puts it this way: "If the victory of God accomplished in Jesus was a victory over violence and nationalism, then all subsequent Christian accommodations of violence and nationalism are betrayals of Jesus' agenda, surrenders of territory won for us by the one we call Lord" (1999, 158).

ties in which they lived without possessing or seeking military power. Thus "Jewish minorities, within a few generations of their arrival, almost everywhere they went, came to be valued as specialists in cross-cultural communication. Sometimes that meant leadership in trade, sometimes in literacy or language, sometimes in diplomacy" (2003, 172). In other words, such Jewish (and early Christian) communities became concrete witnesses to God's peacemaking in the world.

Ezra and Nehemiah, like the messianic pretenders who assisted the disastrous military rebellions against the Roman Empire in the first and second centuries AD in hopes of regaining a political kingship over the territory of preexilic Judah, represent for Yoder the opposite path of a return to the patterns of violent religion, patterns that (as God showed through the prophecies of Jeremiah and the exile) had failed. Having given up claims to a political kingship, postexilic Jews and early Christians could display "the paradox of the power of weakness" (2003, 174). This power is also "the power of promise" or hope that God will triumph over the fallenness of the world's political structures. Jesus embodies this approach: "Jesus defeated the powers not by being better than they at their trade of domination, but by refusing to meet them on that terrain, at the cost of his life" (2003, 175). The alleged realism of worldly political maneuvering leads to more and more violence so as to preserve the "peace" of militaristic polities, whereas abandoning such alleged realism—"our refusal to play the game by the agreed rules" (2003, 175)—reveals the power of God to overturn even crucifixion.

Yoder argues that trusting in God's power rather than military strength to accomplish peace and bring order out of disorder is the distinctive mark of postexilic Jews and early Christians. This witness provides hope for a justice not based upon the injustices intrinsic to the use of military force. He says, therefore: "It may be the case not only by happenstance but by a deep inner logic, if God is God, that the sub-community's fidelity to its own vocation will 'contribute to state policy' more strongly—and certainly more authentically—than if they worried about just how and why to go about compromising their principles in order to be effective" (2003, 175). Postexilic Jews and early Christians contribute to the upbuilding of the state both by witnessing to the true justice toward which the state purportedly aims and by witnessing to the all-powerful God who governs all human societies and yet who has chosen to be present in fallen societies not through power but through weakness.

This mission, which Jeremiah's prophecies and the exile revealed in full to the Jews, was rejected by Ezra and Nehemiah, who sought to revive the failed military pretensions of the corrupt kingship, not recognizing that God had destined the Davidic kingship toward a far greater—and nonviolent—fulfillment in the "weakness" of Jesus of Nazareth. Both Constantinian Christendom and, in certain of its forms, Zionism continued the error of Ezra and Nehemiah, according to Yoder. Yoder appeals in this regard to "the orthodox Jewish perspective of the *neturei karta,* which does not acknowledge the State of Israel because it was not established by the Messiah, but by human initiative" (Yoder 2003, 174–75; cf. Yoder 1984, 135–47). For Yoder, the books of Ezra and Nehemiah depict an effort of Jews to "be in charge" once again and thus are tragic books, failing to recognize the movement of God's work in history and mistakenly rejecting the "robust alternative holistic social system" (2003, 172) of "not being in charge" that characterized the exilic Jews.

In their responses to this aspect of Yoder's thought, Jewish philosopher/ theologian Peter Ochs and Christian theologian Michael Cartwright seek to reclaim the books of Ezra and Nehemiah. Ochs argues that "not being in charge" for postliberal Jews within the rabbinic tradition stands alongside numerous other virtues. Not all communities need to "specialize" in the same particular virtues. Thus postliberal Jews, Ochs says, "would therefore not expect the radical [Protestant] reformers to bear the same responsibilities for landedness that Jews bear, just as much as they would not expect most Jews to bear the same responsibility for pacifism that the radical reformers bear" (in Yoder 2003, 179). For Ochs, then, Ezra and Nehemiah's commitment to the covenantal landedness of Israel should not be set in opposition to later Protestants' commitment to pacifism. Both are true virtues, but the rabbinic tradition accepts that no finite community is able to display all the virtues. Yoder did not, Ochs suggests, grasp the Jews' covenantal landedness and thus reads "Zionism" in much too flat-footed a manner. Postliberal rabbinic Jews

> would, above all, not reduce the broad spectrum of nineteenth- to twenty-first-century Jewish theo-political options under the rubrics of "Zionism" and "non-Zionism." They know that the biblical record ties them to the land of Israel, whether they like it or not, in ways that Exilic Judaism never abrogated and in ways with which all disciples of the gospels are not burdened. But to be burdened with the land of Israel is not simply to apply a very modernist notion of national-political-ethnic sovereignty to that land. Nor is it to reduce all discussions of the land to the single issue of political governance. There are issues of home, of "autochthonous religiosity" (to use one of Yoder's own terms), of the linguistic and historical traditions that bind members of this covenant to that land, of the physical survival of the bodies of the people Israel and of the place of land in that survival, of the unique burdens of Jewish life in nineteenth- and twentieth-century life in Europe, and much more. (in Yoder 2003, 180)

In short, Yoder's marginalization of Ezra and Nehemiah misunderstands the covenantal bonds of Israel to the land, bonds that possess an extraordinary range of meanings and that are by no means rejected by Jeremiah or the practices of diaspora Judaism.[10]

10. For an excellent account of Israel and the land from a Christian perspective, see Vall forthcoming.

Similarly, Michael Cartwright agrees with Douglas Harink's argument that "Yoder has 'occluded' the doctrine of the election of Israel in favour of offering a 'moral history' of Israel's obedience through his [Yoder's] reading of the Jewish diaspora history since the exile" (in Yoder 2003, 211).[11] Cartwright observes that Yoder's essay contains his fullest account of a normative "Jeremianic turn," that is, pacifism from a Jewish perspective (in Yoder 2003, 215–16). Yoder focuses upon the synagogue, the Torah, and the rabbinate, but as Cartwright points out, "there is no reference to 'land' in this definition—synagogues can take shape 'wherever' the requisite minimum of households come together" (in Yoder 2003, 215). Nor is there for Yoder a synagogue worship other than the nonauthoritative remembering and reading provided by the rabbis. Cartwright finds, then, that Yoder "gives short shrift to the prospect of any kind of Jewish 'return from exile' in favour of his own view that the best narrative framework to account for Jewish existence is to be found in *galut* as the proper form of 'missionary' vocation of the Jewish people" (in Yoder 2003, 218).[12] Thus Yoder emphasizes that the books of Ezra and Nehemiah do not require the Jews to possess either a Davidic kingship or military control of the territory of Israel, and so "return to the land" comes to mean (metaphorically) return to faith.[13] Cartwright observes that "by making the 'return to Zion' mythic, Yoder effectively disengages from the deeply rooted complex of Jewish theological claims that see the land of eretz yisrael as the locus of the sacred and thereby displaces the theological unity of election, covenant, and God's promise of redemption from exile" (in Yoder 2003, 219).

As a contrast to the weaknesses of Yoder's position, Cartwright points to the work of David Weiss Halivni. Yoder holds that the books of Ezra and Nehemiah stand outside the main biblical narrative, which flows through the "Jeremianic turn" and does not reward Ezra and Nehemiah's restorationist project. Quite differently, Halivni argues that the main biblical narrative flows through the books of Ezra and Nehemiah. For Halivni, indeed, it is Ezra who rescues, restores, and shapes the main biblical narrative. Although Ezra is not able to recover revelation in its perfect form, his prophetic authority enables him to produce a canonical text of the Torah that adequately, despite its er-

---

11. See also Harink 2003, 151–207. For similar criticisms of Yoder's position, see also Reimer 1999 and Schlabach 1999. For an Anabaptist defense of Yoder's position that seeks to offer (in Cartwright's words) "a non-supersessionist 'orthodox' theological critique of Zionism" (in Yoder 2003, 213), see Weaver 2001. Cartwright also points to the significance of Wyschogrod 1983.

12. Regarding the "Jeremianic turn," Cartwright quotes from Yoder's essay "See How They Go with Their Face to the Sun": "Yoder believes that the move from Zion to Babylon 'was not a two-generation parenthesis, after which the Davidic and Solomonic project was supposed to take up again where he had left off. It was rather the beginning, under a fresh prophetic mandate, of a new phase of the Mosaic project'" (in Yoder 2003, 218).

13. Cartwright draws here upon Yoder's "See How They Go with Their Face to the Sun." Yoder is indebted to Stephan Zweig's early-twentieth-century play *Jeremiah*, which does not envision a return to geographic Jerusalem.

rors, expresses the original divinely revealed Torah. Cartwright summarizes the value of Halivni's work: "Halivni is able to account for key instances of Jewish disobedience and infidelity described in the biblical history while also displaying the constitutive power of the restoration of the Torah in the context of the re-covenanting of Israel brought about by Ezra and Nehemiah, which in turn enabled Israel to continue as a people" (in Yoder 2003, 224 [emphasis original]; see Halivni 1997). Ezra and Nehemiah, and the return to the land (Zion), here play a profoundly positive role in the reception of the Torah (Sinai). According to Cartwright, the affirmation of the importance of Ezra and Nehemiah also exposes the difficulties endured by "the peoples of the land" and thereby serves as a resource for upholding justice toward the peoples of the land today, the Palestinians (in Yoder 2003, 225–26).

Much historical-critical scholarship also gives a significant role to the figure of Ezra. In *Who Wrote the Bible?* Richard Elliot Friedman remarks that during the period of the rebuilt temple "the Aaronid priests were in authority. There were no more kings. Rival priesthoods had been superseded. It is really no surprise that an Aaronid priest of the second Temple days should have been the redactor of the final work. This was the time, as never before, that the priests had the authority to promulgate the work—and to enforce it" (1987, 223). Friedman notes that Ezra appears to have had such authority more than any other Aaronid priest. As a scribe, Ezra shows a particular interest in the Torah. Friedman does not claim to have demonstrated that Ezra was the final editor of the Torah, but he nonetheless makes a lengthy argument that it was indeed Ezra who "took on the enormous, intricate, and ironic task of combining these alternative versions of the same stories into one work" (1987, 226). If so, then efforts to downplay the importance of the books of Ezra and Nehemiah are all the more misguided.

For Yoder, the biblical story can indeed be read as a unity—under the rubric of "not being in charge"—but large portions of the Bible, including the books of Ezra and Nehemiah, unconsciously and falsely present the very opposite message as if it were blessed and sanctioned by God. For von Balthasar, Ezra and Nehemiah unconsciously expose the abrupt end of sacred history and the rise of Judaism, although von Balthasar holds that precisely their emptiness can be seen from the perspective of the new covenant to have christological undertones. For their part, Cartwright and Halivni (and in his way Friedman too) affirm that the main biblical narrative flows through Ezra, within whose mission Nehemiah takes on its positive value as well.

Did Ezra and Nehemiah, in their efforts to reconstitute Israel cultically and politically, take a wrong turn or at least a dead-end? To probe this question further requires setting forth on our task—that of commenting on the books of Ezra and Nehemiah—and thereby recalling, with Ezra, "the word of the Lord by the mouth of Jeremiah."

THE BOOK OF EZRA

Introduction to the Book of Ezra

If the main theme of the book of Ezra is the struggle to rebuild the temple, how does this theme relate to Ezra's other themes: the return to the land (Ezra 1–2), the renewal of sacrifice (Ezra 3), the struggle against the "peoples of the land" (Ezra 4–5), the renewal of the festival of passover (Ezra 6), the journey of Ezra the Scribe and his followers from Babylon to Jerusalem (Ezra 7–8), and the purification of the returned exiles who had mingled with the peoples of the land (Ezra 9–10)? Insight into this question is obtained by appreciating the depth of the meaning of the terms "land" and "people" in the Old Testament. I will briefly trace the basic covenantal narrative with respect to land and people[1] and then explore the applicability of this covenantal narrative to the book of Ezra.

Adam and Eve are created as holy people. Connected with this holiness is their dwelling with God in the land of Eden. When they sin, they not only lose their holiness but are also expelled from the land where they dwell with God. God's covenant with Noah makes clear his intention to restore human beings to a state of blessing, a new Eden (and a new Adam and Eve). God's covenant with Abraham takes the first steps in this direction, promising Abraham both land and descendents who will be a blessing to all nations. Neither this land nor Abraham's descendents, however, are as yet particularly holy, as the narrative goes on to show. Thus before God leads the descendents of Abraham into the promised land, God makes a further covenant with Moses. In this covenant God gives Israel a law, a pattern of holiness for the people. Second, God makes himself present in the midst of the people in the ark of the covenant, which

---

1. For a detailed discussion, see Dauphinais and Levering 2005.

becomes the true focal point of the land, as is made clear when the Philistines later dare to steal it away.

The experience of Israel during the period of the judges shows that not only does Israel fail radically to follow the law, but also that this failure is in some sense connected with the apparent lack of a king, since the role of a king is to establish justice in his land. Under the judges, the land of Israel is an unjust and idolatrous place. Although the Israelites should ideally have recognized God as their king and obeyed the law, God gives the Israelites another covenant, the covenant with David. This covenant provides for a Davidic king who will reign forever in Jerusalem and establish the people in justice/holiness, as well as a temple in which God will place his name, thereby constituting Israel by divine indwelling as holy land.

While God thus sets in place the lineaments of the renewal of Eden, something is lacking: God's increasing gifts to Israel display all the more how far short Israel falls due to sin. Just as Adam and Eve are exiled from Eden, Israel incurs the covenantal curse, exile from the land (and more importantly the flight of God's presence from the temple). Yet, through the prophets, God promises a restoration that will finally accomplish the new Eden.

Various themes intertwine in God's promise through the prophets regarding the eschatological restoration of Israel: the return of the Davidic king as Messiah, the eschatological banquet with God, the Suffering Servant, the entrance of the Son of man into the divine throne, the forgiveness of sins, the new temple, God's perfect indwelling in a new covenant that gives a "heart of flesh," the nations streaming to Mount Zion to worship the Lord, a radically new creation, and so forth. The main point is that Israel will become a holy people because God will dwell within them: the marriage of God and humankind!

It might seem from this brief survey of salvation history that the events recorded in the book of Ezra are neither fish nor fowl. The great covenants of salvation history, along with the great prophecies, have been already given; all that remains is anticipation of the messianic fulfillment, and any other labor—including any project of temporal restoration of Israel's Torah and temple after the exile—is irrelevant. I expect that this is what Hans Urs von Balthasar means when, as noted in the introduction, he states that Ezra and Nehemiah are "like a brook in the process of drying up" (1991, 370). On this view, Ezra and Nehemiah are at best Lenten reading. They are like the last chapter of the biography of an eminent man, when the great deeds are done, senility has arrived, and only the promise of eternal life provides hope for the story. Were the people of Israel to go down the dead-end charted by Ezra and Nehemiah, they would—to continue the analogy—remain in the period of senility forever.

A more positive way of putting it would be to say that if the great deeds and the great men and women of Israel's past prefigure Christ's active life, the book of Ezra prefigures the dryness and waiting that Christ endured in his perfect kenosis, the cross. Like Christ bearing the scourging from the Roman soldiers, the Israelites suffer under the Babylonians, Persians, and Samaritans. The book of Ezra, then, shows Israel in its stage of kenotic enduring, as Israel comes to realize that God alone can accomplish the restoration and that no human efforts (other than patient suffering of the oppression from the surrounding nations) will avail. Jeremiah says before the exile: "O daughter of my people, gird on sackcloth, and roll in ashes; make mourning as for an only son, most bitter lamentation" (Jer. 6:26). The book of Ezra is a period of sackcloth and ashes, a necessary purification so that Israel's idolatrous pride in its gifts might be peeled away in penitence and neediness and the people be thereby prepared to receive their Lord.

Clearly there is much truth to such a reading. In the book of Ezra, the greatly diminished people of Israel have to endure a lot, and Ezra also makes clear that the people, due to their sinfulness and weakness, cannot accomplish the eschatological restoration that the prophets foretell. Abraham received the promises of land and countless descendents, but after generations of expansion the people of Israel are now contracting, and the land is ruled by foreign kings. There is certainly a kenosis here (as there has always been, to varying degrees, throughout Israel's difficult history as a small people caught between powerful nations). There is also required, on the part of the reader, an ascesis or purifying of mind so as to read patiently and attentively about events that trudge on, by and large, to no dramatic conclusion.

Yet this kenotic interpretation should not be the primary one of the book of Ezra (or of Nehemiah). It overlooks that what Ezra the Scribe—and before him Sheshbazzar, Zerubbabel, Jeshua, Haggai, Zechariah, and other great leaders, priests, and prophets—accomplishes is absolutely extraordinary and constitutes a crucial continuation of salvation history, not merely a penitential pause. Why should the rebuilding of the temple and the renewal of obedience to the Torah, despite the diminishment of the splendor of the temple and the continuing failure fully to observe the Torah, be counted as small things, as the "drying up" of the stream of salvation history? It seems to me, on the contrary, that the rebuilding of the temple and the renewal of obedience to the Torah are precisely the kind of wrestling to be faithful to God's gifts that one would expect from true sons and daughters of Jacob. A spiritually weak people would not have bothered to reclaim their temple and Torah, but would instead have been content gradually to blend into the wealthy and powerful society of Babylon religiously, economically, and politically. His wrestling with God at the threshold of the holy land may leave Jacob/Israel permanently limping (Gen. 32:31)—perhaps even more so in the books of Ezra and Nehemiah than elsewhere—but this is a glorious wound, not a sign of drying up. Obedience to the Torah and worship at the temple actually increase in the centuries after Ezra as compared to the centuries prior to the exile.

Not only should the renewal of temple and Torah be counted as magnificent personal and communal acts of commitment to God's covenantal gifting, but also how could salvation history have proceeded without the great acts recorded in Ezra? Without Ezra the Scribe's reclamation of the Torah, could the Sermon on the Mount be imagined? Jesus says: "Think not that I have come to abolish the law and the prophets; I have come not to abolish them but to fulfil them. For truly, I say to you, till heaven and earth pass away, not an iota, not a dot, will pass from the law until all is accomplished" (Matt. 5:17–18). Without Zerubbabel and Jeshua, Haggai and Zechariah, could Jesus have enacted the return of YHWH to Zion? On Palm Sunday Jesus triumphantly enters the rebuilt Jerusalem in fulfillment of Zechariah's prophecy. From there he cleanses the temple and, seated in the rebuilt temple, heals the blind and lame (21:12–14). Could Jesus have done this, to the same effect, from the ziggurat of Babylon? What would it have meant for Jesus to claim to *be* the temple—to be the holy land in the flesh—had there been no actual temple? What would it have meant for Jesus to claim to fulfill and consummate the Torah had there been no communal effort to obey the Torah? In a nutshell, the downplaying of the active contribution to salvation history of the leaders described in the book of Ezra runs on parallel tracks with the dehistoricizing of Jesus, the classical liberal reading of Jesus that removes him from his historical context and turns him into a mouthpiece for Enlightenment projects.

From this perspective, we must reclaim a positive vision of the deeds recorded in Ezra as the ongoing and powerful activity of God in Israel. The book of Ezra begins with the return to the land to rebuild the temple. Because of the Edenic overtones that the reality of the covenantal land possesses, certainly this land cannot be what it is without the temple (as the locus of the promised divine indwelling); and yet the temple cannot be understood outside the land. The return to the land, therefore, is not a mere geographical journey: it is a new exodus that can be fulfilled only when the people arrive at a new temple, where once again the Lord's passover can be celebrated. This is why the returning exiles cannot allow the peoples of the land to rebuild the temple with them. Were the peoples of the land to assist in the rebuilding of the temple, then no return to the land could actually take place, because the land becomes itself (that is, suffused with the promise of divine indwelling) only when the returning exiles seek it for the purpose of true worship. Not geopolitical issues, but true worship, marks out this land. This story is told in Ezra 1–6.

Yet, since true worship is what is required for divine indwelling, neither can the rebuilding of the temple be efficacious without holiness on the part of the people. Therefore the remainder of the book, Ezra 7–10, contextualizes the rebuilding of the temple within the purification required of the people of Israel. This purification has two aspects. On the one hand, the people must know that their return is a journey of faith, a pilgrimage, not a mere effort to reclaim property owned by their ancestors. This accounts for the almost liturgical formalism of the account of the returning exiles under Ezra the Scribe in Ezra 7–8. On the other hand, the people must know that the mingling of returned exiles with the peoples of the land—and thus with other gods, destroying the purity of the temple worship—makes a mockery of the very purpose toward which the return to the land aims. However economically or socially valuable, such mingling with the peoples of the land makes the land into no land at all by destroying through idolatry the holiness of the people.

In short, Ezra 1–6 reaches a climax with the rebuilding of the temple and the celebration of passover and presents the restoration of the holy land in terms of the achievement of the rebuilding of the foundations of the temple and the renewal of its liturgical life. Ezra 7–10 teaches that this achievement, and the restoration of the holy land, cannot happen without the attainment of the holiness of the people, measured by their absolute commitment to the worship of the God of Israel as opposed to the gods of the peoples of the land.

Looking forward, the story of Ezra connects with the theology of St. Paul. Whereas the striving of the Israelites in Ezra has to do with the renewal of the temple and Torah after the destruction of the Babylonian exile, Paul's striving takes shape around the fulfillment of the temple and Torah in Christ, in light of Paul's own experience of being dead or exiled in sin. Paul cries out: "Wretched man that I am! Who will deliver me from this body of death? Thanks be to God through Jesus Christ our Lord!" (Rom. 7:24–25). By revealing sin, the law reveals Paul's spiritual death, just as the law's covenantal curse revealed exile for Israel. By his perfect obedience and victory over death, Jesus fulfills the law. On this basis Paul remarks: "Do we then overthrow the law by this faith [in Jesus Christ]? By no means! On the contrary, we uphold the law" (3:31)—by being enabled to fulfill it. The indwelling of the Holy Spirit, through faith in Christ, makes this possible: "Do you not know that your body is a temple of the Holy Spirit within you, which you have from God? You are not your own; you were bought with a price. So glorify God in your body" (1 Cor. 6:19–20). But the striving does not thereby come to an end; like the people of Israel in the book of Ezra, we must strive to share in Christ's fulfillment of Torah and temple. Paul tells the Corinthians regarding this striving: "I do not run aimlessly, I do not box as one beating the air; but I pommel my body and subdue it, lest after preaching to others I myself should be disqualified" (9:26–27).

Looking backward, the story of Ezra takes its bearings from the theology of Jeremiah and through Jeremiah from the covenantal theology of Abraham, Moses, David, and the exile. Jeremiah's prophecies make clear that the striving recorded by the book of Ezra has its place only in the context of the recognition that God alone can bring about the eschatological restoration. My commentary on Ezra will focus primarily on this backward connection, so as to draw the reader into the narrative and worldview of Ezra, from within which Paul (and Christ Jesus) must be understood.

PART I

EZRA 1–6: THE RESTORATION OF THE HOLY LAND, UNITED BY THE TEMPLE

Ezra 1–6 introduces us to a number of extraordinary people: King Cyrus of Persia, well known in world history for his military exploits; the Israelite leaders Sheshbazzar (whom Ezra calls a "prince of Judah"; 1:8), Zerubbabel of the Davidic line, Jeshua of the Aaronic priesthood; Kings Xerxes, Artaxerxes, and Darius of Persia, whose exploits against the Greeks were chronicled by the first Greek historians; the prophet Haggai and the great prophet Zechariah; and various local functionaries, hangers-on, and troublemakers such as Bishlam, Mithredath, Rehum, Shimshai, Tattenai, and Shethar-bozenai. God ordains that these diverse personages shape the story of the Israelites' return to the land and rebuilding of the temple. With the book of Ezra, we will take Jeremiah's prophecies as our guide to understanding this restoration of the holy land.

EZRA 1

Return to the Land

The opening sentence of the book of Ezra is also the concluding sentence of 2 Chronicles.[1] After his conquest of Babylon in 539 BC, *Cyrus king of Persia* encouraged by edict the return of peoples conquered by Babylon to their lands. Although historians disagree about who wrote the edict that we find in the book of Ezra (it is widely thought that the Chronicler reconstructed the edict), there is little disagreement that some Jews under *Sheshbazzar* made the journey back to Jerusalem around 538. *The word of the* LORD *by the mouth of Jeremiah* clearly refers, then, to Jeremiah's prophecy of the end of the Babylonian exile.

Commenting on Ezra 1 thus requires exploring Jeremiah's prophecy and its background. What is included within *the word of the* LORD *by the mouth of Jeremiah*, and how can it *be accomplished*?

The Covenantal Curse of Exile and the Promised Restoration

In the book of Jeremiah, God says *by the mouth of Jeremiah* that because the people of Israel have not listened to God, but instead have continued in their idolatrous evil ways: "I will send for all the tribes of the north, says the LORD, and for Nebuchadnezzar the king of Babylon, my servant, and I will bring them against this land and its inhabitants, and against all these nations round about; I will utterly destroy them, and make them a horror, a hissing, and an everlasting reproach" (Jer. 25:9). Through Jeremiah, God explains to the people

---

1. Davies observes that this connection between Ezra and 2 Chronicles "is a redactional stitch tying the two books together to give a textual dimension to a theological idea," namely, the continuity of the postexilic people and God with the preexilic people and God (1999, 4).

the nature and scope of the exile: "This whole land shall become a ruin and a waste, and these nations shall serve the king of Babylon seventy years. Then after seventy years are completed, I will punish the king of Babylon and that nation, the land of the Chaldeans, for their iniquity" (25:11–12). For seventy years, the land shall be no land, after which time Babylon itself shall fall.

The first sentence of the book of Ezra tells us that the seventy years prophesied by Jeremiah are now at an end. When Cyrus conquers Babylon in the fall of 539 BC, seventy years have passed since the ascension to the Davidic throne of King Jehoiakim. These seventy years, of course, can be interpreted in different ways. We can observe with the Venerable Bede the numbers seven and ten, which play important roles throughout the scripture. Bede's mystical reading of the seventy years brings out clearly the connection between the true end of exile and human holiness: "For there are seven gifts of the Holy Spirit which the prophet Isaiah enumerates and clearly distinguishes, but the sum of all the divine law is contained in the ten commandments, and seven multiplied by ten is seventy" (2006, 8). By violating God's commandments, the people of Israel became exiles, and the exile will not fully end until the people's holiness in the land is attained.

Why do the seventy years of exile begin with Jehoiakim's ascension to the throne? Jehoiakim was a Davidic king reigning in Jerusalem. Why then would his ascension mark the beginning of exile?

Josiah, Jehoiakim's father, was the last good king, and during his reign a copy of the Torah was discovered in the temple by the high priest Hilkiah (2 Kgs. 22:8) and the scope of Israel's disobedience to God became clear. Despite Josiah's desperate efforts to renew the covenant, Pharaoh Necho defeated and killed him in battle at Megiddo. Three months later he deposed Josiah's son Jehoahaz and installed Jehoiakim as a puppet king. Jehoiakim's "reign" was therefore already bondage. Jehoiakim's eighteen-year-old son reigned after him but spent only three months on the throne before being carried off to Babylonian exile.

It might seem that we have traveled somewhat far from Jeremiah, but we have not. Jeremiah lived during these times. In the fourth year of Jehoiakim's reign, Jeremiah prophesied the coming destruction and exile of Judah to Babylon. For these words King Jehoiakim severely persecuted the prophet, but Jeremiah's words were the truthful harbinger of the arrival of the covenantal curse.

Nonetheless, the Lord also says through Jeremiah: "When seventy years are completed for Babylon, I will visit you, and I will fulfil to you my promise and bring you back to this place. For I know the plans I have for you, says the LORD, plans for welfare and not for evil, to give you a future and a hope" (Jer. 29:10–11). What is this future and hope? It is a restored Israel: "For I will restore health to you, and your wounds I will heal, says the LORD, because they have called you an outcast: 'It is Zion, for whom no one cares!'" (30:17). Not only shall Israel "return and have quiet and ease" (30:10), but also Israel "shall serve the LORD their God and David their king, whom I will raise up for them" (30:9). Since the purpose of a king is to establish peace and justice in the land, the Davidic king that God "will raise up for them" will make the land truly a place for the indwelling of God. The restored reign of the Davidic king is joined, in Jeremiah's prophecy, to an interior transformation that accomplishes a new passover: "Behold, the days are coming, says the LORD, when I will make a new covenant with the house of Israel and the house of Judah, not like the covenant which I made with their fathers when I took them by the hand to bring them out of the land of Egypt, my covenant which they broke, though I was their husband, says the LORD" (31:31–32). Israel's death will be followed by resurrection.

The "Covenant Which They Broke"

At the beginning of the exodus, the Lord takes the whole people of Israel as his bride—unimaginable intimacy—when he saves them by the blood of the lamb and by water (prefiguring the Eucharist and baptism that flow from Christ's side on the cross): "Then Moses called all the elders of Israel, and said to them, 'Select lambs for yourselves according to your families, and kill the passover lamb. Take a bunch of hyssop and dip it in the blood which is in the basin, and touch the lintel and the two doorposts with the blood which is in the basin'" (Exod. 12:21–22). Marked by the passover lamb's blood, the people are spared the penalty of death that follows from sin and that the Egyptians endure. Having saved them through blood, the Lord in their flight saves them by water, which like blood otherwise evokes death: "The LORD said to Moses, 'Why do you cry to me? Tell the people of Israel to go forward. Lift up your rod, and stretch it out over the sea and divide it, that the people of Israel may go on dry ground through the sea. And I will harden the hearts of the Egyptians so that they shall go in after them, and I will get glory over Pharaoh and all his host, his chariots, and his horsemen'" (14:15–17). "But one of the soldiers pierced his side with a spear, and at once there came out blood and water" (John 19:34).

After God teaches Israel the law of holiness at Mount Sinai (Exod. 20), God seals this teaching by a covenant renewal at the foot of Mount Sinai, just as Christ Jesus's Sermon on the Mount is sealed by his sacrificial death. After reading to the people "the book of the covenant," Moses splashes half of the sacrificial blood upon the altar and the other half upon the people. The people swear a covenantal oath: "All that the LORD has spoken we will do, and we will be obedient" (24:7). The sacrificial blood confirms this covenantal oath: "And Moses took the blood and threw it upon the people, and said, 'Behold the blood of the covenant which the LORD has made with you in accordance with all these words'" (24:8).

After the sacrificial blood confirms the covenantal promises, Moses, Aaron and his sons, and the seventy elders ascend Mount Sinai. There "they saw the

God of Israel; and there was under his feet as it were a pavement of sapphire stone, like the very heaven for clearness. And he did not lay his hand on the chief men of the people of Israel; they beheld God, and ate and drank" (24:10–11). This covenantal meal, completing the covenantal sacrifice, so unites them to God that they "beheld God." The intimate union between Moses and God is such that when Moses, as mediator, communes with God, "the skin of his face shone because he had been talking with God" (34:29).

This covenantal meal prefigures the eschatological banquet of the Eucharist. Consider also the Lord's promise through Isaiah: "On this mountain the LORD of hosts will make for all peoples a feast of fat things, a feast of wine on the lees, of fat things full of marrow, of wine on the lees well refined" (Isa. 25:6). This feast for "all peoples" hardly consists of mere food. Rather, God promises through Isaiah something far greater, including the forgiveness of sins and the final destruction of death: "He will destroy on this mountain the covering that is cast over all peoples, the veil that is spread over all nations. He will swallow up death for ever, and the Lord GOD will wipe away tears from all faces, and the reproach of his people he will take away from all the earth, for the LORD has spoken" (25:7–8).

Jeremiah's Prophecy of a New Covenant

In prophesying a new covenant, what Jeremiah looks forward to is the fulfillment of what God offers Israel at Sinai. When the exiles return to the land, in order *that the word of the LORD by the mouth of Jeremiah might be accomplished*, what must therefore be accomplished is Israel's perfection as holy people in a communion with God that is so intimate as to be marital. "You shall no more be termed Forsaken, and your land shall no more be termed Desolate; but you shall be called My delight is in her, and your land Married; for the LORD delights in you, and your land shall be married" (Isa. 62:4). Because of God's indwelling, the land will become the holy bride of God: "Again I will build you, and you shall be built, O virgin Israel! Again you shall adorn yourself with timbrels, and shall go forth in the dance of the merrymakers" (Jer. 31:4). This comes after both Israel and Judah had, by their idolatrous worship of the gods of the surrounding peoples, "played the harlot" (3:8) and "polluted the land, committing adultery with stone and tree" (3:9).

Jeremiah describes the restoration of "virgin Israel" as consisting in the reality that God's law of holiness will be written on their hearts: "But this is the covenant which I will make with the house of Israel after those days, says the LORD: I will put my law within them, and I will write it upon their hearts; and I will be their God, and they shall be my people" (31:33). The law will fill the people with wisdom and charity, and they will no longer be spiritually dead in their sins. Speaking through Jeremiah, God continues: "And no longer shall each man teach his neighbor and each his brother, saying, 'Know the LORD,' for they shall all know me, from the least of them to the greatest, says the LORD; for I will forgive their iniquity, and I will remember their sin no more" (31:34). Perfect holiness will comprise a knowing of the Lord that will truly attain to him and a loving of the Lord that will be perfect due to the peace of God's forgiveness of sins.

Already Jacob had received an intimation of this marital communion between God and Israel. Journeying away from his home in the promised land, Jacob "dreamed that there was a ladder set up on the earth, and the top of it reached to heaven; and behold, the angels of God were ascending and descending on it!" (Gen. 28:12). At the heart of this communion between heaven and earth, Jacob discovers, is the covenantal promise that "by you and your descendants shall all the families of the earth bless themselves" (28:14). This ladder, this blessing, is Christ Jesus: "Truly, truly, I say to you, you will see heaven opened, and the angels of God ascending and descending upon the Son of man" (John 1:51).

Cyrus: The New Exodus

The reference in Ezra 1:1 to the accomplishment of *the word of the LORD by the mouth of Jeremiah*, therefore, places in view a return to the holy land that encompasses far more than material bounty or conquest. The instrument of this return is Cyrus, inspired by the Lord: "Thus says the LORD to his anointed, to Cyrus. . . . For the sake of my servant Jacob, and Israel my chosen, I call you by your name, I surname you, though you do not know me. I am the LORD, and there is no other, besides me there is no God; I gird you, though you do not know me, that men may know . . . that there is none besides me" (Isa. 45:1, 4–6). Cyrus will ensure that the temple is rebuilt, because the Lord "says of Cyrus, 'He is my shepherd, and he shall fulfil all my purpose'; saying of Jerusalem, 'She shall be built,' and of the temple, 'Your foundations shall be laid'" (44:28). Let us note four things about Cyrus.

First, in contrast to Pharaoh's spirit in the days of Moses, when "the heart of Pharaoh was hardened, and he did not let the people go" (Exod. 9:7)—and even after Pharaoh does let them go, he repents and sends soldiers after them—Cyrus's spirit is *stirred up* by the Lord to do good.[2] Ezra suggests that Cyrus, unlike Pharaoh, is moving toward a deeper understanding of God: *The LORD, the God of heaven, has given me all the kingdoms of the earth.* Only an almighty God, not a merely local god, could give *all the kingdoms of the earth*, and only one God could be *the God of heaven*.

2. Cf. Davies's comment that "the Return from Exile announced here [Ezra 1] is described in terms that allude to the escape from Egypt" (1999, 10).

Do Cyrus's words suggest humility or pride? The Venerable Bede recognizes a hint of both. On the side of pride, he remarks that perhaps now that Cyrus "had conquered, destroyed, and brought to an end as mighty and ancient a kingdom as that of the Chaldeans, he believed that no one in the whole world could oppose his rule" (2006, 14). On the side of humility, Bede finds that Cyrus's words agree "with the majesty of him who says: *All power is given to me in heaven and in earth* [Matt. 28:18]" (2006, 14). Israel's God is the God of all human beings, not merely a local god (1 Kgs. 8:27), and even foreign rulers will come to confess this reality. From Pharaoh to Cyrus we thus observe an ascending movement, one that culminates in St. Paul's mission to the Gentiles.

Second, as Isaiah prophesies, God inspires Cyrus to rebuild the temple in Jerusalem, the center of the holy land as the locus of God's indwelling. It is Cyrus now, not Solomon, who says that the Lord *has charged me to build him a house at Jerusalem, which is in Judah.* "Foreigners shall build up your walls, and their kings shall minister to you; for in my wrath I [the LORD] smote you, but in my favor I have had mercy on you. Your gates shall be open continually; day and night they shall not be shut; that men may bring to you the wealth of the nations, with their kings led in procession" (Isa. 60:10–11). The salvation of all nations is drawing near, now that God has moved the Persian king Cyrus to build God's *house.*

Third, God inspires Cyrus to gather together the people of Israel, the holy people, so that they might return to the land. Cyrus proclaims: *Whoever is among you of all his [the LORD's] people, may his God be with him, and let him go up to Jerusalem, which is in Judah, and rebuild the house of the LORD, the God of Israel—he is the God who is in Jerusalem.* Because this God *who is in Jerusalem* is the transcendent *God of heaven,* Cyrus's work of restoration of the people and the land ultimately will lead to a universal blessing. "It shall come to pass in the latter days that the mountain of the house of the LORD shall be established as the highest of the mountains, and shall be raised above the hills; and all the nations shall flow to it, and many peoples shall come, and say: 'Come, let us go up to the mountain of the LORD, to the house of the God of Jacob; that he may teach us his ways and that we may walk in his paths'" (Isa. 2:2–3). Through Cyrus, God is moving toward fulfillment of his covenant with Abraham, in which God promised that "by you [Abraham] all the families of the earth shall bless themselves" (Gen. 12:1–3; cf. 22:18). "Salvation is from the Jews" (John 4:22).

Fourth, in contrast to the exodus, when not Pharaoh but rather fear caused by the plagues allowed the Israelites to despoil the Egyptians of jewelry and clothing (Exod. 12:36), Cyrus freely commands regarding the Israelites: *Let each survivor, in whatever place he sojourns, be assisted by the men of his place with silver and gold, with goods and with beasts, besides freewill offerings for the house of God which is in Jerusalem.* Of course there was no *house of God* in Jerusalem yet; the Babylonians under Nebuchadnezzar had destroyed the temple, and so

Cyrus the king also brought out the vessels of the house of the LORD *which Nebu-chadnezzar had carried away from Jerusalem and placed in the house of his gods. Cyrus king of Persia brought these out in charge of Mithredath the treasurer, who counted them out to Sheshbazzar the prince of Judah.* The Lord had also *stirred* the spirits of the Israelites *to go up to rebuild the house of the* LORD, and so they were able to take with them sufficient instruments for the sacrificial worship of the temple: *A thousand basins of gold, a thousand basins of silver, twenty-nine censers, thirty bowls of gold, two thousand four hundred and ten bowls of silver, and a thousand other vessels; all the vessels of gold and of silver were five thousand four hundred and sixty-nine.*

An Accomplishment beyond Human Powers

In light of Cyrus's proclamation and God's promises through the prophets, it may have seemed to some of the exiles that the restoration of Israel was at hand, by which God would establish Israel in holiness, so as to bless the entire world. This perspective cannot be dismissed, since Cyrus and the exiles were preparing for the restoration that in fact did occur through *the God [who] is in Jerusalem.* "The Word became flesh and dwelt among us, full of grace and truth; we have beheld his glory, glory as of the only Son from the Father" (John 1:14).

EZRA 2

Return of the Holy People to the Land

Much has occurred between the end of Ezra 1 and the beginning of Ezra 2. After a thirty-year public career that took him from being a vassal of King Astyages of the Medians to the establishment of his own empire, Cyrus died in 529 BC while waging war in the mountains of India (Fensham 1982, 11, 42). Sheshbazzar, leader of the first group of returning exiles, is not mentioned in Ezra 2. Instead we now meet Zerubbabel and Jeshua's group of returning exiles. It is unclear when they departed from Babylon for Judea. In 523 the Persians conquered Egypt, and perhaps this would have been an auspicious time for the return of a party of exiles to Judea (Fensham 1982, 11; cf. 49).

A Depleted People without a King

Ezra 1 sets in motion the Israelites' return to the land where Israel dwells with God. Cyrus issues a proclamation commanding the rebuilding of the temple and the return of the exiles to the land. The land is in a radically depleted condition: at present Israel does not dwell there, and there is no temple.

Ezra 2 turns to the almost equally depleted condition of the people. In the time of David—even allowing for exaggeration—"in Israel there were eight hundred thousand valiant men who drew the sword, and the men of Judah were five hundred thousand" (2 Sam. 24:9). Similarly Moses had found that "the whole number of the people of Israel, by their fathers' houses, from twenty years old and upward, every man able to go forth to war in Israel—their whole number was six hundred and three thousand five hundred and fifty" (Num. 1:45–46), not counting the Levites. By contrast the returned exiles, including a much reduced number of priests and Levites, amount to *forty-two thousand three hundred and sixty*. Bede compares this remnant to the small number of the early church, arguing that the remnant was of one heart and one soul (cf. Acts 2:44; 4:32) (2006, 30–31). Perhaps Bede is being somewhat optimistic here, however. After all, when they finally arrived in Jerusalem, only *some of the heads of families* gave money to assist in the rebuilding of the temple.

No Davidic king returns to the land, but a member of the royal house does return: *Zerubbabel*. We may be glad that he did return, because he appears, in fact, in the lineage of Christ Jesus: "And after the deportation to Babylon: Jechoniah [son of King Josiah] was the father of Shealtiel, and Shealtiel the father of Zerubbabel" all the way down to "Jacob the father of Joseph the husband of Mary" (Matt. 1:12, 16). Similarly Zerubbabel figures in the genealogy of Jesus given in Luke as well, although here Shealtiel's father is named Neri (Luke 3:27). Yet, Zerubbabel is not on the Davidic throne and never ascends to that throne.

Does this constitute a contradiction to God's covenantal promise to King David that "your house and your kingdom shall be made sure for ever before me; your throne shall be established for ever" (2 Sam. 7:16)? "Lord, where is thy steadfast love of old, which by thy faithfulness thou didst swear to David?" (Ps. 89:49). At the time of King Solomon's consecration of the temple, the Lord qualifies this covenant with David. The Lord tells Solomon: "I have consecrated this house [the temple] which you have built, and put my name there for ever; my eyes and my heart will be there for all time" (1 Kgs. 9:3). But the Lord now makes this promise conditional: "And as for you [Solomon], if you will walk before me, as David your father walked, with integrity of heart and uprightness, doing according to all I have commanded you, and keeping my statutes and my ordinances, then I will establish your royal throne over Israel for ever, as I promised David your father, saying, 'There shall not fail you a man upon the throne of Israel'" (9:4–5; cf. Ps. 132). If Solomon or his descendents sin, however—and they certainly do sin!—God will cast them aside even unto the destruction of Solomon's Temple: "But if you turn aside from following me, you or your children, and do not keep my commandments and my statutes which I have set before you, but go and serve other gods and worship them, then I will cut off Israel from the land which I have given them; and the house which I have consecrated for my name I will cast out of my sight" (1 Kgs. 9:6–7).

The Lord also warns, through Jeremiah, that the people should not trust solely in the Davidic covenant without holiness: "Thus says the LORD of hosts, the God of Israel, Amend your ways and your doings, and I will let you dwell in this place. Do not trust in these deceptive words: 'This is the temple of the LORD, the temple of the LORD, the temple of the LORD'" (Jer. 7:3–4). But as we have seen, the Lord mercifully gives a promise regarding the end of exile: "It shall come to pass in that day, says the LORD of hosts, that I will break the yoke from off their neck, and I will burst their bonds, and strangers shall no more make servants of them. But they shall serve the LORD their God and David their king, whom I will raise up for them" (30:8–9). The failure of the kings to establish a holy people will lead not to the destruction of Israel, but to their purification through affliction and their ultimate eschatological restoration.

At this stage, however, no messianic Davidic king has yet been "raised up" by the Lord for this eschatological restoration, although Zerubbabel remains a candidate. The curse spoken by the Lord through Jeremiah thus remains at least partially true: "Say to the king and the queen mother: 'Take a lowly seat, for your beautiful crown has come down from your head.' The cities of the Negeb are shut up, with none to open them; all Judah is taken into exile, wholly taken into exile" (Jer. 13:18–19). The people of Israel must still take a lowly seat because they have no beautiful crown. The exile will continue until this crown is restored in Christ Jesus.

They Came to the House of the Lord

Although *they returned to Jerusalem and Judah, each to his own town*, their arrival in the land is announced by the book of Ezra with the remark that *they came to the house of the LORD which is in Jerusalem*—meaning by this the *site* of the destroyed temple. The land is thus, for Ezra, far more than the territories or towns of the tribes of Israel. The land is the locus of dwelling with God, and thus true arrival in the land means arrival in Jerusalem and particularly the temple mount.

Again, the Israelites' return to the land, so *that the word of the LORD by the mouth of Jeremiah might be accomplished*, cannot be understood solely geopolitically. The arrival points to the blessing that will extend to all peoples, once the full prophecy of Jeremiah has been accomplished. In the spiritual sense, Bede interprets Jerusalem as the universal church and the towns as the local churches (2006, 26). For Bede the land is none other than the church, the body and bride of Christ, locus of God's perfect dwelling.

The journey to the land, however, cannot be a return from exile if some of the people who attempt to return are not Israelites. The task of preserving the integrity of the people—their connection to the covenantal family of Abraham, Isaac, and Jacob—thereby becomes a paramount condition of the restoration. The necessary goal is to preserve the particularity of God's covenantal people from whom universal blessing will arise. This particularity undergirds the particularity of Christ Jesus: "By this you know the Spirit of God: every spirit which confesses that Jesus Christ has come in the flesh is of God, and every spirit which does not confess Jesus is not of God" (1 John 4:2–3). That it is God's covenantal people who return, and not a different people, keeps in view that redemption proceeds from within human flesh, not from "on high." God's love is universal because it is concentrated.

A number of people, including people who claim to be of priestly families, *came up from Telmelah, Telharsha, Cherub, Addan, and Immer, though they could not prove their fathers' houses or their descent, whether they belonged to Israel.* The book of Ezra makes clear that the very efficacy of the temple sacrificial worship is endangered by the possibility that it will be performed by priests who do not truly belong to the covenantal people: *These sought their registration among those enrolled in the genealogies, but they were not found there, and so they were excluded from the priesthood as unclean; the governor told them that they were not to partake of the most holy food [from the sacrificial offerings], until there should be a priest to consult Urim and Thummim.* Not anyone, but only those who wear the "wedding garment" (Matt. 22:11–12), may celebrate the (nuptial) divine sacrifice.

In the list of the returning exiles, *Nehemiah* is mentioned after *Zerubbabel* and *Jeshua,* but either this is not the Nehemiah who later in the fifth century BC becomes governor of Judea, or else it is an honorific insertion of his name. The list of the priests, which begins with *the sons of Jedaiah, of the house of Jeshua,* connects the leading postexilic priestly family of Jeshua with the preexilic priestly family of Jedaiah (1 Chr. 24:7), descended from Aaron.

Only a small number of Levites return. In contrast to the priests' work, the labor of the Levites is onerous. Through the prophet Ezekiel, the Lord lays a curse upon some of the families of the Levites: "But the Levites who went far from me, going astray from me after their idols when Israel went astray, shall bear their punishment" (Ezek. 44:10). The punishment is that while they can no longer be priests, they will have to do all the work of the maintenance of the temple. God says through Ezekiel: "They shall not come near to me, to serve me as priest, nor come near any of my sacred things and the things that are most sacred; but they shall bear their shame, because of the abominations which they have committed. Yet I will appoint them to keep charge of the temple, to do all its service and all that is to be done in it" (44:13–14). No wonder few of them came back, although this does not excuse them. "Only, let every one lead the life which the Lord has assigned to him, and in which God has called him" (1 Cor. 7:17).

EZRA 3

Laying the Foundations of the Temple:
Joy and Weeping

The Festivals of God

Ezra 3 is devoted to worship and culminates in the rebuilding of the foundations of the temple. It is not for nothing that we now fast-forward to *the seventh month*. The liturgical calendar of Israel (whose development is recorded in Num. 28–29; Lev. 23; Deut. 16; Exod. 12; 23) begins in the first month with passover; but the seventh month, with three central feasts, could be viewed as the preeminent month. Bede observes in the spiritual sense that "the seventh month suggests the grace of the Holy Spirit, which is described as sevenfold in the prophet Isaiah and in the Apocalypse of Saint John" (2006, 40–41). The Holy Spirit is at work in the seventh month through a series of divinely ordained festivals.

The first day of the seventh month is a one-day feast of praise to God. The tenth day of the month is the great day of expiation. Beginning on the fifteenth day of the month and extending for seven days is the feast of booths, regarding which God instructs the people: "You shall dwell in booths for seven days; all that are native in Israel shall dwell in booths, that your generations may know that I made the people of Israel dwell in booths when I brought them out of the land of Egypt: I am the LORD your God" (Lev. 23:42–43). The feast of booths thus commemorates the passover. Jesus celebrates the feast of booths: "About the middle of the feast Jesus went up into the temple and taught" (John 7:14; cf. 7:2). He teaches that the Holy Spirit is going to be poured out through faith in him: "On the last day of the feast, the great day, Jesus stood up and proclaimed, 'If any one thirst, let him come to me and drink. He who believes in me, as the scripture has said, "Out of his heart shall flow rivers of living water."' Now this he said about the Spirit, which those who believed in him were to receive" (7:37–39).

For its part, the great day of expiation—which Christ's cross fulfills—prepares the people to experience the holiness of the true exodus. Only once a year could the high priest come into the holy place, "before the mercy seat which is upon the ark" (Lev. 16:2). On this day of expiation, the high priest must enter the holy place "with a young bull for a sin offering and a ram for a burnt offering" (16:3). After offering the bull as a sin offering for his own sins, the high priest must come to the door of the tent of meeting with two goats: one to be offered in sacrifice to the Lord, the other to be sent forth "into the wilderness to Azazel" (16:10) bearing the sins of the people: "Aaron shall lay both his hands upon the head of the live goat, and confess over him all the iniquities of the people of Israel, and all their transgressions, all their sins; and he shall put them upon the head of the goat, and send him away into the wilderness by the hand of a man who is in readiness. The goat shall bear all their iniquities upon him to a solitary land" (16:21–22). This priestly expiation is joined to the people's penitence so as to cleanse the people from sin.

The seventh month provides the context for the solemn return of the people of Israel, who must become the holy people, to the land that is intended to be holy as the locus of divine indwelling through the people's covenantal worship in and through the temple. Ezra 1–2 describes the journey toward the land and the remnant of God's people who are able to make this journey. Ezra 3 then places the return to the land in the context of the original "return"—the exodus—with its hopes for the establishment of a holy people who dwell with God in the land by holy worship.

The New Exodus and the Peoples of the Land

When the seventh month came, and the sons of Israel were in the towns, the people gathered as one man to Jerusalem. Recalling the preexilic leadership of Israel, *Zerubbabel* (a member of the house of David although not king) and the priest *Jeshua the son of Jozadak* take charge. Following the commands of the Torah, *they built the altar of the God of Israel . . . and they kept the feast of booths, as it is written,* with the sacrificial offerings. Because it truly is a new exodus—even if in reverse, due to the sins that brought upon their fathers the covenantal curse—their first celebration in the land is the feast of booths, *and after that the continual burnt offerings, the offerings at the new moon and all the appointed feasts of the Lord, and the offerings of every one.* Bede finds a mystical meaning in their prompt construction of a temporary altar: "We too perform this today in the Church in a spiritual manner when above all we place faith in our Lord's incarnation and passion in our heart and hand this faith over to our hearers that it may be received before anything else and rooted in their inmost heart" (2006, 42). Our first gift must be what is due to God.

The returned exiles find their position in the land, however, to be perilous: not so much geopolitically, although this too will soon pose difficulties for the return, but religiously. *They set the altar in its place, for fear was upon them because of the peoples of the lands.* Some historians, on the basis of Jer. 41:5, think that in order to build this altar, the returned exiles had to tear down one that had been in place since the destruction of the temple and thereby incurred the anger of the local people (Fensham 1982, 59). The returned exiles appear to be already facing conflict over true worship.

The peoples of the lands—most significantly the Samaritans, whom we will discuss further on—worshiped other gods along with the God of Israel. But the worship of various gods could not be accommodated into Israel's worship of the Lord, since in justice only the Lord, the Creator, should receive worship. Preserving and nourishing the seed of this truth about God had been precisely the point in separating Israel for holiness. The first commandments at Sinai state: "I am the LORD your God, who brought you out of the land of Egypt, out of the house of bondage. You shall have no other gods before me. You shall not make for yourself a graven image, or any likeness of anything that is in heaven above, or that is in the earth beneath, or that is in the water under the earth; you shall not bow down to them or serve them, for I the LORD your God am a jealous God" (Exod. 20:1–5).

God or Idols?

There can be no unity between the returned exiles and the *peoples of the lands* on the matter of true worship. Joshua teaches the people of Israel upon their first entrance into the holy land: "Now therefore fear the LORD, and serve him in sincerity and in faithfulness; put away the gods which your fathers served beyond the River, and in Egypt, and serve the LORD" (Josh. 24:14). Joshua is aware that some of the people of Israel will not remain faithful, but will mingle worship of Israel's God with worship of other gods. Thus Joshua calls the people of Israel to make a choice: "And if you be unwilling to serve the LORD, choose this day whom you will serve, whether the gods your fathers served in the region beyond the River, or the gods of the Amorites in whose land you dwell; but as for me and my house, we will serve the LORD" (24:15). Without meaning to be unfaithful to their oath, the people swear that they, too, will serve only the Lord, even though Joshua warns them that "if you forsake the LORD and serve foreign gods, then he will turn and do you harm, and consume you, after having done you good" (24:20). God's holiness is connected to his jealousy, because a people can know him only by becoming holy; when people fall into idolatry, they cannot know the Lord.

Admittedly, from the time of Joshua through all the kings and right up to the day of Babylonian exile, many members of the people of Israel worshiped a variety of gods and did so even after King Josiah tried to centralize and renew the worship of the Lord. Egypt was a place of high culture, as was Babylon; and in these centers of culture, many gods were worshiped. Indeed, the most cultured king of Israel, Solomon, whose wisdom was considered to excel "all the kings of the earth" (1 Kgs. 10:23), fell enthusiastically into idolatry, and his idolatry was mixed up with his intermarriages with the daughters of leading foreign potentates: "Now King Solomon loved many foreign women: the daughter of Pharaoh, and Moabite, Ammonite, Edomite, Sidonian, and Hittite women, from the nations concerning which the LORD had said to the people of Israel, 'You shall not enter into marriage with them, neither shall they with you, for surely they will turn away your heart after their gods'" (11:1–2). No one ever had so many unfortunate marriages as King Solomon, whose wisdom in this regard was mere worldly wisdom, seeking political alliances: "He had seven hundred wives, princesses, and three hundred concubines; and his wives turned away his heart. For when Solomon was old his wives turned away his heart after other gods; and his heart was not wholly true to the LORD his God, as was the heart of David his father" (11:3–4). This regarding the builder of the temple!

The terrible extent of Solomon's idolatry, linked to his intermarriages with the daughters of the neighboring peoples, shows how the wise become fools by seeking to please the world rather than God: "For Solomon went after Ashtoreth the goddess of the Sidonians, and after Milcom the abomination of the Ammonites. . . . Then Solomon built a high place for Chemosh the abomination of Moab, and for Molech the abomination of the Ammonites, on the mountain east of Jerusalem. And so he did for all his foreign wives, who burned incense and sacrificed to their gods" (1 Kgs. 11:5, 7–8). What Paul says of the Gentiles—and indeed, to various degrees, of all human beings—applies to Solomon: "So they are without excuse; for although they knew God they did not honor him as God or give thanks to him, but they became futile in their thinking and their senseless minds were darkened. Claiming to be wise, they became fools, and exchanged the glory of the immortal God for images resembling mortal man or birds or animals or reptiles" (Rom. 1:20–23). To the extent that such explicit idolatry, prevalent in Solomon's Temple, no longer plagues the temple in Jesus's day, one sees the fruits of the labors depicted in the book of Ezra.

We cannot proceed without again asking: Who is this immortal God? He is identifiable through his covenantal relationships. Moses, in his first encounter with the Lord, hears him say that "I am the God of your father, the God of Abraham, the God of Isaac, and the God of Jacob" (Exod. 3:6). He is not however a god trapped in time or space; he creates and governs time and space. Thus he also names himself to Moses as the one who simply is, the one who can name himself (as no creature can) simply "I AM" (3:14). It is as "I AM" that God wishes to be first named to the Israelites in Egyptian slavery. His name is not a mere appellation, but indicates his very nature: "Then Moses said to God, 'If I come to the people of Israel and say to them, "The God of your fathers has sent me to you," and they ask me, "What is his name?" what shall I say to them?' God said to Moses, 'I AM WHO I AM.' And he said, 'Say this to the people of Israel, "I AM has sent me to you"'" (3:13–14). This name "I AM" is the great medicine for idolatry, since mere creatures exist only contingently and fallibly.

"I AM" is YHWH, "the God of your fathers, the God of Abraham, the God of Isaac, and the God of Jacob" (3:15), a covenantal name that God, as Savior, will possess forever. This Lord is also Creator: "In the beginning God created the heavens and the earth" (Gen. 1:1). In his transcendent glory, he is "perfect" (Matt. 5:48) and "good" (Mark 10:18). "God is light and in him is no darkness at all" (1 John 1:5). "God is love" (4:16).

The Foundations of the New Temple

If King Solomon himself could go astray from this God due to the influence of living among worshipers of gods, then no wonder that, as Ezra says with regard to the returning Israelites, *fear was upon them because of the peoples of the lands.* This fear is primarily that the returning Israelites will lapse from the Torah's precepts for true worship. The book of Ezra assures us that this does not happen, at least at the beginning. Even so, *the foundation of the temple of the LORD was not yet laid.* The main problem seems to be lack of money, which is no surprise given the relative poverty and small number of those who returned. But the book of Ezra reports (without comment) that only "some of the heads of families . . . made freewill offerings for the house of God, to erect it on its site" (Ezra 2:68). One wonders whether some of the returned exiles already do not recognize their fundamental mission as the people of God.

The lack of money is eventually overcome, however. The returned exiles use *the grant which they had from Cyrus king of Persia* to pay for *the masons and the carpenters, and food, drink, and oil to the Sidonians and the Tyrians to bring cedar trees from Lebanon to the sea, to Joppa.* The material and much of the labor for Solomon's Temple likewise came from Tyre and Lebanon: "And Hiram [king of Tyre] sent to Solomon, saying, 'I have heard the message which you have sent me; I am ready to do all you desire in the matter of cedar and cypress timber. My servants shall bring it down to the sea from Lebanon'" (1 Kgs. 5:8–9; for Sidon and Tyre see 1 Chr. 22:4). It is no surprise that the returning Israelites seek to build a temple that mirrors Solomon's Temple; and yet Solomon's Temple will be impossible to duplicate.

In the second year of their coming to the house of God at Jerusalem, in the second month, the leaders begin the actual work of rebuilding the temple. Although the book of Ezra names *Zerubbabel the son of Shealtiel and Jeshua the son of Jozadak* as the leaders responsible for the rebuilding, other indications suggest that these original foundations were laid in the second year, that is, 538 BC, by Sheshbazzar (cf. Ezra 5:16); and Hag. 2:15–18 confuses the matter still more by implying a later date (for further discussion see Fensham 1982, 61–63, 85). However this may be, the Levites, among the twelve tribes of Israel, had been set aside for God's work: "The LORD said to Moses, 'Take the Levites instead of all the first-born among the people of Israel, and the cattle of the Levites instead of their cattle; and the Levites shall be mine: I am the LORD'" (Num. 3:44–45). And so, in obedience, the returned exiles *appointed the Levites, from twenty years old and upward, to have the oversight of the work of the house of the LORD.*

Having *laid the foundation of the temple of the LORD,* they rejoice solemnly with psalms and shouts of praise: *The priests in their vestments came forward with trumpets, and the Levites, the sons of Asaph, with cymbals, to praise the LORD, according to the directions of David king of Israel; and they sang responsively, praising and giving thanks to the LORD, "For he is good, for his steadfast love endures for ever toward Israel."* By these actions, the returned exiles express their awareness that the laying of the foundations for the new temple renews the hope of a universal blessing coming through the particular people and land promised to Abraham, a people and land separated by God to manifest in holiness his indwelling.

Moses teaches the people of Israel: "For you are a people holy to the LORD your God; the LORD your God has chosen you to be a people for his own possession, out of all the peoples that are on the face of the earth" (Deut. 7:6). Why Israel? Moses answers that God's choice was entirely free: "It was not because you were more in number than any other people that the LORD set his love upon you and chose you, for you were the fewest of all peoples; but it is because the LORD loves you, and is keeping the oath which he swore to your fathers, that the LORD has brought you out with a mighty hand, and redeemed you from the house of bondage" (7:7–8). "For when I am weak, then I am strong" (2 Cor. 12:10). "What then shall we say to this? If God is for us, who is against us? He who did not spare his own Son but gave him up for us all, will he not also give us all things with him? Who shall bring any charge against God's elect?" (Rom. 8:31–33).

This weakness and smallness of Israel—"the fewest of all peoples"—now, after the exile, is true more than ever; indeed the noise of the trumpets, cymbals, singing, and the *great shout, when they praised the LORD, because the foundation of the house of the LORD was laid,* are here mixed with the sound of weeping. We are very far indeed from the original triumphant exodus, when after the destruction of the Egyptian army "Miriam, the prophetess, the sister of Aaron, took a timbrel in her hand; and all the women went out after her with timbrels and dancing" (Exod. 15:20). During the dedication of Solomon's Temple, "a cloud filled the house of the LORD, so that the priests could not stand to minister because of the cloud; for the glory of the LORD filled the house of the LORD" (1 Kgs. 8:10–11). Rather ominously, this cloud of glory does not return.

The weeping during the laying of the new temple's foundations does not indicate rebellion against the mission of the returned exiles, unlike when "the whole congregation of the people of Israel murmured against Moses and Aaron in the wilderness" (Exod. 16:2). Rather, because of the temple foundation's much reduced status due to the covenantal curse, *many of the priests and Levites and heads of fathers' houses, old men who had seen the first house [Solomon's Temple], wept with a loud voice when they saw the foundation of this house being laid.* Bede gives a spiritual sense: "Those who by repenting have risen up from the death of the soul also exult in their own salvation, and they weep that they have at any time lost the life of the soul by sinning" (2006, 67). Having sinned, the returned exiles weep bitter tears, and yet they also rejoice in God's mercy. Thus the joy of the people predominates: *Many shouted aloud for joy; so that the people could not distinguish the sound of the joyful shout from the sound of the people's weeping, for the people shouted with a great shout, and the sound was heard afar.* "Our holy and beautiful house, where our fathers praised thee, has been burned by fire, and all our pleasant places have become ruins. Wilt thou restrain thyself at these things, LORD? Wilt thou keep silent, and afflict us sorely?" (Isa. 64:11–12).

The Lord is no longer restraining himself. It must have seemed that the day of restoration had arrived or would soon arrive. Recall the bitterness of the psalmist: "But now thou hast cast off and rejected, thou art full of wrath against thy anointed. Thou hast renounced the covenant with thy servant; thou hast defiled his crown in the dust. Thou has breached all his walls; thou hast laid his strongholds in ruins" (Ps. 89:38–40). For the psalmist in his agony, it seemed that Israel, the holy land, was no more now that the temple and Davidic king were gone: "Thou hast removed the scepter from his hand, and cast his throne to the ground. Thou hast cut short the days of his youth; thou hast covered him with shame. How long, O LORD? Wilt thou hide thyself for ever? How long will thy wrath burn like fire?" (89:44–46). Could it be that this agony is coming to an end, now that the exiles have returned to the temple mount and built up the foundations anew? "How often would I have gathered your children together as a hen gathers her brood under her wings, and you would not!" (Matt. 23:37).

EZRA 4

Obstacles to Rebuilding the Temple

The Peoples of the Land: The History of the Samaritans

Ezra 4 recounts the threat to the rebuilding project posed *by the adversaries of Judah and Benjamin*. It is from Abraham's seed that the blessing to all nations will come, as God promised Abraham after he showed trust in God to the point of being willing to sacrifice Isaac, the son on whom the promise rested. By not counting his son as gain for himself, but instead by recognizing that his son is God's gift, Abraham makes manifest his profound faith, his stance of receptivity toward the Lord. The Lord tells him: "By myself I have sworn, says the LORD, because you have done this, and have not withheld your son, your only son, I will indeed bless you, and I will multiply your descendants as the stars of heaven and as the sand which is on the seashore" (Gen. 22:16–17). The Lord again promises that through Abraham blessing will come not only to Abraham's descendants, but to all nations: "And your descendants shall possess the gate of their enemies, and by your descendants shall all the nations of the earth bless themselves, because you have obeyed my voice" (22:17–18). But who and where are Abraham's descendents?

This question of who constitutes the true Israel becomes paramount when the adversaries of Judah and Benjamin heard about the efforts to build a new temple. These adversaries claim to be friends: *Let us build with you; for we worship your God as you do, and we have been sacrificing to him ever since the days of Esarhaddon king of Assyria who brought us here.*[1]

1. Some historians doubt the account of the origin of these adversaries as presented in Ezra 4 and 2 Kgs. 17; see Davies 1999, 17–18.

The reference to the king of Assyria locates the adversaries of Judah and Benjamin within the covenantal history. Under the arrogant and foolish King Rehoboam, son of Solomon, the twelve tribes of Israel—united under Saul, David, and Solomon—were divided into north and south: Israel and Judah. The threat of division had already plagued King David, who ruled for seven years over only the southern tribes before finally defeating the family of Saul in a civil war and thereby reuniting the twelve tribes (2 Sam. 5:3–5). The division in Rehoboam's time occurred through a dispute over taxes and proved intractable due partly to the strong leadership of Jeroboam, now king over Israel (the north), with Rehoboam king of Judah (the south). At the root of the split was Solomon's idolatry (1 Kgs. 11:9–14), which poisoned the unity of the land.

The split had effects far more serious than the geopolitical ones. One of the first acts of Jeroboam as king of the north was aimed at destroying the unity of worship that the Lord had ordained to strengthen Israel's separation from the idolatry of the surrounding peoples. In Deuteronomy, Moses bestows his blessing upon this centralization or unification of Israel's worship. He commands that the people of Israel, when they are established in the holy land, take their firstfruits "to the place which the LORD your God will choose, to make his name to dwell there. And you shall go to the priest who is in office at that time, and say to him, 'I declare this day to the LORD your God that I have come into the land which the LORD swore to our fathers to give us'" (Deut. 26:2–3). The place that the Lord chooses to "make his name to dwell" is Jerusalem—and specifically Solomon's Temple (1 Kgs. 8:29). Jeroboam, then, consciously rebels not only against Rehoboam, but also against the name of the Lord: "And Jeroboam said in his heart, 'Now the kingdom will turn back to the house of David; if this people go up to offer sacrifices in the house of the LORD at Jerusalem, then the heart of this people will turn again to their lord, to Rehoboam king of Judah, and they will kill me and return to Rehoboam king of Judah'" (12:26–27). Jeroboam's shrewd solution is to make two golden calves for his people to worship: "And he said to the people, 'You have gone up to Jerusalem long enough. Behold your gods, O Israel, who brought you up out of the land of Egypt.' And he set one in Bethel, and the other he put in Dan" (12:28–29). Bethel and Dan were the southern and northern limits of his new kingdom, making it easy for his entire people to commit idolatry, which they proceeded to do over the course of two centuries.

The book of Ezra assumes that nothing in human history escapes the governance of God, and Jeroboam's rebellion is a case in point. Already during the reign of King Solomon, the prophet Ahijah met Jeroboam and, as a symbolic depiction of what was to come, tore his own clothes into twelve pieces, giving ten to Jeroboam. Ahijah prophesied to Jeroboam: "For thus says the LORD, the God of Israel, 'Behold, I am about to tear the kingdom from the hand of Solomon . . . because he has forsaken me, and worshiped Ashtoreth the goddess of the Sidonians, Chemosh the god of Moab, and Milcom the god of the Ammonites'" (11:31, 33). (The Lord goes on to say through Ahijah that the kingdom will be divided in the time of Solomon's son.) "Are not two sparrows sold for a penny? And not one of them will fall to the ground without your Father's will. But even the hairs of your head are all numbered" (Matt. 10:29–30).

Two consequences result from the northern kingdom's rebellion and corresponding fall into idolatry. On the one hand, great prophets are raised up to fight for the Lord. During the time of King Ahab, Elijah single-handedly defeats at Mount Carmel, by the power of God, "the four hundred and fifty prophets of Baal and the four hundred prophets of Asherah, who eat at Jezebel's table" (1 Kgs. 18:19), and Elisha raises the dead son of the Shunammite woman. On the other hand, two centuries after Jeroboam, God allows the Assyrian Empire to conquer the northern kingdom.

This has a profound effect on the situation depicted in the book of Ezra. Many Israelites of the northern tribes went into exile in Assyria, from which they never truly returned, while "the king of Assyria brought people from Babylon, Cuthah, Avva, Hamath, and Sepharvaim, and placed them in the cities of Samaria instead of the people of Israel" (2 Kgs. 17:24). At first these foreigners did not worship the God of Israel, but when lions (whose presence is ascribed to the Lord) killed some of the newcomers, "the king of Assyria was told, 'The nations which you have carried away and placed in the cities of Samaria do not know the law of the god of the land; therefore he has sent lions among them'" (17:26). In response the Assyrian ruler sent back to the northern kingdom one of the priests of the Lord, but this action had little effect: the people simply "feared the LORD but also served their own gods, after the manner of the nations from among whom they had been carried away" (17:33), thus treating the God of Israel as merely another god.

The adversaries of Judah and Benjamin who meet the returned exiles, therefore, have already been inhabitants for at least two hundred years of the northern part of what was originally the promised land given by God to the twelve tribes of Israel. In a certain sense they do worship the Lord, but they worship him as a god among gods. For this reason, the leaders of the returned exiles reject their petition to assist in the rebuilding of the temple, whose significance for "all the nations of the earth" depends upon the Abrahamic particularity—linear descent from Abraham and inclusion among those who received the Mosaic and Davidic covenants—of the renewed people of Israel: *You have nothing to do with us in building a house to our God; but we alone will build to the LORD, the God of Israel, as King Cyrus the king of Persia has commanded us.* The particularity of salvation does not undermine its ability to be offered to all. On the contrary, the more particular, the more universal. "And the Word became flesh and dwelt among us, full of grace and truth" (John 1:14).

The Lord Will Build It

In order to understand the remainder of Ezra 4, one might recall the foolishness of King David, who, having built himself a cedar palace, decides that it is time to build a temple for the Lord, since "the ark of God dwells in a tent" (2 Sam. 7:2). David's ambition suggests that David thinks that he provides for the living God rather than vice versa. For this mistaken perspective, David is thoroughly chastised by the Lord through the prophet Nathan: "Go and tell my servant David, 'Thus says the LORD: Would you build me a house to dwell in? I have not dwelt in a house since the day I brought up the people of Israel from Egypt to this day, but I have been moving about in a tent for my dwelling. In all places where I have moved with all the people of Israel, did I speak a word with any of the judges of Israel, whom I commanded to shepherd my people Israel, saying, 'Why have you not built me a house of cedar?'" (7:5–7).

The Lord issued no such command to the judges, who ruled the twelve tribes for two hundred years, but David might well have wondered why the Lord failed to do so. By the end of the period of the judges—such a woeful time—"every man did what was right in his own eyes" (Judg. 21:25). This recipe for chaos was embodied by such dreadful acts as the rape and murder of a Levite's concubine while he and she were guests at a home in Gibeah in the tribe of Benjamin (which led to war among the tribes). When the last judge of the twelve tribes, Samuel, was a boy in the house of the priest Eli, ministering before the ark of the Lord, "the word of the LORD was rare in those days; there was no frequent vision" (1 Sam. 3:1). When "the word of the LORD" is not heard, all Israel suffers: it is not Israel who provides for the Lord, but the Lord who provides for Israel.

David is right, therefore, that the temple should be built, but the builder must be God himself: "Unless the LORD builds the house, those who build it labor in vain" (Ps. 127:1). Similarly, the returned exiles rightly seek to rebuild, but these efforts bear fruit only slowly. Even though the rebuilders of the temple are assisting in the accomplishment of *the word of the LORD by the mouth of Jeremiah*, God permits them to undergo adversity. Immediately after the rebuilders boldly proclaim that *we alone will build to the LORD*, they learn that the success of the labor will not be due to their own strength. *Then the people of the land discouraged the people of Judah, and made them afraid to build, and hired counselors against them to frustrate their purpose, all the days of Cyrus king of Persia, even until the reign of Darius king of Persia*. These counselors make the returned exiles *afraid to build*. Work stops on the new temple after the foundation had been laid. *Then the work on the house of God which is in Jerusalem stopped; and it ceased until the second year of the reign of Darius king of Persia*, that is, until 520 BC.

The Weakness of Israel

It seems incredible that the same returned exiles who had "shouted with a great shout, when they praised the LORD, because the foundation of the house of the LORD was laid" (Ezra 3:11), discontinue work on the temple for fifteen years. How could fear stop such holy zeal? We have already observed evidence of a certain lack of fervor, namely, when only "some of the heads of families, when they came to the house of the LORD which is in Jerusalem, made freewill offerings for the house of God, to erect it on its site" (2:68).

In fact, the experience of the returned exiles conforms to the pattern of all the covenant renewals of Israel, due to the sinfulness and weakness of the human partners in the covenants. Their actions strive toward a fulfillment that is as yet beyond them because they are not yet holy people: they await the accomplishment (in Christ Jesus) of *the word of the LORD by the mouth of Jeremiah*, that "I [the LORD] will put my law within them, and I will write it upon their hearts; and I will be their God, and they shall be my people" (Jer. 31:33).

We find the pattern of weakness already in Abraham. Having received the covenantal promise of a son by his wife Sarah (Gen. 17), he jeopardized everything by fearfully pretending to King Abimelech of Gerar (where Abraham was sojourning) that Sarah was not his wife but his sister. It took God's intervention to avert Abimelech's sexual coupling with Sarah, which would have called into question whether the promised son was Abraham's or Abimelech's: "God came to Abimelech in a dream by night, and said to him, 'Behold, you are a dead man, because of the woman whom you have taken; for she is a man's wife.' Now Abimelech had not approached her. . . . Then God said to him in the dream, 'Yes, I know that you have done this in the integrity of your heart, and it was I who kept you from sinning against me; therefore I did not let you touch her'" (20:3–4, 6).

Likewise, even Moses—having led Israel out of Egypt, given them the law, and found such favor that "the LORD used to speak to Moses face to face, as a man speaks to his friend" (Exod. 33:11)—nonetheless could not enter the promised land but could only look upon it from Mount Nebo (Deut. 34), because Moses "broke faith with me [the LORD] in the midst of the people of Israel at the waters of Meribath-kadesh, in the wilderness of Zin; because you [Moses] did not revere me as holy in the midst of the people of Israel" (32:51) but instead in a fit of pride took credit for God's work (cf. Num. 20:10–12).

Again, almost immediately after God proclaimed his covenant with David, David committed adultery with Bathsheba, had her husband Uriah the Hittite killed, and stirred up a nest of incest, revenge, attempted parricide, and civil war among his own children—so that the temple had to wait until Solomon's time.

In this context, the returned exiles' failure to continue to act upon their initial impulse makes clear that, like those who have gone before them, they too await from God's Messiah the fulfillment of the covenantal promises, so that they might be holy and dwell in marital intimacy with the Lord. They are not yet what they should be.

Persecuting the Returned Exiles

The book of Ezra stresses that the persecution that temporarily stopped construction is by no means a mere trifle; its impact grows in the next century. Ezra cites some letters from provincial officials instigating such persecution. These letters were written in the fifth century BC, whereas otherwise the book of Ezra treats the sixth century BC. Why does Ezra include these letters here?

Three letters are described. First, *in the reign of Ahasuerus* (485–465 BC), *in the beginning of his reign, they [the people of the land] wrote an accusation against the inhabitants of Judah and Jerusalem.* Second, *in the days of Artaxerxes* (464–424 BC), *Bishlam and Mithredath and Tabeel and the rest of their associates wrote to Artaxerxes king of Persia.*[2] Third, the peoples of the land sent another letter to Artaxerxes, from *Rehum the commander, Shimshai the scribe, and the rest of their*

2. Blenkinsopp comments: "In the long section dealing with opposition which begins here it is particularly important to grasp the logic of the narrative. After the resumptive 4:24, 5:1–2 continues 4:1–5 and takes us down to the second year of Darius (520). The intervening passage 4:6–23, dealing with opposition under Ahasuerus/Xerxes (485–465) and Artaxerxes (464–424), is obviously out of chronological order. This is not unusual in ancient historiography and neither calls for a theory of interpolation nor requires us to conclude that the author was ignorant about the correct order of the early Achaemenids. Having just dealt with opposition under Cyrus, he simply wished to carry this theme through the reigns of Darius (4:5), Xerxes (4:6), and Artaxerxes (4:7–23)—in the correct chronological order—omitting Cambyses, for whose reign he probably had no comparable information. He then doubled back to continue the account of the rebuilding under Darius, including Tattenai's intervention, the imperial edict reaffirming the authorization and, finally, the completion and dedication of the temple in the sixth year of his reign" (Blenkinsopp 1988, 105–6). By contrast Davies suggests that Ezra 4:6–7 are confused: "The identity of the writers is unclear. Their names are detailed, but confused. Perhaps an irregularity in the transmission of the text has resulted in the combination of two letters under two Persian kings signed by people whose names vary. Did they write 'in the beginning of the reign of Ahasuerus' (v. 6) or 'in the days of Artaxerxes' (v. 7)? Are Bishlam, Mithredath, Tabeel, and 'the rest of the associates' (v. 7) the same group as in v. 9—Rehum the chancellor, Shimshai the scribe, and the rest of their associates listed by rank and nationality including all the nations deported by the Assyrians?" (1999, 19–20). Davies agrees with Halpern 1990, 110, that the ambiguity may be intentional. See also Davies's postmodern reflections on Ezra 4–6: "History is not computable or even sequential here. It is prismatic. An event can be recounted in different forms that provide both continuity and plasticity. New realities are brought into focus by shifting the optic on the past" (1999, 30). Blenkinsopp, I think, has the better of this argument. Like the Revised Standard Version, Fensham 1982, 71–72, holds that "Bishlam" is a proper noun, against other interpretations that take its meaning to be "in accord with" (Blenkinsopp 1988, 109) or "in the matter of Jerusalem."

associates, the judges, the governors, the officials, the Persians, the men of Erech, the Babylonians, the men of Susa, that is, the Elamites, and the rest of the nations.

The letter that Rehum and Shimshai send to Artaxerxes receives significant attention from Ezra. In addressing their letter, Rehum and Shimshai recall *the great and noble Osnappar,*[3] the king of the Assyrians who two centuries earlier bore responsibility for exiling the peoples of the land into the northern kingdom (displacing the ten tribes of Israelites). Rehum and Shimshai suggest that Artaxerxes should follow the example of Osnappar, rather than continuing to allow the returned exiles to establish a quasi-independent nation.

Their letter warns that *the Jews who came up from you to us have gone to Jerusalem. They are rebuilding that rebellious and wicked city; they are finishing the walls and repairing the foundations.*[4] In short, the returned exiles are becoming strong again. In the distant background is Hezekiah's defeat of the forces of the Assyrian Empire, due to the power of the Lord (cf. 2 Kgs. 19:5–7); even lowly Jehoiakim had tried to avoid paying taxes to Babylon. For this reason the letter warns that *if this city is rebuilt and the walls finished, they will not pay tribute, custom, or toll, and the royal revenue will be impaired.* Rehum and Shimshai present themselves as the king's loyal functionaries, seeking the king's interests: *Now because we eat the salt of the palace and it is not fitting for us to witness the king's dishonor, therefore we send and inform the king, in order that search may be made in the book of the records of your fathers. You will find in the book of the records and learn that this city is a rebellious city, hurtful to kings and provinces, and that sedition was stirred up in it from of old. That is why this city was laid waste.*

None of this could be denied by the returned exiles; indeed it is a mark of honor and a manifestation of the power of the Lord. As a counterweight to the image of weakness given earlier by the description of how *the people of the land*

---

3. "Osnappar" is Ashurbanipal, who as the last king of Assyria ruled 668–627 BC. See Fensham 1982, 73.

4. Blenkinsopp comments on this verse: "The wording of the opening sentence would more naturally refer to an aliyah during the reign of Artaxerxes I Long Hand (465–424) rather than to the return under Cyrus. In all probability, Ezra and his caravan arrived in Jerusalem in the seventh year of this reign (458) and Nehemiah thirteen years later (445). The allusion could not be to the latter, who received personal authorization from the king to rebuild the city" (1988, 113). If it does not refer to Ezra the Scribe, Blenkinsopp adds: "Another possibility is suggested by the report of Hanani to his brother Nehemiah in the twentieth year of the reign that the wall had been broken down and its gates burnt (Neh. 1:3). Since the natural assumption is that this had happened quite recently—it was news to Nehemiah—the action of the authorities in Samaria may have taken place shortly before Nehemiah's mission (in 446 . . .). In that case the correspondence could have been occasioned by the revolt of Megabyzus, satrap of Abar-nahara, some three years before Nehemiah's mission, which would also explain why the complaint was lodged by a provincial official without reference to the governor of the satrapy. That the king reversed his decision soon after at the request of Nehemiah does not rule out this possibility, especially since the revolt was of brief duration and Megabyzus won his way back into favor. Reversal is also contemplated in the king's reply (Ezra 4:21)" (1988, 113–14).

discouraged the people of Judah, and made them afraid to build, the book of Ezra rejoices in this image of preexilic Israel's power. Ezra describes Artaxerxes as almost afraid of the Israelites. In his reply to Rehum and Shimshai, Artaxerxes observes that *mighty kings have been over Jerusalem* and commands that *this city be not rebuilt, until a decree is made by me. And take care not to be slack in this matter; why should damage grow to the hurt of the king?*

By the mid-fifth century BC the Persian Empire was in gradual decline. Heavy taxes and a scarcity of gold imposed an increasing burden upon the subjugated peoples. Both the Greeks and the Egyptians were fighting the Persians. Megabyzus, the Persian general who put down the Egyptian rebellion, later took offense against his king and in 449 BC successfully rebelled against Artaxerxes (Fensham 1982, 15–16, 73). Artaxerxes takes seriously the possibility of a rebellion in Jerusalem. Upon receiving the king's answer, Rehum and Shimshai *went in haste to the Jews at Jerusalem and by force and power made them cease* the work of rebuilding the city.

Why does Ezra include these fifth-century letters in the midst of discussing the rebuilding of the temple in the late sixth century BC? He thereby recalls the power of the people of God despite their seeming weakness in the midst of persecution. Their power depends solely upon God, who has acted and will act again through his people.

The power-in-weakness of Israel is a theme present already in the person of Abraham, and one that extends through Jacob into slavery in Egypt and even to the person of Moses. Often as a rebuke, one finds it throughout the history of the judges and kings. In Jeremiah, the Lord explicitly addresses it: "Then I said, 'Ah, Lord God! Behold, I do not know how to speak, for I am only a youth.' But the Lord said to me, 'Do not say, "I am only a youth"; for to all to whom I send you you shall go, and whatever I command you you shall speak. Be not afraid of them, for I am with you to deliver you, says the Lord'" (Jer. 1:6–8). This power-in-weakness points forward to Christ Jesus, whose power is hidden in weakness: "Therefore I will divide him a portion with the great, and he shall divide the spoil with the strong; because he poured out his soul to death, and was numbered with the transgressors; yet he bore the sin of many, and made intercession for the transgressors" (Isa. 53:12).

Power in Weakness

The returned exiles no longer possess the divinely given power that they had under Moses and Joshua "to go in to take possession of the land which the Lord your God gives you to possess" (Josh. 1:11). Even under Moses and Joshua, however, the people of Israel participated in the working out of God's plan not as a powerful nation but as a weak people: "It was not because you were more in number than any other people that the Lord set his love upon you and chose you, for you were the fewest of all peoples; but it is because the LORD loves you, and is keeping the oath which he swore to your fathers, that the LORD has brought you out with a mighty hand, and redeemed you from the house of bondage" (Deut. 7:7–8). Moses says to Joshua: "You shall not fear them; for it is the LORD your God who fights for you" (3:22). Regarding the returned exiles, one could say with even more truth that they are "the fewest of all peoples," but they do not receive military power from the Lord.

Their weakness instead displays their dependence on the Lord: "Fear not, stand firm, and see the salvation of the LORD, which he will work for you today. . . . The LORD will fight for you, and you have only to be still" (Exod. 14:13–14). It will be in weakness that the power of Jeremiah's new covenant is brought about through the Messiah's holy embodiment of Israel's people and land; and in weakness, too, that Christ's followers will find their strength in the Lord: "And Agrippa said to Paul, 'In a short time you think to make me a Christian!' And Paul said, 'Whether short or long, I would to God that not only you but also all who hear me this day might become such as I am—except for these chains'" (Acts 26:28–29).

Only God can accomplish *the word of the LORD by the mouth of Jeremiah*. By working through the human striving that Ezra records, God raises up a Messiah out of the people of Israel worshiping at the temple in Jerusalem. The risen Lord says to his apostles: "'These are my words which I spoke to you, while I was still with you, that everything written about me in the law of Moses and the prophets and the psalms must be fulfilled.' Then he opened their minds to understand the scriptures" (Luke 24:44–45).

EZRA 5

The Prophets of God and the Completion of the Temple

After God, through King Cyrus, fulfilled Jeremiah's promise that the exiles would return from Babylon after seventy years, the returned exiles set about obeying Cyrus's command to rebuild the temple. The rebuilding of the temple, however, is hampered by fear and even apathy. Ezra 5 introduces the late-sixth-century prophets Haggai and Zechariah, who recalled the returned Israelites to their temple-building vocation. How did these two prophets conceive of the accomplishment of *the word of the LORD by the mouth of Jeremiah*?

Haggai and Zechariah: Kenosis and Glory

Haggai, prophesying in the second year of King Darius, who reigned 521–486 BC, warns the people that God will no longer tolerate their delay in rebuilding the temple: "Is it a time for yourselves to dwell in your paneled houses, while this house lies in ruins?" (Hag. 1:4). This barb should not be taken to mean that the returned exiles now lived in wealth; on the contrary, Haggai continues by offering (in the name of the Lord) increased wealth if only the people would first rebuild the temple, whose neglected state explains why "the heavens above you have withheld the dew, and the earth has withheld its produce" (1:10; cf. 2:18–19). In addition to the ongoing poverty, Haggai also addresses the reduced state of the new temple in contrast with Solomon's Temple. Lest the returned exiles give up in shame because the new temple is so inferior, Haggai promises in the name of the Lord, "I will shake all nations, so that the treasures of all nations shall come in, and I will fill this house with splendor, says the LORD of hosts. The silver is mine, and the gold is mine, says the LORD of hosts. The latter splendor of this house shall be greater than the former" (2:7–9). Lastly, the problem of the present lack of a Davidic king is dealt with by an allusion to future glory for Zerubbabel, who possesses the crucial Davidic lineage: "I am about to shake the heavens and the earth, and to overthrow the throne of kingdoms. . . . On that day, says the LORD of hosts, I will take you, O Zerubbabel my servant, the son of Shealtiel, says the LORD, and make you like a signet ring; for I have chosen you, says the LORD of hosts" (2:21–23).

Are Haggai's words merely propaganda aimed at renewing the people's stalled labors on the construction of the temple? Will the rebuilding of the temple assist in reversing the poverty of the returned exiles? Is "the latter splendor" of the temple in fact "greater than the former"? Is Zerubbabel actually chosen and made "like a signet ring" by God?

With regard to the temple, Bede offers a historical explanation of Haggai's prophecy: "That the few surviving captives were able to accomplish such a great undertaking even as their enemies were opposing them was a greater and more obvious miracle of divine power than that a very rich king who had no adversaries at all but rather the very powerful and wealthy king of Tyre as a collaborator, did this with most accomplished craftsmen, just as he desired" (Bede 2006, 66). But this comparison seems rather flat-footed. A better explanation consists in the renewed people and temple, along with Zerubbabel, pointing toward fulfillment in the kenotic suffering and glorious resurrection of Christ Jesus. This perspective enables one to affirm that Haggai's seemingly exaggerated promises come true. Christ Jesus enters (and embodies) the rebuilt temple, and so its splendor is greater than that of Solomon's Temple. Zerubbabel is "like a signet ring" because he is the ancestor of the Messiah (Luke 3:27).

How do Zechariah's prophecies differ from Haggai's? In their estimation of the situation, the two prophets are in agreement, but what Zechariah adds is important. Zechariah says with regard to the rebuilding of the temple in Jerusalem: "Thus says the LORD, I have returned to Jerusalem with compassion; my house shall be built in it" (Zech. 1:16). The new temple will be at least as good as the original one, since, the Lord promises: "I will return to Zion, and will dwell in the midst of Jerusalem, and Jerusalem shall be called the faithful city, and the mountain of the LORD of hosts, the holy mountain" (8:3). Zerubbabel will be given honor: "The hands of Zerubbabel have laid the foundation of this house; his hands shall also complete it" (4:9). The Lord also promises through Zechariah that due to the rebuilding of the temple "there shall be a sowing of peace; the vine shall yield its fruit, and the ground shall give its increase, and the heavens shall give their dew; and I will cause the remnant of this people to possess all these things. And as you have been a byword of cursing among the nations, O house of Judah and house of Israel, so will I save you and you shall be a blessing" (8:12–13). The people's poverty, in other words, will abate. More importantly, through the renewed people and land (centered upon its temple), God will complete his promise to Abraham to make this people a blessing to all nations.

Thus Zechariah's prophecies contain the same three elements that comprise the prophecies of Haggai: removal of poverty, the new temple as a place of honor rather than disgrace in comparison with Solomon's, and the uplifting of Zerubbabel. But Zechariah, addressing the situation in which Israel finds itself with respect to the peoples of the land, goes further by recalling the promise that Abraham's seed will bring blessing to all nations: "Sing and rejoice, O daughter of Zion; for lo, I come and I will dwell in the midst of you, says the LORD. And many nations shall join themselves to the LORD in that day, and shall be my people" (2:10–11). Similarly, the Lord promises through Zechariah that "I will remove the guilt of this land in a single day" (3:9), just as we saw in Jeremiah that "I [the LORD] will forgive their iniquity, and I will remember their sin no more" (Jer. 31:34). Lastly, Zechariah's image of "my servant the Branch" (Zech. 3:8) as accomplishing this renewal of the land in holiness opens up the expectation of a Messiah: "There shall come forth a shoot from the stump of Jesse, and a branch shall grow out of his roots. And the Spirit of the LORD shall rest upon him. . . . In that day the root of Jesse shall stand as an ensign to the peoples; him shall the nations seek, and his dwellings shall be glorious" (Isa. 11:1–2, 10). "You are the Christ" (Mark 8:29).

Describing one of his prophetic visions, Zechariah says: "And a second time I said to him [the angel], 'What are these two branches of the olive trees, which are beside the two golden pipes from which the oil is poured out?' He said to me, 'Do you not know what these are?' I said, 'No, my lord.' Then he said, 'These are the two anointed who stand by the Lord of the whole earth'" (Zech. 4:12–14). Although Zechariah refers to "the two anointed," the "Branch" seems to be the priest Jeshua; at least Jeshua symbolically serves to represent the royal and priestly Branch. The Lord commands through Zechariah: "Take from them silver and gold, and make a crown, and set it upon the head of Joshua, the son of Jehozadak, the high priest; and say to him, 'Thus says the LORD of hosts, "Behold, the man whose name is the Branch: for he shall grow up in his place, and he shall build the temple of the LORD"'" (6:11–12). The Lord says that this one man, the Branch who is both high priest and king, shall be the temple-builder. He will be served by priests: "And there shall be a priest by his throne, and peaceful understanding shall be between them both" (6:13).

Lest this appear to be a rejection of Haggai's prophetic elevation of Zerubbabel, earlier Zechariah prophesies: "What are you, O great mountain? Before Zerubbabel you shall become a plain; and he shall bring forward the top stone amid shouts of 'Grace, grace to it!'" (4:7). However one interprets the roles of Zerubbabel and Jeshua, it is clear that Zechariah has added to the elements of Haggai's prophecy three further elements: the fulfillment of the promise to Abraham of a blessing to all nations through Israel, the forgiveness of "the guilt of this land" in a single day, and the "Branch" who will accomplish this work. For Zechariah, in other words, the rebuilding of the temple has a significance that points forward, as it does in Jeremiah, to a radical fulfillment and transformation.

The last part of the book of Zechariah—which historians generally suppose was written by a later prophet—is intelligible in this light. In Zech. 9–14 the prophet proclaims that "a day of the LORD is coming" (14:1) when "there shall be a fountain opened for the house of David and the inhabitants of Jerusalem to cleanse them from sin and uncleanness" (13:1). On this day of victory, which will be an unending "continuous day" (14:7), the Lord's "feet shall stand on the Mount of Olives" (14:4), and "the LORD will become king over all the earth; on that day the LORD will be one and his name one" (14:9). Then all the nations, not only Israel, will stream to Jerusalem to participate in the "feast of booths," the celebration of the final exodus won by the Lord's passover (14:16). This day of victory will also be a day of mourning and repentance for sin: "And I will pour out on the house of David and the inhabitants of Jerusalem a spirit of compassion and supplication, so that, when they look on him whom they have pierced, they shall mourn for him, as one mourns for an only child" (12:10–11). Before this day, the Lord will be rejected, according to the prophetic symbolism, for "thirty shekels of silver . . . cast . . . into the treasury in the house of the LORD" (11:13). Yet Israel is to rejoice, because "lo, your king comes to you; triumphant and victorious is he, humble and riding on an ass, on a colt the foal of an ass. . . . He shall command peace to the nations; his dominion shall be from sea to sea, and from the River to the ends of the earth" (9:9–10). On the day of victory, "the house of David shall be like God" and all Jerusalem "shall be like David" (12:8).

These then are *the prophets, Haggai and Zechariah the son of Iddo,* who *prophesied to the Jews who were in Judah and Jerusalem, in the name of the God of Israel who was over them,* and whose words strongly supported *Zerubbabel the son of Shealtiel and Jeshua the son of Jozadak*—member of the house of David and Aaronic priest, respectively—when Zerubbabel and Jeshua *arose and began to rebuild the house of God which is in Jerusalem* in the second year of Darius's reign, after a cessation of work of some years. The book of Ezra says of the returned exiles: *With them were the prophets of God, helping them.* These prophets of God, particularly Zechariah, saw the work of rebuilding the temple as belonging to the divinely ordained path leading ultimately to a radical consummation of the covenants.

"Jesus answered them, 'Destroy this temple, and in three days I will raise it up.' The Jews then said, 'It has taken forty-six years to build this temple, and will you raise it up in three days?' But he spoke of the temple of his body" (John 2:19–21).

From Prophecy to Political Action

The opposition by the peoples of the land to the rebuilding of the temple, an opposition that years earlier had made the people afraid to build, remains a problem, but this time the returned exiles deal directly with the Persian officials.

Bede explains: "The former letter was sent by the Samaritans, undoubtedly the enemies of the Jews, whereas this one was sent by the governor of the region beyond the river (i.e., lower Syria and Phoenicia) and by his companions, who harboured no personal hatred against the Jews but merely tried to know and carry out the will of the king" (2006, 84). *Tattenai the governor of the province Beyond the River [also called Trans-Euphrates] and Shethar-bozenai and their associates came to them and spoke to them thus, "Who gave you a decree to build this house and to finish this structure?"*[1] This time the returned exiles withstand the bureaucratic pressure and refuse to stop until King Darius has judged the case.

In a letter to Darius, Tattenai and Shethar-bozenai describe the strength of the new temple. Tattenai and Shethar-bozenai also pass along the response that the returned exiles had given them. In defense of their rebuilding project, the returned exiles argue that Cyrus had approved the work under *Sheshbazzar*, who *came and laid the foundations of the house of God which is in Jerusalem; and from that time until now it has been in building, and it is not yet finished.* The returned exiles ask that the Persian archives be searched to prove their claim. Tattenai and Shethar-bozenai conclude: *Therefore, if it seem good to the king, let search be made in the royal archives there in Babylon, to see whether a decree was issued by Cyrus the king for the rebuilding of this house of God in Jerusalem. And let the king send us his pleasure in this matter.*

1. There is some historical confusion regarding Tattenai. Fensham notes that at this time Ushtani served as satrap or governor of the Trans-Euphrates province, although "later in the reign of Darius, Tattenai was appointed as satrap, according to a Babylonian document" (1982, 80). Davies draws attention to other possible ambiguities in Ezra 5–6: "Cyrus is quoted quite differently in ch. 6 than in ch. 1, and in Aramaic, not Hebrew. Ezra 5:11 and 6:3, 7 are explicit that the project is a reconstruction of the Temple on the old site. Ezra 1:1–4 does not mention the place. There is another possible contradiction: Ezra 5:14 calls Sheshbazzar the 'governor'; Ezra 1:8 names him the 'prince'" (1999, 31–32).

EZRA 6

The Temple and the Passover

Ezra 6 brings the first part of the book of Ezra to a glorious conclusion with the completion of the new temple and the celebration of the passover.

Discovering the good wishes that Cyrus had for the exiles from Judah, Darius assists in bringing these good wishes to fruition. After receiving the letter from Tattenai and Shethar-bozenai, Darius orders a search of the archives, first in *Babylonia* and then in *Ecbatana*.[1] When the search locates Cyrus's decree, with its command that the temple in Jerusalem must be rebuilt and *the cost be paid from the royal treasury*, Darius upholds this decree and adds that a portion of *the tribute of the province from Beyond the River* must go to pay for *the rebuilding of this house of God*. Furthermore, he rules that the province must pay the daily cost of providing *whatever is needed—young bulls, rams, or sheep for burnt offerings to the God of heaven, wheat, salt, wine, or oil, as the priests at Jerusalem require*. Darius does this because he wants to propitiate *the God of heaven*. Darius also includes a curse: *May the God who has caused his name to dwell there overthrow any king or people that shall put forth a hand to alter this, or to destroy this house of God which is in Jerusalem*.

Is it any wonder, as we read in Isaiah, that "the LORD, who made all things, . . . says of Cyrus, 'He is my shepherd, and he shall fulfil all my purpose'; saying of Jerusalem, 'She shall be built,' and of the temple, 'Your foundation shall be laid'" (Isa. 44:24, 28) and that the Lord calls Cyrus his "anointed" or "messiah" (45:1)? Ezra underscores as well the contribution of *the prophesying of Haggai the prophet and Zechariah the son of Iddo*, who were active around the same time as

---

1. Fensham comments: "According to Xenophon's *Cyropaedia* (viii.6.22), however, in the winter Cyrus lived in Babylon, in the spring in Susa, and in the summer in Ecbatana. It is thus probable that Darius started his search in the city of Babylon" (1982, 86).

Darius's decree.[2] The Lord's activity through his prophets brings to fruition his activity in the hearts of Cyrus and Darius, so that *the elders of the Jews built and prospered*. "The LORD, the LORD, a God merciful and gracious, slow to anger, and abounding in steadfast love and faithfulness" (Exod. 34:6)!

In 515 BC, *this house was finished on the third day of the month of Adar*, the twelfth month of Israel's year. *And the people of Israel, the priests and the Levites, and the rest of the returned exiles, celebrated the dedication of this house of God with joy*. Far from the "drying up" of salvation history, therefore, the book of Ezra records the preparations for the eschatological restoration of Israel. This is emphasized by Bede through a mystical interpretation of the temple's dedication in Adar: the temple "was begun at the beginning of the seventh month because it is with the grace of the Holy Spirit leading us that we begin every good thing we do and with it accompanying us that we complete it. But it was completed in the twelfth month in order to signify the perfection that is contained in this number" (2006, 94). Bede has in view Christ's body the church as the fulfillment of the temple, since twelve is "the number of the apostles, in whose faith and teaching the Church is completed" (2006, 95).

Even so, when Solomon dedicated the First Temple, he "offered as peace offerings to the LORD twenty-two thousand oxen and a hundred and twenty thousand sheep" (1 Kgs. 8:63). The reduced scale of the returned exiles is sorely apparent despite the triumph of rebuilding: *They offered at the dedication of this house of God one hundred bulls, two hundred rams, four hundred lambs, and as a sin offering for all Israel twelve he-goats, according to the number of the tribes of Israel*. Yet the reduced scale is still sufficient for Israel's sacrificial worship to function: an adequate number of *the priests in their divisions and the Levites in their courses* are present, so that *the service of God at Jerusalem* accords with the Torah's laws about the temple service: "And the surviving remnant of the house of Judah shall again take root downward, and bear fruit upward; for out of Jerusalem shall go forth a remnant, and out of Mount Zion a band of survivors. The zeal of the LORD will do this" (2 Kgs. 19:30–31). "Then I will gather the remnant of my flock out of all the countries where I have driven them, and I will bring them back to their fold" (Jer. 23:3).

The returned exiles keep the passover *on the fourteenth day of the first month*. Having purified themselves, the Levitical priests *killed the passover lamb for all the returned exiles, for their fellow priests, and for themselves*. Ezekiel receives an instruction in his prophetic vision of the rebuilt temple: "In the first month, on the fourteenth day of the month, you shall celebrate the feast of the passover, and for seven days unleavened bread shall be eaten" (Ezek. 45:21). This

---

2. Fensham holds that "the prophecies of Haggai written in the biblical book of Haggai were delivered not later than the beginning of 519 B.C. Those of Zechariah could not have been pronounced later than 518 B.C." (1982, 92).

glorious event now takes place, even if the eschatological temple that Ezekiel foresees is not yet present.

Against our temptation to take for granted the rebuilding of the temple and the celebration of passover at the rebuilt temple, note that without the Lord's words through the prophets Haggai and Zechariah, the rebuilding of the temple might never have happened. The people had abandoned the project for a time, but fear and apathy had not won the day. The formidable opposition of the peoples of the land had been overcome. Moses wrote prior to the entrance into the promised land: "You shall not be afraid of them [the nations occupying the land], but you shall remember what the Lord your God did to Pharaoh and to all Egypt, the great trials which your eyes saw, the signs, the wonders, the mighty hand, and the outstretched arm, by which the Lord your God brought you out" (Deut. 7:18–19). The returned exiles had been afraid, and yet the Lord their God had brought them out once again to the promised land.

In their first passover at the rebuilt temple, moreover, the returned exiles reenact and participate in their fathers' being saved by the sacrificial blood. This sacrificial blood is more powerful than all the military might on which the nations foolishly depend. Jeremiah prophesies in the name of the Lord: "Babylon must fall for the slain of Israel, as for Babylon have fallen the slain of all the earth" (Jer. 51:49). On the very site of the former temple, which was destroyed by the now-eclipsed military might of Babylon, the returned exiles rebuild the temple and celebrate the Lord's passover, recalling the Lord's promise that "when I see the blood, I will pass over you, and no plague shall fall upon you to destroy you" (Exod. 12:13): "We have heard with our ears, O God, our fathers have told us, what deeds thou didst perform in their days, in the days of old: . . . for not by their own sword did they win the land, nor did their own arm give them victory; but thy right hand, and thy arm, and the light of thy countenance; for thou didst delight in them" (Ps. 44:1, 3).

Even with the support of Darius and the encouragement of the prophets Haggai and Zechariah, however, the returned exiles remain terribly weak. But their weakness provides an opportunity for God to manifest his power. Compare the prophet Elijah's single-handed struggle against idolatry in the northern kingdom. Worn out and despairing of improvement in the northern kingdom (which indeed went into permanent exile a century later), Elijah "went a day's journey into the wilderness, and came and sat down under a broom tree; and he asked that he might die, saying, 'It is enough; now, O Lord, take away my life; for I am no better than my fathers'" (1 Kgs. 19:4). Instead of taking away his life, the Lord twice gave him food and drink, and Elijah "went in the strength of that food forty days and forty nights to Horeb the mount of God" (19:8). At Mount Horeb—also called Mount Sinai—where the Lord appeared to all Israel in "thunders and lightnings, and a thick cloud upon the mountain, and a very loud trumpet blast" (Exod. 19:16), the Lord manifests himself to Elijah in "a still small voice" (1 Kgs. 19:12).

Why a still small voice? The Lord thereby combats the world's notion of power. Adam and Eve accepted the serpent's contention that they could grasp autonomous power: "You will not die. For God knows that when you eat of it your eyes will be opened, and you will be like God" (Gen. 3:4–5). They imagined that to be god is to have arbitrary power, and they desired that power for themselves so as to be "like God." In so doing they hid themselves from true divine power, which is self-giving rather than self-aggrandizing: "And they heard the sound of the LORD God walking in the garden in the cool of the day, and the man and his wife hid themselves from the presence of the LORD God among the trees of the garden" (3:8). Rather than becoming like God, they separated themselves from the source of life and handed themselves over to the power of death.

How does God overcome this separation? *On the fourteenth day of the first month the returned exiles kept the passover. . . . So they killed the passover lamb for all the returned exiles, for their fellow priests, and for themselves.* "Behold the Lamb of God, who takes away the sins of the world!" (John 1:29).

The returned exiles' celebration of the passover—much reduced though it is and despite their lack of a Davidic king—underscores that the sacrificial weakness of Israel has again prevailed over the military power of the nations. In their weakness one can recognize the "still small voice" that later reveals itself as "the power of God for salvation to every one who has faith, to the Jew first and also to the Greek" (Rom. 1:16). Not only has the Lord's plan for his people not failed despite the consequences of their sins, but the Lord's power governs the king to whom Israel is subject: God *had turned the heart of the king of Assyria [Darius] to them, so that he aided them in the work of the house of God, the God of Israel.*[3] "The king's heart is a stream of water in the hand of the LORD; he turns it wherever he will" (Prov. 21:1).

In this celebration the passover lamb *was eaten by the people of Israel who had returned from exile, and also by every one who had joined them and separated himself from the pollutions of the peoples of the land to worship the LORD, the God of Israel.*[4] Regarding non-Israelites who wanted to partake of the passover meal in order to worship the Lord, Moses was instructed: "When a stranger shall sojourn with you and would keep the passover to the LORD, let all his males be circumcised, then he may come near and keep it; he shall be as a native of the land. But no uncircumcised person shall eat of it" (Exod. 12:48). Ezra specifies that everyone could keep the passover who had *separated himself from the pollutions of the peoples of the land*—idolatrous practices—because Israel is a people

---

3. Various explanations of this reference to Darius as "king of Assyria" have been given, ranging from a mistake made by the author (generally thought to be the Chronicler) to Darius also being king of Assyria since he was king of the Persian Empire. See Fensham 1982, 96–97.

4. Fensham observes that the identity of "every one who had joined them" is not known for certain: "They might have been Israelites of the former northern kingdom or Jews who were not exiled, or proselytes (cf. Exod. 12:44, 48). The last possibility seems best" (1982, 96).

separated from the surrounding nations so as to obey God's commandments of holiness. "You shall therefore keep all my statutes and all my ordinances, and do them; that the land where I am bringing you to dwell may not vomit you out. . . . I have said to you, 'You shall inherit their land, and I will give it to you to possess, a land flowing with milk and honey.' I am the LORD your God, who have separated you from the peoples" (Lev. 20:22, 24). Together with those *who had joined them*, therefore, the returned exiles *kept the feast of unleavened bread seven days with joy; for the LORD had made them joyful.* "For he remembered his holy promise, and Abraham his servant. So he led forth his people with joy, his chosen ones with singing" (Ps. 105:42–43).

Thus after long years of exile followed by the absence of a temple in Jerusalem, Moses's words once more apply to the people of God: "But when you go over the Jordan, and live in the land which the LORD your God gives you to inherit, and when he gives you rest from all your enemies round about, so that you live in safety, then to the place which the LORD your God will choose, to make his name dwell there, thither you shall bring all that I command you" (Deut. 12:10–11). When the people bring to the temple their tithes and offerings, Moses says: "You shall rejoice before the LORD your God" (12:12). The passover has been kept in the temple; the people again "live in the land which the LORD your God gives you to inherit." Their joy is no longer, as on the day the foundations were laid, tempered with weeping. "Rejoice in the LORD always; again I will say, Rejoice" (Phil. 4:4).

Even so, there will be weeping again soon, and for good reason. The fulfillment of *the word of the LORD by the mouth of Jeremiah* has not yet arrived.

PART II

EZRA 7–10: THE HOLY PEOPLE, UNITED BY THE TORAH

The rebuilding of the temple seems to bring to completion the struggle of the people of Israel to return to the land from Babylonian exile. In fact, however, for the land to be what it truly is, it requires not merely the temple but the indwelling of God. This indwelling is impossible unless the people are holy. By giving the people the Torah at Mount Sinai, God charted the pattern of human holiness. Ezra the Scribe's mission, as described in Ezra 7–10, is to renew this pattern of holiness in the lives of the people, although he is aware that such holiness cannot by itself accomplish the restoration of Israel. According to Jeremiah and the other prophets, a messianic Davidic king is needed, as is the forgiveness of sins and a radical transformation of heart. In order to prepare for what God will accomplish, Ezra the Scribe calls upon the people of Israel not only to worship in the temple but also to separate themselves strictly from the idolatrous practices of the nations and thus to become a holy people fit for such a land.

In Ezra 7–10 the "lamentation and bitter weeping" (Jer. 31:15) of "Rachel" for the children of Israel continues because of their lack of holiness, and yet Ezra also has in view God's promise: "Keep your voice from weeping, and your eyes from tears; for your work shall be rewarded, says the LORD, and they shall come back from the land of the enemy. There is hope for your future" (31:16–17).

EZRA 7

The Mission of Ezra the Scribe

Why Ezra the Scribe?

Not all the exiled Jews returned from Babylon during the time of the rebuilding of the temple. Fifty-seven years after the dedication of the new temple, during *the reign of Artaxerxes king of Persia* (464–424 BC), Ezra and his group come to Jerusalem. In addition to being a priest, Ezra *was a scribe skilled in the law of Moses which the LORD the God of Israel had given.* Ezra is also a powerful advocate before Artaxerxes: *The king granted him all that he asked, for the hand of the LORD his God was upon him.*

Once the temple has been built and sacrificial worship to the Lord takes place there, why is Ezra's mission necessary? The answer is that the returned exiles are not yet a holy people because they do not follow the Torah. Thus, the land cannot yet be a holy land. The book of Ezra is keyed particularly to Jeremiah's prophecies: the return to the land takes place so that *the word of the LORD by the mouth of Jeremiah might be accomplished.* For the temple's sacrificial worship truly to embody holy land (divine indwelling), the people have to be holy, in right relationship with God. In this vein Jeremiah warns: "Thus says the LORD of hosts, the God of Israel, Amend your ways and your doings, and I will let you dwell in this place. Do not trust in these deceptive words: 'This is the temple of the LORD, the temple of the LORD, the temple of the LORD'" (Jer. 7:3–4).

Some further comments about the land to which Ezra returns are in order. Judah is the tribe of David, and its preeminent place among the tribes of Israel is established prophetically by Jacob/Israel himself: "The scepter shall not depart from Judah, nor the ruler's staff from between his feet, until he comes to whom it belongs; and to him shall be the obedience of the peoples. Binding his foal to the vine, and his ass's colt to the choice vine, he washes his garments in wine and his vesture in the blood of grapes; his eyes shall be red with wine, and his teeth white with milk" (Gen. 49:10–12). Zechariah prophesied that "the LORD will inherit Judah as his portion in the holy land, and will again choose Jerusalem" (Zech. 2:12) on the day that the Lord again dwells with his people. The significance of Jerusalem also appears in Isaiah's prophecy: "For Zion's sake I will not keep silent, and for Jerusalem's sake I will not rest, until her vindication goes forth as brightness, and her salvation as a burning torch" (Isa. 62:1). The Lord promises through Isaiah: "You shall no more be termed Forsaken, and your land shall no more be termed Desolate; but you shall be called My delight is in her, and your land Married; for the LORD delights in you, and your land shall be married" (62:4).

This marital intimacy between God and the people of Israel is the meaning of holy land. The Israelites' return to the land aims ultimately at the accomplishment of this marriage with God, divine indwelling. Although only God can accomplish such a marriage, the yearning for its accomplishment is what makes the rebuilding of the temple so important: just as earlier God "dwelt" among Israel in the ark of the covenant and the tent of meeting, God had said that his unique dwelling among the people of Israel would continue in the temple, where he placed his name (1 Kgs. 8). True worship offered in the temple brings God into the midst of Israel.

Before the Babylonian exile, however, the prophet Ezekiel had seen in visions the presence of the Lord abandoning the temple due to the people's idolatry: "Then the cherubim lifted up their wings, with the wheels beside them; and the glory of the God of Israel was over them. And the glory of the LORD went up from the midst of the city, and stood upon the mountain which is on the east side of the city" (Ezek. 11:22–23). Through Ezekiel, the Lord had also prophesied that after the exile the Lord would gather Israel again and would restore them to the land where "I [the LORD] will give them one heart, and put a new spirit within them . . . that they may walk in my statutes and keep my ordinances and obey them; and they shall be my people, and I will be their God" (11:19–20). Yet the presence of the Lord had not been seen, by either Haggai or Zechariah, reentering the new temple. Neither had the people received a new spirit of obedience to God's law.

In addition, the new temple was not of the size and scope of the new temple that Ezekiel sees in visions (Ezek. 40–48). Ezekiel sees life-giving water "issuing from below the threshold of the temple toward the east (for the temple faced east); and the water was flowing down from below the south end of the threshold of the temple, south of the altar" (47:1). In Ezekiel's visions, the water flowing from the temple constitutes a large river that gives life to the desert with miraculous power: "And on the banks, on both sides of the river, there will grow all kinds of trees for food. Their leaves will not wither nor their fruit fail, but they will bear fresh fruit every month, because the water for them flows from the sanctuary. Their fruit will be for food, and their leaves for healing" (47:12). The imagery of this new temple, with its miraculous life-giving water of reconciliation and peace, clearly goes beyond what any rebuilt temple could literally accomplish and has in view an eschatological fulfillment.

Thus until God writes the law upon the people's hearts and establishes the eschatological temple, the people's task is to strive to be holy by rebuilding God's temple and by obeying God's law to the fullest degree possible. They must do what they can to restore the right relationship to God lost by sin, while at the same time awaiting God's transformative fulfillment. Until the time of fulfillment, the patterns inscribed by the Mosaic and Davidic covenants—law and king to make the people holy, sacrificial temple as the locus of the divine indwelling in the land—need to be sustained and nourished as much as possible. This is the task of Ezra the Scribe.

Ezra and Artaxerxes

As *a scribe skilled in the law of Moses*, Ezra leaves a prominent position in Babylon in order to recall his fellow Israelites, who have rebuilt the temple in Jerusalem, to obedience to the law: *For Ezra had set his heart to study the law of the* LORD, *and to do it, and to teach his statutes and ordinances to Israel.* Zerubbabel and Jeshua, heirs to the Davidic and Aaronic lines respectively, sought to restore the holy land by returning from exile and rebuilding the temple. Ezra the Scribe seeks to restore the holy people formed by the Torah, so that Israel will experience more fully the blessings (present and future) of a covenantal relationship with God, rather than undergoing once again the covenantal curses. "Give me understanding, that I may keep thy law and observe it with my whole heart. Lead me in the path of thy commandments, for I delight in it. Incline my heart to thy testimonies, and not to gain!" (Ps. 119:34–36).

Assuming that the sacred writings kept in the temple were destroyed when the Babylonians burned down the temple, Bede venerates Ezra as the one who rewrote both the Torah and the other preexilic books (2006, 109).[1] It should also be noted that in these three figures—Zerubbabel, Jeshua, Ezra—one finds the triad that Christ Jesus unites in himself, namely, king, priest, and lawgiver/prophet.

Ezra returns from Babylonian exile around 458 BC, *in the seventh year of Artaxerxes the king* (for discussion see Blenkinsopp 1988, 139–44). His arrival

---

1. See Scott DeGregorio's footnote to this passage of Bede: "Although the latter [Ezra's restoration of the sacred writings] is mentioned by Jerome (*Prologus in Regum* 364) and Isidore (*Etymologiae* 6.3.2), the story itself derives ultimately from apocryphal sources, mainly 4 Esdras 14:9–48. . . . These verses tell of a vision in which Ezra is divinely inspired to restore the Law that was destroyed when Nebuchadnezzar sacked Jerusalem in 587 BC" (in Bede 2006, 109n6).

in Jerusalem takes place with symbolic weight *on the first day of the fifth month
. . . for the good hand of his God was upon him.* "In the fifth month, on the
seventh day of the month, . . . Nebuzaradan, the captain of the bodyguard, a
servant of the king of Babylon, came to Jerusalem. And he burned the house of
the LORD" (2 Kgs. 25:8–9). In a reversal of Nebuzaradan's destructive mission,
Ezra leads a group of reformers, including *some of the people of Israel, and some
of the priests and Levites, the singers and gatekeepers, and the temple servants.*

Artaxerxes provides Ezra with a letter of support outdoing even Cyrus's
edict for the first return. Artaxerxes attends primarily to the provision of the
temple, because the temple is the place where occurs the sacrificial worship
of the Lord, whom Artaxerxes desires to placate: *I, Artaxerxes the king, make
a decree to all the treasurers in the province Beyond the River: Whatever Ezra the
priest, the scribe of the law of the God of heaven, requires of you, be it done with
all diligence, up to a hundred talents of silver, a hundred cors of wheat, a hundred
baths of wine, a hundred baths of oil, and salt without prescribing how much.
Whatever is commanded by the God of heaven, let it be done in full for the house
of the God of heaven, lest his wrath be against the realm of the king and his sons.*[2]
Whereas Artaxerxes seems primarily to desire to placate God by stocking the
temple, Ezra the Scribe has the primary goal of increasing the people's obedience to the Torah.

Artaxerxes describes Ezra as *sent by the king and his seven counselors to make
inquiries about Judah and Jerusalem according to the law of your God, which is in
your hand.*[3] The law, and not specifically the temple service, stands at the center

2. Blenkinsopp notes that Artaxerxes' decree "like those of Cyrus (6:3–5) and Darius (6:6–
12) is in Aramaic" (1988, 146). After surveying the scholarly controversy over the authenticity
of the letter, Blenkinsopp concludes: "The mission of Ezra, like that of Udjahorresnet in Egypt
under Darius I, is certainly historical. The purpose of the mission, as mandated in an imperial
firman, was to restore the Jerusalem cultus and put the administration of the Jewish law on a firm
basis, and this in the interests of peace and stability in the province and perhaps elsewhere in the
satrapy. With or without editorial retouching, the decree was incorporated into Ezra's personal
account of his tour of duty, from which it was subsequently excerpted by C [the Chronicler] who,
as elsewhere in the history, did not scruple to engage in extensive rewriting" (1988, 147).

3. Throntveit observes with regard to Artaxerxes' decree: "The Aramaic word *dat*, translated
as 'law' in these chapters (7:12, 14, 21, 25, 26), usually relates to royal decrees, as seen in the
books of Esther and Daniel, and so should not be taken to be an Aramaic equivalent for Torah"
(1992, 43). He adds: "Historically his [Ezra the Scribe's] mission was secular in nature as was his
office as a scribe or secretary in the Persian court. The description of the law as being 'in [his]
hand' (7:14, 25) is not to be taken literally, as though he actually carried a scroll from Babylon,
but figuratively with the meaning 'which you possess' (cf. NRSV). Nevertheless, it is also clear
that the compiler has capitalized on the differing ways the terms 'scribe,' 'law,' and 'in your hand'
would be heard by his community and invites the reader to hear this text as if it were a report of
Ezra, the scribe (in the later Jewish sense) mandated to implement the Torah of his God. This
theological claim of the text, regardless of its historical accuracy, is at the heart of the passage
as we now have it and will control the reading of Ezra's subsequent reforms in both Ezra 9–10
and Nehemiah 8–10" (1992, 44). See also Blenkinsopp 1988, 152–57, who concludes: "Our
survey would therefore suggest the conclusion that 'the law' in Ezra-Nehemiah, and therefore

of Ezra's mission. Bede says: "The Law of God was in Ezra's hand because he not only preached it with his tongue but fulfilled it by his action" (2006, 120). Yet the temple service commanded by the law is also highly important to Ezra, and he accepts *the silver and gold which the king and his counselors have freely offered to the God of Israel, whose dwelling is in Jerusalem,* so he can *buy bulls, rams, and lambs, with their cereal offerings and their drink offerings.*

Artaxerxes gives free rein to Ezra's mission to establish the law in the land of Israel: *And you, Ezra, according to the wisdom of your God which is in your hand, appoint magistrates and judges who may judge all the people in the province Beyond the River, all such as know the laws of your God; and those who do not know them, you shall teach.* This authority to make appointments gives Ezra the ability to spread the observance of the Torah throughout the communities of the returned exiles. Although God has not yet written the law "upon their hearts" so that "no longer shall each man teach his neighbor and each his brother, saying, 'Know the LORD'" (Jer. 31:33–34), God here acts so as to make the Torah better known through Artaxerxes' support of Ezra the Scribe. In addition to this authority to make appointments, Ezra even more importantly receives the power to punish those who disobey the law: *Whoever will not obey the law of your God and the law of the king, let judgment be strictly executed upon him, whether for death or for banishment or for confiscation of his goods or for imprisonment.*[4]

The book of Ezra now shifts to Ezra as the first-person narrator.[5] The narrator Ezra's first words acknowledge what the Lord has done for Israel through Artaxerxes. The first half of this acknowledgement concerns the temple: *Blessed be the LORD, the God of our fathers, who put such a thing into the heart of the king, to beautify the house of the LORD which is in Jerusalem.* The second half of the acknowledgement pertains to Ezra's own role: the Lord *extended to me [Ezra] his steadfast love before the king and his counselors, and before all the king's mighty officers.* This role will have primarily to do with the Torah, the restoration of

---

Ezra's law *as understood by the redactor,* refers basically to Deuteronomic law supplemented by ritual legislation in the Pentateuchal corpora conventionally designated P and H. This conclusion is, however, complicated by another factor: those indications in Ezra-Nehemiah of practice in accord with neither Deuteronomic nor Priestly law. The clearest example is the observance of a day of repentance and fasting on the twenty-fourth rather than the tenth of Tishri, the latter being the date fixed for Yom Kippur in the Priestly laws (Neh. 9:1; cf. Lev. 16:29; 23:27–32; Num. 29:7–11). The most natural explanation would be that at that point in time Yom Kippur was either unknown or at least not firmly established" (1988, 155).

4. Blenkinsopp 1988, 151–52, defends the historical credibility of this passage and notes that "the second penalty is often translated 'banishment' (e.g., by RSV), but this appears to be mistaken since the Persian word from which it derives means something different (1 Esd. 8:24, which has *timōria,* physical punishment, points in the right direction)" (1988, 152). On the basis of the list of penalties, he holds that "it seems that the Persian penal code was invoked even for infractions of traditional Jewish law" (1988, 152).

5. For discussion of the various viewpoints regarding this shift, see Fensham 1982, 4–5.

the holy people. "Then we cried to the LORD the God of our fathers, and the LORD heard our voice" (Deut. 26:7).

A New Moses?

As a giver of the Torah, Ezra appears to some degree as a new Moses, despite being blessed with Artaxerxes' support rather than faced with the stubborn opposition of Pharaoh. Ezra remarks: *I took courage, for the hand of the LORD my God was upon me, and I gathered leading men from Israel to go up with me.* The Lord likewise gives Moses courage for his mission to Pharaoh, since Moses at first says: "Oh, my Lord, send, I pray, some other person" (Exod. 4:13). Just as Artaxerxes instructs Ezra to appoint judges, Moses appoints judges for the people at the urging of his Midianite father-in-law, Jethro. Ezra is sustained by *the hand of the LORD my God.* The Lord similarly tells Moses: "I know that the king of Egypt will not let you go unless compelled by a mighty hand. So I will stretch out my hand" (3:19–20).

When Ezra says, *I gathered leading men from Israel to go up with me,* this reminds us that a number of exiled Israelites still remained in Babylon. In the first deportation of exiles to Babylon "he [Nebuchadnezzar] carried away all Jerusalem, and all the princes, and all the mighty men of valor, ten thousand captives, and all the craftsmen and the smiths; none remained, except the poorest people of the land" (2 Kgs. 24:14). These talented people succeeded in wealthy Babylon, and many did not return to an impoverished and decimated Israel when they had the opportunity to do so under Cyrus. The psalmist's words condemn such sluggishness: "How shall we sing the LORD's song in a foreign land? If I forget you, O Jerusalem, let my right hand wither! Let my tongue cleave to the roof of my mouth, if I do not remember you, if I do not set Jerusalem above my highest joy!" (Ps. 137:4–6). Could the exiled Israelites accept their exile, like the Israelites of old who, despite their slavery, grew attached to the fleshpots of Egypt (Exod. 16:3)?

Surely to "sing the LORD's song" requires participating in the ongoing effort to bring about the prophesied restoration and forgiveness of sins. Ezra leads his followers from Babylon to Jerusalem with this purpose in view. "With weeping they shall come, and with consolations I will lead them back, I will make them walk by brooks of water, in a straight path in which they shall not stumble; for I am a father to Israel" (Jer. 31:9).

EZRA 8

The Holy People

Ezra 8 lists those who share in Ezra's mission to restore Israel to a holy people and describes their journey to Jerusalem and the temple. The list of Ezra's companions conveys, through its symbolism, what God is doing through Ezra.[1] Ezra's companions provide almost all that is needed for the full replanting of the remnant of Israel in the land: two Aaronic priests, a member of the house of David, and twelve other families, symbolic of the twelve tribes (Throntveit 1992, 46).

Priestly Purity

Ezra first mentions the two members of priestly families: *Of the sons of Phinehas, Gershom. Of the sons of Ithamar, Daniel.* Phinehas, "the son of Eleazar, son of Aaron the priest" (Num. 25:7), is responsible during the exodus for preserving the purity of the community of the Israelites as descendants of Abraham. Since this will be such a large theme for Ezra as well, it is no wonder that Gershom, a priestly descendent of Phinehas, receives first mention in Ezra's genealogy of his companions.

---

1. For discussion see Fensham 1982, 110–11. Fensham points out that "Ezra's choice of twelve families might be attributed to his belief that such a complete number would invest blessing for his journey to Jerusalem" (1982, 111). Blenkinsopp comments: "As for the number twelve, reminiscent of the twelve leaders of the first return (2:2), and sometimes taken as evidence of an artificial and fictive schematizing: if it necessitated some editorial arrangement of the data (as with the twelve 'minor' prophets in the canon), this would not impugn the essential authenticity of the list" (1988, 161).

To understand Phinehas's role, we must remember that Moses himself married foreign women. Moses's first wife was a Midianite, Zipporah (Exod. 2:21), and Aaron and Miriam challenged his authority over the people of Israel on the grounds that "he had married a Cushite woman" (Num. 12:1). Moses is inviolable: God turns Miriam leprous for her audacity. Yet, intermarriage quickly becomes forbidden for the people. First, once they are no longer slaves in Egypt, they are more attractive candidates for intermarriage. Second, the stakes of intermarriage are profoundly increased once the true God has revealed his identity as "I AM" and given the law commanding worship of God alone. Once Israel has been separated for the worship of the true God as the covenantal people through whom the blessing to all families of the earth is to flow, there is always the risk that Israel's distinctiveness will dissolve and the people will turn entirely to the idolatrous worship of local gods, as very many of them do: "So the people of Israel dwelt among the Canaanites, the Hittites, the Amorites, the Perizzites, the Hivites, and the Jebusites; and they took their daughters to themselves for wives, and their own daughters they gave to their sons; and they served their gods" (Judg. 3:5–6).

Moses seeks to preserve Israel's separateness as a people consecrated to the Lord. During the exodus "the people began to play the harlot with the daughters of Moab. These invited the people to the sacrifices of their gods, and the people ate, and bowed down to their gods. So Israel yoked himself to the Baal of Peor" (Num. 25:1–2). At stake is the very survival of Israel, since Israel's "play[ing] the harlot with the daughters of Moab" has brought upon the people a disastrous plague: "Moses said to the judges of Israel, 'Every one of you slay his men who have yoked themselves to Baal of Peor'" (25:5).

The first leader to do this is Phinehas, scandalized by the audacity of a union between an Israelite man and a Midianite woman in a time of threat to the people's existence. While the people of Israel "were weeping at the door of the tent of meeting" (25:6), Phinehas follows the man and woman to their tent and kills them in the act of intercourse; although the plague then abated, it killed "twenty-four thousand" (25:9). The Lord rewards Phinehas with a promise of "my covenant of peace; and it shall be to him, and to his descendants after him, the covenant of perpetual priesthood, because he was jealous for his God, and made atonement for the people of Israel" (25:12–13).

Ithamar too, from whom Ezra's companion Daniel was descended, was a son of Aaron (Exod. 38:21). Under King Solomon, however, the house of Eleazar found more favor than did the house of Ithamar (1 Chr. 24). At first David's priest was Abiathar the son of Ahimelech of the house of Ithamar. When David was fleeing Saul, Abiathar "fled to David to Keilah" (1 Sam. 23:6). Upon David's ascension to the united throne of Israel, Abiathar shared the priesthood with Zadok of the house of Eleazar (2 Sam. 8:17). Both Abiathar and Zadok remained loyal to David during Absalom's rebellion (17:15), but Abiathar and Zadok took differing sides during the struggle between Adonijah and Solomon over who was to succeed David as king. Zadok supported Solomon, with the eventual result, not surprisingly, that Solomon "put Zadok the priest in the place of Abiathar" (1 Kgs. 2:35).

Ezra's mention of both Gershom and Daniel may indicate a reconciliation among the competing priestly families, although the house of Eleazar still receives first mention. Certainly such a reconciliation would serve the unification of the people of Israel that Ezra seeks.

The names of the leaders of the twelve families as well as the member of David's house—*Hattush*, who is not heard from again in any role of significance (for discussion see Blenkinsopp 1988, 162), despite his eminent lineage (1 Chr. 3:17–22)—can be passed over. These leaders are otherwise unremembered. "For of the wise man as of the fool there is no enduring remembrance, seeing that in the days to come all will have been long forgotten. How the wise man dies just like the fool!" (Eccl. 2:16).

The Role of the Levites

Ezra soon discovers that one necessary component of Israel is missing among his companions: *I gathered them to the river that runs to Ahava, and there we encamped three days. As I reviewed the people and the priests, I found there none of the sons of Levi.* There were already some Levites in Israel who had returned under Zerubbabel and Jeshua, but Ezra desires that his group be complete. He therefore gathers the leaders and sends them to *Iddo and his brethren the temple servants at the place Casiphia*, Levites who still lived in Babylon: *And by the good help of our God upon us, they brought us a man of discretion, of the sons of Mahli the son of Levi, son of Israel, namely Sherebiah with his sons and kinsmen, eighteen; also Hashabiah and with him Jesaiah of the sons of Merari, with his kinsmen and their sons, twenty; besides two hundred and twenty of the temple servants, whom David and his officials had set apart to attend the Levites.*

In addition to the importance of the Levites in the temple service, why does Ezra so much desire to have Levites among his companions on his return to the land of Judah and to the temple? The Levites, like Phinehas the priest, were exalted under Moses for their defense of the integrity of Israel as a people set apart for the Lord. When Moses spent many days with the Lord on the top of Mount Sinai, where he received "the two tables of the testimony, tables of stone, written with the finger of God" (Exod. 31:18) along with detailed instructions about how to worship the Lord, "the people gathered themselves together to Aaron, and said to him, 'Up, make us gods, who shall go before us; as for this Moses, the man who brought us up out of the land of Egypt, we do not know what has become of him'" (32:1). Aaron then made for them, from their golden jewelry, a golden calf to worship. Seeing his handiwork, "they said, 'These are your gods, O Israel, who brought you up out of the land of

Egypt!' When Aaron saw this, he built an altar before it" (32:4–5). Already, in other words, the entire people had departed from the Lord and begun to serve the gods of the nations, as they would do so often. At this very moment Moses returns from Mount Sinai and calls for those on the side of the Lord to come to his aid: "Moses stood in the gate of the camp, and said, 'Who is on the Lord's side? Come to me.' And all the sons of Levi gathered themselves together to him" (32:26). Moses commands them to go into battle against the idolaters among the people of Israel: "And the sons of Levi did according to the word of Moses; and there fell of the people that day about three thousand men. And Moses said, 'Today you have ordained yourself for the service of the Lord, each one at the cost of his son and of his brother, that he may bestow a blessing upon you this day'" (32:28–29).

Thus, in defense of Israel's mission as a people separated by the Lord for the worship of the Lord alone, a people constituted by the covenants that they and their fathers had received, the Levites were willing to support Moses in a civil war without which the covenantal people of the Lord might well not have survived. For this service, the Lord gives them special privileges among the people, as guardians of the people's worship: "And the Lord said to Moses, 'Bring the tribe of Levi near, and set them before Aaron the priest, that they may minister to him. They shall perform duties for him and for the whole congregation before the tent of meeting, as they minister at the tabernacle; they shall have charge of all the furnishings of the tent of meeting, and attend to the duties for the people of Israel as they minister at the tabernacle'" (Num. 3:5–8). Ezra himself, to engage in his own mission of purification of the people according to the laws of the Torah, needs the valor of the Levites.

In the Hands of God

Before leaving Babylon, Ezra proclaims a fast so as to ask God's blessings upon the journey, for Ezra and his companions undertake the dangerous journey without military protection. *Then I proclaimed a fast there, at the river Ahava, that we might humble ourselves before our God, to seek from him a straight way for ourselves, our children, and all our goods. For I was ashamed to ask the king for a band of soldiers and horsemen to protect us against the enemy on our way; since we had told the king, "The hand of our God is for good upon all that seek him, and the power of his wrath is against all that forsake him."*

Is Ezra's claim that *the hand of our God is for good upon all that seek him* true? The teachers of wisdom in Israel recognized its truth: "For the upright will inhabit the land, and men of integrity will remain in it; but the wicked will be cut off from the land, and the treacherous will be rooted out of it" (Prov. 2:21–22). Without denying its truth, the psalmist, desperate over the plight of Israel, nonetheless calls it into question: "Rise up, O judge of the earth; render to the proud their deserts! O Lord, how long shall the wicked, how long shall the wicked exult? They pour out their arrogant words, they boast, all the evildoers. They crush thy people, O Lord, and afflict thy heritage. They slay the widow and the sojourner, and murder the fatherless; and they say, 'The Lord does not see; the God of Jacob does not perceive'" (Ps. 94:2–7). Trust in God's providence ultimately rests upon the assurance that his wisdom and love will prevail and are prevailing, even when we cannot understand the suffering that human beings endure: "How great are thy works, O Lord! Thy thoughts are very deep! The dull man cannot know, the stupid cannot understand this: that, though the wicked sprout like grass and all evildoers flourish, they are doomed to destruction for ever, but thou, O Lord, art on high for ever" (92:5–8).

Because the vindication of the righteous has an eschatological dimension—the righteous suffer in their earthly lives—Ezra understands that he and his companions are truly in danger. Even so, Ezra embraces God's providence and places the hopes of his party in God's hands. He does this not only because otherwise the party would be shamed before Artaxerxes; in light of his particular mission, the entrance into the land must be entrusted entirely to God's power. Ezra models his work upon the words that God spoke to Joshua, who first led Israel into the land. Obedience to the Torah is paramount: "Be strong and very courageous, being careful to do according to all the law which Moses my servant commanded you; turn not from it to the right hand or to the left, that you may have good success wherever you go" (Josh. 1:7). Obedience enables Ezra to follow God's command to Joshua to "be not frightened, neither be dismayed; for the Lord your God is with you wherever you go" (1:9). Thus Ezra and his party fast and pray for God's guidance and deliverance during the journey: *So we fasted and besought our God for this, and he listened to our entreaty.*

The precedents for Ezra's fast include King Hezekiah, who, when Assyrian troops arrived at the gates of Jerusalem, "rent his clothes, and covered himself with sackcloth, and went into the house of the Lord" (2 Kgs. 19:1). This penitence proves to be Judah's strength, warding off exile. Likewise, Jacob/Israel fasts and prays before his potentially fatal encounter with his brother Esau in the promised land. Like the people of the land who oppose the returned exiles, Esau has reason to hate Jacob and is stronger in military power than Jacob. Before crossing into the promised land, Jacob prays: "O God of my father Abraham and God of my father Isaac, . . . I am not worthy of the least of all the steadfast love and all the faithfulness which thou hast shown to thy servant, for with only my staff I crossed this Jordan; and now I have become two companies. Deliver me, I pray thee, from the hand of my brother, from the hand of Esau, for I fear him, lest he come and slay us all" (Gen. 32:9–11). It is on that very night that Jacob wrestles with "a man" from whom he receives a blessing and a new name, "Israel," given to Jacob because "you have striven with God and with men, and have prevailed" (32:28). Jacob/Israel at dawn rejoices that "I have seen God face to face, and yet my life is preserved" (32:30).

What could be more emblematic of the people of Israel than this tenacious wrestling to know the name of God? Ezra too is wrestling so that his people might come closer to full knowledge of the name of God. After his wrestling at the brink of the promised land, Jacob/Israel walks with a limp. "When I am weak, then I am strong" (2 Cor. 12:10). This limp from the encounter with God marks Israel as separated from the other nations, as a people whose power is hidden in God. "For you have died, and your life is hid with Christ in God" (Col. 3:3).

The Offering for the Lord

Ezra ensures that if his party does get attacked by robbers in the land, at least the robbers should know that they are attacking not merely a party of returning exiles but Artaxerxes himself, whose sacred offerings Ezra's party is carrying. For this reason, Ezra places all the silver, gold, and vessels in the hands of the priests: *Then I set apart twelve of the leading priests: Sherebiah, Hashabiah, and ten of their kinsmen with them. And I weighed out to them the silver and the gold and the vessels, the offering for the house of our God which the king and his counselors and his lords and all Israel there present had offered.* Interpreting this passage in the mystical sense, Bede remarks on the transference of valuables from Babylon to Jerusalem: "It has frequently been said that the silver and gold and the vessels that were being sent from Babylon to Jerusalem designate souls that are converted to the Lord from the confusion and sins of this world" (2006, 129–30, following Jerome). It follows that the priests should carry the valuables, because the sacramental ministry of priests brings souls into the church.

This mystical sense resonates with Ezra's goal of making his people holy. By giving the valuables to the twelve priests (probably twelve priests and the twelve Levites),[2] Ezra underscores the goal of the journey. He tells the priests and Levites: *You are holy to the LORD, and the vessels are holy; and the silver and the gold are a freewill offering to the LORD, the God of your fathers. Guard them and keep them until you weigh them before the chief priests and the Levites and the heads of fathers' houses in Israel at Jerusalem, within the chambers of the house of the LORD.* The gifts thus already belong to the Lord. "What have you that you did not receive? If then you received it, why do you boast as if it were not a gift?" (1 Cor. 4:7).

God had promised the Israelites at Mount Sinai that "you shall be to me a kingdom of priests and a holy nation" (Exod. 19:6) if only they would obey God's law. Far from obeying, however, the people became so corrupt that in the

---

2. Fensham notes that "almost all modern scholars" read "here a conjunction *waw*," giving the sentence this meaning: "I chose from the leaders of the priests twelve men, as well as Sherebiah and Hashabiah and with them from their kinsmen, ten men" (1982, 117).

Davidic kingdom before the exile even the priests were untrustworthy. When King Jehoash commanded that all the taxes and gifts given to the temple should go for repairs to the temple, Jehoash trusted that the priests would spend the money on repairs. Yet "by the twenty-third year of King Jehoash the priests had made no repairs on the house" (2 Kgs. 12:6). The Lord also issued an admonition through Jeremiah: "When one of this people, or a prophet, or a priest asks you, 'What is the burden of the LORD?' you shall say to them, 'You are the burden, and I will cast you off, says the LORD'" (Jer. 23:33). By contrast, Ezra trusts the priests with God's gifts, thereby signaling his hopes for restoration.

From Babylon to Jerusalem

After these preparations, says Ezra, *we departed from the river Ahava on the twelfth day of the first month, to go to Jerusalem; the hand of our God was upon us, and he delivered us from the hand of the enemy and from ambushes by the way.* The tenth day of the first month is the feast of passover, and on the fourteenth day of the month the people eat unleavened bread for seven days (Exod. 12). On the tenth day of the first month the Hebrew slaves slaughtered the sacrificial lambs of passover; on the eleventh day they were finally permitted to leave Egypt (12:37). After these events, "the LORD said to Moses, 'Consecrate to me all the first-born; whatever is the first to open the womb among the people of Israel, both of man and beast, is mine'" (13:1–2). Ezra's party begins their journey on the twelfth day of the first month, expressive of Ezra's desire to consecrate all Israel to the Lord through a new exodus.[3]

At this stage Ezra's paschal pattern shifts and evokes not the exodus but Christ's passion: *We came to Jerusalem, and there we remained three days.* Ezra's party stayed longer than three days in Jerusalem, and so why does Ezra speak of remaining three days? Three days was the length of time that King Rehoboam, son of Solomon, took to destroy the unity of the twelve tribes: "Jeroboam and all Israel came and said to Rehoboam, 'Your father made our yoke heavy. Now therefore lighten the hard service of your father and his heavy yoke upon us, and we will serve you.' He said to them, 'Come to me again in three days'" (2 Chr. 10:3–5). By contrast to these three days that accomplished disunity, Ezra's mission is to unify all Israel in obedience to the Torah, so that they can be the holy people who truly dwell with God in the land. In addition, the Israelites requested, while enslaved in Egypt, "a three days' journey into the wilderness, that we may sacrifice to the LORD our God" (Exod. 3:18). After three days, Ezra's party present their gifts to the Lord: *On the fourth day, within*

---

3. For discussion of the book of Ezra's use of the theme of a new exodus, see Throntveit 1992, 44–46. Throntveit observes that the book of Ezra has in view the "fulfillment of the exilic prophecy of Second Isaiah (42:13–16; 43:14–21; 52:1f., 11f.)" (1992, 44).

the house of our God, the silver and the gold and the vessels were weighed into the hands of Meremoth the priest, son of Uriah, and with him was Eleazar the son of Phinehas, and with them were the Levites, Jozabad the son of Jeshua and Noadiah the son of Binnui. The whole was counted and weighed, and the weight of everything was recorded. The significance of the three days appears when the pasch of the Messiah accomplishes the unification of humankind: "For as Jonah was three days and three nights in the belly of the whale, so will the Son of man be three days and three nights in the heart of the earth'" (Matt. 12:40). Bede says that "the three days of tarrying in Jerusalem are the excellent virtues of faith, hope and love that all the faithful should possess" (2006, 133).

After they deliver their gifts, Ezra and his party offer sacrificial offerings in the temple: *At that time those who had come from captivity, the returned exiles, offered burnt offerings to the God of Israel, twelve bulls for all Israel, ninety-six rams, seventy-seven lambs, and as a sin offering twelve he-goats; all this was a burnt offering to the* LORD. The numbers of the sacrificial animals express Ezra's quest for the unity of the holy people: twelve (or eight times twelve equals ninety-six) and seventy-seven, two sevens. These numbers, indicating perfection, convey Ezra's hopes for the new creation of Israel.

Having offered the sacrifices, they attend to their business as representatives of King Artaxerxes: *They also delivered the king's commissions to the king's satraps and to the governors of the province Beyond the River.* During that time *they aided the people and the house of God.* In this interlude all is peaceful. "And day by day, attending the temple together and breaking bread in their homes, they partook of food with glad and generous hearts, praising God and having favor with all the people" (Acts 2:46–47).

EZRA 9

The Purification of the People

Intermarriage and Idolatry

Ezra 9 tells the sad tale of intermarriage and idolatry. All is not well with the people of Israel—nor, of course, had Ezra thought it to be when he set out on his mission "to make inquiries about Judah and Jerusalem according to the law of your God" (Ezra 7:14). Ezra does not need to inquire; some leaders come to him with the truth: *The officials approached me and said, "The people of Israel and the priests and the Levites have not separated themselves from the peoples of the lands with their abominations, from the Canaanites, the Hittites, the Perizzites, the Jebusites, the Ammonites, the Moabites, the Egyptians, and the Amorites."*[1] As so often in Israel's history, the problem consists in the idolatry brought about by intermarriage with non-Israelites. If things continue in this way, Israel will dissolve into the peoples of the land, and God's covenantal bride, recipient of the promises given to Abraham, Moses, and David, will be no more. Israel's disappearance as a distinct people would be disastrous not only for Israel, but indeed for "all the families of the earth" who are to receive God's blessing through the seed of Abraham. First Peter describes this economy, in which Israel's separation serves the whole world: "The prophets who prophesied of the grace that was to be yours searched and inquired about this salvation; they inquired what person or time was indicated by the Spirit of Christ within them when predicting the

---

1. Throntveit comments: "The Hittites, Perizzites, Jebusites, and Ammonites were no longer in existence at this time. By taking action specifically against marriages with Israel's old enemies of the wilderness and conquest periods, the narrative seeks to reestablish in Ezra's day the 'conquest' of the Promised Land. The otherwise inexplicable addition of 'the Egyptians' to this list strengthens the reader's perception that the list is a 'flashback' to the similar situation that existed at the time of the first exodus (cf. Exod. 3:8; 13:5; Deut. 7:1; 20:17)" (1992, 51).

sufferings of Christ and the subsequent glory. It was revealed to them that they were serving not themselves but you" (1 Pet. 1:10–12).

The *officials* tell Ezra that the Israelites *have taken some of their [i.e., the peoples of the lands'] daughters to be wives for themselves and for their sons; so that the holy race has mixed itself with the peoples of the lands. And in this faithlessness the hand of the officials and chief men has been foremost.* If the people do not care to preserve their distinctiveness, then Ezra's effort to get them to follow the Torah will be fruitless, no matter how much power he receives from Artaxerxes.

The preservation of distinctiveness is crucial also for the economy in Christ. The first Christians are "aliens and exiles" who must "abstain from the passions of the flesh that wage war against your soul" (1 Pet. 2:11). Christians must keep free from those who "entice with licentious passions of the flesh men who have barely escaped from those who live in error" (2 Pet. 2:18). Paul similarly warns the Corinthians: "I wrote to you not to associate with any one who bears the name of brother if he is guilty of immorality or greed, or is an idolater, reviler, drunkard, or robber—not even to eat with such a one" (1 Cor. 5:11).

We have already discussed what consequences flow from intermarriage. Only after a plague has killed twenty-four thousand Israelites does the priest Phinehas's action spare the people of Israel. King Solomon, supremely wise due to God's gift, becomes in old age supremely foolish due to his many marriages with non-Israelite women. After Israel's conquest of the land, Joshua had urged: "Take good heed to yourselves, therefore, to love the LORD your God" (Josh. 23:11). Israel swears as a community to obey God's law, and this law applies to every individual in the community: their vocation (individually and collectively) is to be a separated people for the Lord, and so they are not free as individuals to intermarry with the idolatrous nations that surround them. For this reason Joshua continues: "For if you turn back, and join the remnant of these nations left here among you, and make marriages with them, so that you marry their women and they yours, know assuredly that the LORD your God will not continue to drive out these nations before you; but they shall be a snare and a trap for you . . . till you perish from off this good land which the LORD your God has given you" (23:12–13). What Joshua warns against, of course, later happens. Ezra is trying to ensure that it does not happen again with the returned exiles, so that finally, eventually, *the word of the LORD by the mouth of Jeremiah might be accomplished.* "Do not be mismated with unbelievers. For what partnership have righteousness and iniquity? Or what fellowship has light with darkness? What accord has Christ with Belial?" (2 Cor. 6:14–15).

Ezra Appalled

Even though only the Messiah can accomplish the salvific conjunction of divine indwelling and human holiness (the fulfillment of Israel's temple and law), the Messiah must come from and to the people of Abraham, Isaac, and Jacob on the land promised to Abraham, so that "all the families of the earth" (Gen. 12:3) will be blessed. Thus Ezra's response to the rampant intermarriage is hardly inappropriate: *When I heard this, I rent my garments and my mantle, and pulled hair from my head and beard, and sat appalled. Then all who trembled at the words of the God of Israel, because of the faithlessness of the returned exiles, gathered round me while I sat appalled until the evening sacrifice.*

Ezra's action is the traditional one of mourning and repentance. For instance, when Jacob was notified falsely of his beloved son Joseph's death, he "rent his garments, and put sackcloth upon his loins, and mourned for his son many days" (Gen. 37:34). Similarly, King Hezekiah, supposing the conquest of Judah to be near, "rent his clothes, and covered himself with sackcloth, and went into the house of the LORD" (2 Kgs. 19:1; cf. Isa. 37:1). Just as Judah was then threatened with destruction, so now intermarriage threatens to destroy the ability of the returned exiles to be the people of God. "Keep me as the apple of the eye; hide me in the shadow of thy wings, from the wicked who despoil me, my deadly enemies who surround me" (Ps. 17:8–9). The returned exiles are their own deadly enemies.

In addition to being a sign of mourning and repentance, Ezra's rending of his clothes connects him to Joshua, the first to lead the people into the land. Like Ezra, Joshua was protesting how easily the people of Israel are impressed by the peoples of the land. During the exodus, Moses sent spies to the land, who came back with exaggerated reports of the prowess of the peoples of the land. In their fear the people of Israel "said to one another, 'Let us choose a captain, and go back to Egypt.' Then Moses and Aaron fell on their faces before all the assembly of the congregation of the people of Israel. And Joshua the son of Nun and Caleb the son of Jephunneh, who were among those who had spied out the land, rent their clothes" (Num. 14:4–6). The congregation responded to Joshua and Caleb's rending of their clothes by urging that they be stoned, but God intervened on Joshua and Caleb's behalf (14:10). Likewise immediately following their glorious conquest of Jericho after entering the promised land, the Israelites were defeated at Ai because a member of the people has "taken some of the devoted things" (Josh. 7:11), that is, valuables of Jericho that God has commanded be destroyed. "Joshua rent his clothes, and fell to the earth upon his face before the ark of the LORD until the evening" (7:6).

Paul and Barnabas likewise rend their clothes when confronted with idolatry: "And when the crowds saw what Paul had done, they lifted up their voices, saying in Lycaonian, 'The gods have come down to us in the likeness of men!' . . . But when the apostles Paul and Barnabas heard of it, they tore their garments and rushed out among the multitude, crying, 'Men, why are you doing this? We are also men, of like nature with you'" (Acts 14:11, 14–15).

What Ezra Had to Say

As expected, Ezra becomes the leader of the reform movement: *All who trembled at the words of the God of Israel, because of the faithlessness of the returned exiles, gathered round me while I sat appalled.* He ends his silence at *the evening sacrifice* and offers a lengthy prayer, which serves also as a speech to his followers. The prayer/speech emphasizes that the exile in fact has not yet ended, because the same lack of holiness continues today that brought about the people's exile from the land and God's abandonment of the Davidic king and of Solomon's Temple.

Ezra begins with a confession of communal guilt, accepting the justice of the Babylonian exile: *O my God, I am ashamed and blush to lift my face to thee, my God, for our iniquities have risen higher than our heads, and our guilt has mounted up to the heavens. From the days of our fathers to this day we have been in great guilt; and for our iniquities we, our kings, and our priests have been given into the hand of the kings of the lands, to the sword, to captivity, to plundering, and to utter shame, as at this day.* The key is that the "utter shame" still plagues the people "at this day," due to the ongoing presence of what Ezra calls "our guilt." "Behold, the LORD's hand is not shortened, that it cannot save, or his ear dull, that it cannot hear; but your iniquities have made a separation between you and your God, and your sins have hid his face from us, so that he does not hear" (Isa. 59:1–2).

At this point in his prayer/speech, Ezra describes a glimmer of hope for the possibility that God will begin the task of the restoration of Israel, hope caused by the return to the land and the rebuilding of the temple: *But now for a brief moment favor has been shown by the LORD our God, to leave us a remnant, and to give us a secure hold within his holy place, that our God may brighten our eyes and grant us a little reviving in our bondage.* "Bondage" refers to Israel having no Davidic king, but instead laboring under Persian rule. God has yet to "raise up for David a righteous Branch" who "shall reign as king and deal wisely, and shall execute justice and righteousness in the land. In his days Judah will be saved, and Israel will dwell securely" (Jer. 23:5–6). The Branch that Zechariah likewise prophesied has not yet arrived.

Despite the continuing bondage, however, the hope that the remnant of Israel may obtain *a secure hold within his holy place* indicates that God is acting once again on behalf of his people. For one thing, the bondage has of late become a lenient one: *Our God has not forsaken us in our bondage, but has extended to us his steadfast love before the kings of Persia, to grant us some reviving to set up the house of our God, to repair its ruins, and to give us protection in Judea and Jerusalem.* Paul describes the bondage: "For I delight in the law of God, in my inmost self, but I see in my members another law at war with the law of my mind and making me captive to the law of sin which dwells in my members. Wretched man that I am! Who will deliver me from this body of death?" (Rom. 7:22–24).

Ezra suggests that hope of future deliverance comes from the leniency on the part of Cyrus, Darius, and Artaxerxes, who have allowed a remnant to return to the land. Indeed, speaking through the prophets, God promises that he will gather a remnant through whom he will renew Israel. In this vein Jeremiah prophesies: "I will gather the remnant of my flock out of all the countries where I have driven them, and I will bring them back to their fold, and they shall be fruitful and multiply. I will set shepherds over them who will care for them, and they shall fear no more, nor be dismayed, neither shall any be missing, says the LORD" (Jer. 23:3–4). Likewise Isaiah prophesies regarding the remnant: "In that day the remnant of Israel and the survivors of the house of Jacob will no more lean upon him that smote them, but will lean upon the LORD, the Holy One of Israel, in truth. A remnant will return, the remnant of Jacob, to the mighty God" (Isa. 10:20–21). However, Ezra also fears that the leniency of the Persian kings, which has allowed for the return of a remnant and the rebuilding of the temple, will be rendered fruitless due to the people's continued sin, so that there will be further delay of the fulfillment of *the word of the LORD by the mouth of Jeremiah.*

In other words, God is giving Israel a chance to prepare for his work of fulfillment, but Israel, according to Ezra, is failing again. In making his decisive indictment against the returned exiles' intermarriages with the peoples of the land, Ezra offers a pastiche of texts from the Torah:[2] *For we have forsaken thy commandments, which thou didst command by thy servants the prophets, saying, "The land which you are entering, to take possession of it, is a land unclean with the pollutions of the peoples of the lands, with their abominations which have filled it from end to end with their uncleanness. Therefore give not your daughters to their sons, neither take their daughters for your sons, and never seek their peace or prosperity, that you may be strong, and eat the good of the land, and leave it for an inheritance to your children for ever."* Ezra's command that the returned exiles should *never seek their* [i.e., *the peoples of the lands'*] *peace or prosperity* sounds harsh, especially since *the peoples of the lands* initially sought to help Israel rebuild the temple. But in fact seeking to compromise with the peoples of the land, while the easy way toward temporal peace and prosperity (due to the political and economic interrelationships that would be secured), would deal a deathblow to the people of Israel's particular mission among the nations,

---

2. Fensham remarks: "The citations in vv. 11–12 are a conglomeration of expressions borrowed from various parts of Scripture, e.g., Deut. 4:5ff. for *the land you are going to possess*; *unclean* or 'polluted' in Lev. 18:25ff.; 20:22ff. and Lam. 1:17; *their abominations* in Deut. 18:9; 2 K. 16:3; 21:2; 2 Chr. 28:3; 33:2; *filled the land from end to end* in 2 K. 21:16; *your daughters their sons* in Deut. 7:3; *further their welfare and prosperity* in Deut. 23:7; *become strong* in Deut. 11:8; *enjoy the prosperity of the country* in Gen. 45:18; Isa. 1:19; and *inherit it for ever* in Ezek. 37:25. The texts are not literally cited, but the essentials of the thought pattern are there" (1982, 131).

namely, to be a holy people separated for the Lord in the land where he has promised to dwell with them.

What happens, says Ezra, if even the remnant that returns is unrighteous? Taking great mercy on the people of Israel, God has been good to them: they have returned to the land, rebuilt the temple, and enjoyed support from the Persian kings. But far from honoring God in return, the people have once again abandoned the law of God, despite this abandonment bringing about their dreadful troubles in the first place! Ezra asks: *Shall we break thy commandments again and intermarry with the peoples who practice these abominations? Wouldst thou not be angry with us till thou wouldst consume us, so that there should be no remnant, nor any to escape?* Ezra has not yet lost hope that God is fulfilling *the word of the LORD by the mouth of Jeremiah* regarding the restoration of Israel through the remnant. But if even the remnant fails, perhaps God will cast Israel off entirely, and God would not be unjust to do so.

Ezra thus concludes his prayer/speech on a note of profound confession of sin and guilt: *O LORD the God of Israel, thou art just, for we are left a remnant that has escaped, as at this day. Behold, we are before thee in our guilt, for none can stand before thee because of this.*[3] "Out of the depths I cry to thee, O LORD! Lord, hear my voice! Let thy ears be attentive to the voice of my supplications! If thou, O LORD, shouldst mark iniquities, Lord, who could stand?" (Ps. 130:1–3).

Ezra the Mediator

It is important to recognize that since Ezra belongs to the people of Israel, he is mourning and confessing the people's guilt *as his own*. His purpose is to carry on the covenantal relationship between Israel and God, not to justify God in rejecting such a relationship. Ezra thus stands as the mediator between the people of Israel and their God (for further discussion see Fensham 1982, 125, 128). "O Israel, hope in the LORD! For with the LORD there is steadfast love, and with him is plenteous redemption. And he will redeem Israel from all his iniquities" (Ps. 130:7–8).

Abraham sought to mediate on behalf of Sodom, where his nephew Lot lived. Lot had shared Abraham's journey from Haran when the Lord commanded Abram: "'Go from your country and your kindred and your father's

---

3. Drawing upon the theology of Dietrich Bonhoeffer, Throntveit remarks that Ezra's prayer/speech "speaks against an attitude of cheap grace that has counted on God's continual provision but has failed to heed the warnings of scripture or history" (1992, 54). See also Blenkinsopp 1988, 181–85, who observes: "Communal confession of sin, whether in the form of prayer or of sermon, is a prominent form of religious expression in the Second Temple period" (181–82). He adds that the prayer/speech bears the marks of the Chronicler, even if perhaps originally spoken and recorded by Ezra (1988, 182).

house to the land that I will show you. And I will make of you a great nation, and I will bless you, and make your name great, so that you will be a blessing. I will bless those who bless you, and him who curses you I will curse; and by you all the families of the earth shall bless themselves.' So Abram went, as the LORD had told him; and Lot went with him" (Gen. 12:1–4). Abraham asks the Lord whether Sodom could be spared if fifty, or forty-five, or forty, or thirty, or twenty, or even ten righteous people live there—and the Lord promises that he will spare the city, even if only ten righteous people lived there. Thanks to Abraham's intercession, two angels of the Lord enable Lot and his family to be spared.

Similarly, Moses's mediation between the people and God serves as a pattern for Ezra's action here. Moses and Aaron alone could speak directly with the Lord on Mount Sinai, due to the people's lack of holiness. The Lord tells Moses: "Go down, and come up bringing Aaron with you; but do not let the priests and the people break through to come up to the LORD, lest he break out against them" (Exod. 19:24). If the mediator's position is privileged vis-à-vis God, however, the words that the mediator must speak to his own people, in order to bring them closer to the Lord, often cause pain. For example, during their lengthy effort to get Pharaoh to let the people go, Moses and Aaron at first succeed only in persuading Pharaoh to burden the people with more work. When the people of Israel angrily confront Moses and Aaron about this, "Moses turned again to the LORD and said, 'O LORD, why hast thou done evil to this people? Why didst thou ever send me? For since I came to Pharaoh to speak in thy name, he has done evil to this people, and thou hast not delivered thy people at all'" (5:22–23). Often, too, the mediator must simultaneously confront the people with their sin and plead to the Lord for the very survival of the people.

Moses finds himself in this situation when the people make and worship the golden calf while Moses is with the Lord on Mount Sinai. The Lord, seeing the people worshiping the golden calf, tells Moses: "Let me alone, that my wrath may burn hot against them and I may consume them; but of you I will make a great nation" (32:10). Moses intercedes powerfully for the people of Israel, and persuades the Lord to stick with them: "Turn from thy fierce wrath, and repent of this evil against thy people. Remember Abraham, Isaac, and Israel, thy servants, to whom thou didst swear by thine own self" (32:12–13). Moses even goes so far as to say that if the Lord will not forgive the people of Israel, then "blot me, I pray thee, out of thy book which thou hast written" (32:32). His words to God in defense of the people, however, are coupled with angry words to the people—and not only angry words but also a bloody purging of those who had without repentance abandoned the Lord. Moses tells the people: "You have sinned a great sin. And now I will go up to the LORD; perhaps I can make atonement for your sin" (32:30).

Ezra, too, informs the people of Israel that they have "sinned a great sin" and speaks on their behalf before God. Like Moses, Ezra confesses the people's guilt not to condemn the people. Rather, Ezra seeks to accomplish a reconciliation between the people of Israel, whose exile is still ongoing, and the God who has chosen them to be a people consecrated to his worship, dwelling with him in the land.

EZRA 10

The Purification of the People Completed

Ezra 10 records the purification of the people of Israel under Ezra, a purification that comes at great sacrifice. How did this purification come about?

The Torah at Stake

Near the end of the period of the judges, when "there was no king in Israel; every man did what was right in his own eyes" (Judg. 21:25), "a certain Levite was sojourning in the remote parts of the hill country of Ephraim, who took to himself a concubine from Bethlehem in Judah" (19:1). The travels of this Levite take him to Gibeah, of the tribe of Benjamin, to spend the night. But as had happened to the angels of the Lord in Sodom (Gen. 19), the Benjaminites, having fallen as low as Sodom, "beset the house round about, beating on the door; and they said to the old man, the master of the house, 'Bring out the man who came into your house, that we may know him'" (Judg. 19:22). The master of the house refuses to send out the man for them to sodomize, but in his distress he offers them "my virgin daughter and his concubine" (19:24). The Benjaminites repeatedly rape the concubine and at dawn leave her for dead at the doorstep. In order to express his shock and outrage that such acts could be performed unpunished among the tribes of Israel, the Levite divides her body "into twelve pieces," one for each tribe, "and sent her throughout all the territory of Israel" (19:29). While the tribe of Benjamin remains unrepentant, the other tribes are horrified by what has occurred in Israel.

    This story of Israel's awakening to the terrible spread of lawlessness bears upon Ezra's situation: for *a very great assembly of men, women, and children, gathered to him out of Israel; for the people wept bitterly.* Ezra has opened the returned exiles' eyes to their having chosen to live outside God's law; they have chosen to abandon their covenantal obligations to be a distinct people consecrated to the Lord so as to dwell with him in the land through true worship. They have not only refused to obey God themselves, but they have also jeopardized the blessing that will come through them to "all the families of the earth." Their lawlessness is similar to that of the lawlessness during the time of the judges: sexual unions not sanctioned by God's law have the potential to destroy God's people.

Ezra's contemporaries who *wept bitterly* remind us of the Israelites who, in the time of the judges, respond to the sexual lawlessness in their midst. When the tribe of Benjamin would not repent and make restitution, civil war breaks out between the eleven tribes and the tribe of Benjamin. By the end of the second day of the battle, those tribes who are seeking to defend the law of God have suffered great casualties: the Benjaminites have slain forty thousand men. In this time of dreadful crisis, "all the people of Israel, the whole army, went up and came to Bethel [where the ark of the Lord was] and wept; they sat there before the Lord, and fasted that day until evening, and offered burnt offerings and peace offerings before the Lord" (Judg. 20:26). On the third day of the battle, the Israelites, by the power of the Lord, conquer the tribe of Benjamin decisively.

Ezra has, indeed, initiated a time of crisis similar to that of a civil war. Weeping before the Lord is in order, for the crisis of widespread intermarriage—a crisis that threatens to dissolve the people of God into the surrounding nations— can be solved, it appears, only by the dissolving of these marriages that were contracted against the law of the Lord.

The Renewal of the Covenant

The leaders of the people of Israel understand the situation and themselves propose the solution: *And Shecaniah the son of Jehiel, of the sons of Elam, addressed Ezra: "We have broken faith with our God and have married foreign women from the peoples of the land, but even now there is hope for Israel in spite of this. Therefore let us make a covenant with our God to put away all these wives and their children, according to the counsel of my lord and of those who tremble at the commandment of our God; and let it be done according to the law."* Hattush, the descendent of David who comes with Ezra, does not take the lead in this crisis. It falls to Shecaniah (see Blenkinsopp 1988, 188), one of the exiles who had returned earlier, to propose to *make a covenant with our God to put away all these wives and their children.* This proposed action of covenant renewal suggests that the people are still in exile, still in "bondage" as Ezra has said in Ezra 9:8–9.[1]

1. For further discussion of the theme of covenant renewal here, see Fensham 1982, 134; and Blenkinsopp 1988, 188–89. Blenkinsopp states that in the Second Temple period the term

In his solemn renewal of the covenant during the dedication of the new temple, King Solomon depicts the very situation of exile that Israel faced in Babylon: "If they [the Israelites] sin against thee—for there is no man who does not sin—and thou art angry with them, and dost give them to an enemy, so that they are carried away captive to the land of the enemy, far off or near" (1 Kgs. 8:46). Solomon then asks God to forgive the exiled people "if they repent with all their mind and with all their heart in the land of their enemies, who carried them captive, and pray to thee toward their land, which thou gavest to their fathers, the city which thou hast chosen, and the house which I have built for thy name" (8:48). God's forgiveness, says Solomon, should first cause Israel's enemy, in whose land they are captive, to "have compassion on them (for they are thy people, and thy heritage, which thou didst bring out of Egypt, from the midst of the iron furnace)" (8:50–51). Second, God's forgiveness should remind God that he separated "them from among all the peoples of the earth, to be thy heritage, as thou didst declare through Moses, thy servant, when thou didst bring our fathers out of Egypt, O Lord God" (8:53).

Although Israel rejected this relationship and thus endured the punishment of exile, if Israel now repents and recognizes once again its status as God's "heritage," separated from the nations, God will again bless Israel in his mercy. Just as Solomon anticipated the exile in renewing the covenant at the dedication of the temple, so now Ezra seeks to renew the covenant after the exile. Although Shecaniah is a key supporter, the restoration of Israel's separation "from among all the peoples of the earth" requires Ezra's leadership. Shecaniah tells Ezra: *Arise, for it is your task, and we are with you; be strong and do it.* Having obtained the strong support of at least some leading families, Ezra persuades the leaders of the community to swear a covenantal oath: *Ezra arose and made the leading priests and Levites and all Israel take oath that they would do as has been said. So they took the oath.* A similar oath had marked earlier, largely futile efforts to renew the covenant under Kings Asa (2 Chr. 15:8–15), Hezekiah (29:10), and Josiah (34:30–33): "And they entered into a covenant to seek the Lord, the God of their fathers, with all their heart and with all their soul; and that whoever would not seek the Lord, the God of Israel, should be put to death. . . . They took an oath to the Lord" (15:12–14).

Whereas under King Asa the oath is taken "with a loud voice, and with shouting, and with trumpets, and with horns" and produces rejoicing in Judah (15:14–15), under Ezra mourning predominates. Far from rejoicing or encouraging others to rejoice, Ezra himself prolongs his solemn mourning, for which purpose he stays in the room of a leading priestly family, *the chamber of Jehohanan the son of Eliashib, where he [Ezra] spent the night, neither eating*

"covenant" involves "a collective commitment to certain stipulations of law confirmed by an oath" (1988, 188).

bread nor drinking water; for he was mourning over the faithlessness of the exiles.[2] This mourning signals again Ezra's awareness of ongoing exile, in comparison with the preexilic situation. "A voice on the bare heights is heard, the weeping and pleading of Israel's sons, because they have perverted their way, they have forgotten the LORD their God. 'Return, O faithless sons, I will heal your faithlessness'" (Jer. 3:21–22). The *faithlessness of the exiles* can be healed, but only through the painful medicine of the dissolution of the lawless marriages. Thus Ezra spends the night in repentant "weeping and pleading."

What about the Marriages?

And yet, could God truly will that Ezra break up these marriages? The Torah permits divorce and remarriage, with certain limits to the latter. Regarding divorce, the Torah instructs: "When a man takes a wife and marries her, if then she finds no favor in his eyes because he has found some indecency in her," the man is permitted to give her "a bill of divorce" and to send her "out of his house" (Deut. 24:1). She may remarry, but if she is divorced again or her new husband dies, then she may not remarry the former husband (24:2–4). Christ Jesus, however, observes that this precept does not do full justice to the nature of marriage. When Pharisees ask him whether divorce is lawful, Jesus responds that the Torah's precept is imperfect and appeals instead to the order of creation as set forth in Genesis: "For your hardness of heart he [Moses] wrote you this commandment. But from the beginning of creation, 'God made them male and female.' 'For this reason a man shall leave his father and mother and be joined to his wife, and the two shall become one flesh.' So they are no longer two but one flesh. What therefore God has joined together, let not man put asunder" (Mark 10:5–9). Jesus goes on to explain to his disciples: "Whoever divorces his wife and marries another, commits adultery against her; and if she divorces her husband and marries another, she commits adultery" (10:11–12).[3]

A similar position is found in the Apostle Paul: "To the married I give charge; not I but the Lord, that the wife should not separate from her husband (but if she does, let her remain single or else be reconciled to her husband)—and that the husband should not divorce his wife" (1 Cor. 7:10–11). In his own name, Paul goes on to allow for marital separations if one of the partners is not a Christian and that "partner desires to separate" (7:15).

In the case of the intermarriage of the Israelites, God repeatedly proclaims in the Torah that it is unlawful for the Israelites to enter into such marriages. The

2. Chronological problems arise here because of the mention of Eliashib also in the book of Nehemiah. These chronological problems lead some historians to date Ezra's arrival much later than the seventh year of Artaxerxes, 458 BC.

3. For further background on divorce in biblical Israel and on Jesus's condemnation of divorce, see Witherington 2006, 359–63.

Israelites are not free to contract marriages among the nations. The Israelites cannot become "one flesh" (Gen. 2:24) with idolatrous spouses, because "the body is not meant for immorality, but for the Lord" (1 Cor. 6:13).

It may also be worth observing that Ezra makes no mention of remarriage for the Israelites who have intermarried in this way and must now separate from their wives so that Israel might once again remember the Lord. Instead what Ezra commands amounts to separation, whereas Jesus indicates, in his explanation to his disciples, that the sin consists in marrying again while the divorced spouse is still alive.[4] Yet the point is not whether the returned exiles live by the ethics of the new covenant, but rather whether they live in accord with God's insistence that their sexual practices cannot be separated from their faithfulness in worship.

Backed by the King

After Ezra's night of mourning and fasting, *a proclamation was made throughout Judah and Jerusalem to all the returned exiles that they should assemble at Jerusalem, and that if any one did not come within three days by order of the officials and the elders all his property should be forfeited, and he himself banned from the congregation of the exiles.*[5] It does not say who made the proclamation. Perhaps Ezra encourages Shecaniah or other leaders of long-established families of returned exiles to take the lead in proclaiming what must have been an unpopular message, given the harsh penalties for noncompliance that are attached to the message. For those returned exiles who have so abandoned God's law that they would not care about being *banned from the congregation of the exiles*, Ezra's power over the property of the returned exiles serves as a strong inducement. Before Ezra had begun his journey, Artaxerxes commanded: "Whoever will not obey the law of your God and the law of the king, let judgment be strictly

4. Throntveit comments on Ezra 10: "With regard to the question of divorce, contemporary readers of this material are frequently scandalized by the harsh measures taken by the restoration community. It must be admitted at the outset that these measures are extreme by the standards of both Testaments. But the text says nothing about the matter that gives rise to the greatest outrage today, the lack of provision for the divorced women and their children" (1992, 56). After noting that not ethnicity but idolatry is the issue for Ezra 10, Throntveit concludes: "Distasteful as they may be, the marriage reforms must be seen as a purification of the community along priestly lines of separation from all that was unclean. Their intent was to preserve the faith intact and redefine Israel's identity as a religious community. It must also be remembered that this negative strengthening of the community in the law will be paired with Ezra's positive strengthening of the community in the covenant renewal of Nehemiah 8–10" (1992, 57).

5. Regarding these penalties, Blenkinsopp remarks that the confiscated property would "become property of the temple, as is explicitly noted at 1 Esd. 9:4 and by Josephus (*Ant.* 11.148). The other punishment, excommunication from the golah community, is closely related since the province constituted, in effect, a temple community in which title to real estate was contingent on participation in and, of course, support of the cult (cf. Ezek. 11:14–15)" (1988, 190–91).

executed upon him, whether for death or for banishment or for confiscation of his goods or for imprisonment" (Ezra 7:26).

Without this power from Artaxerxes, could Ezra have succeeded? His indebtedness to Artaxerxes calls to mind the book of Esther's depiction of the relationship of Xerxes to Mordecai: "And all the acts of his [Xerxes'] power and might, and the full account of the high honor of Mordecai, to which the king advanced him, are they not written in the Book of the Chronicles of the kings of Media and Persia?" (Esth. 10:2). The book of Esther makes much of this relationship: "For Mordecai the Jew was next in rank to King Ahasuerus [Xerxes], and he was great among the Jews and popular with the multitude of his brethren, for he sought the welfare of his people" (10:3). "He who loves purity of heart, and whose speech is gracious, will have the king as his friend" (Prov. 22:11). Ezra seeks "purity of heart."

Trembling before the Verdict

Given the penalties for noncompliance, it is no surprise that *all the men of Judah and Benjamin assembled at Jerusalem within the three days*. They assemble, it appears, not with particular zeal but out of fear. It is a miserable day for them: *All the people sat in the open square before the house of God, trembling because of this matter and because of the heavy rain.*[6] Many of them have built their lives around disobedience to the law of God, and now they are witnessing the terrible crumbling of these lives. One thinks of the psalmist's words: "Unless the LORD builds the house, those who build it labor in vain" (Ps. 127:1); or of Jesus's description of the "foolish man who built his house upon the sand; and the rain fell, and the floods came, and the winds blew and beat against that house, and it fell; and great was the fall of it" (Matt. 7:26–27). "The LORD reigns; let the peoples tremble!" (Ps. 99:1).

What sort of *trembling* is this? It is the trembling that comes not from a filial fear (i.e., not with a fear of wronging God's love), but from servile fear, fear of God's power—or Ezra's. Such servile fear remains far from the filial fear praised by Israel's wisdom teachers: "In the fear of the LORD one has strong confidence, and his children will have a refuge. The fear of the LORD is a fountain of life, that one may avoid the snares of death" (Prov. 14:26–27). "The fear of the Lord is the crown of wisdom, making peace and perfect health to flourish" (Sirach 1:18). The situation of the Israelites who are *trembling because of this matter and because of the heavy rain* has its remedy in another proverb: "Be not wise in your own eyes; fear the LORD, and turn away from

6. Fensham notes regarding this sentence: "In the English translation the important difference between the two prepositions does not come out, viz., *'al* before 'this matter' and *min* before 'heavy rains.' The preposition *'al* has here a kind of emotional value. *Min* means 'as a result of'" (1982, 139).

evil. It will be healing to your flesh and refreshment to your bones. . . . My son, do not despise the LORD's discipline or be weary of his reproof, for the LORD reproves him whom he loves, as a father the son in whom he delights" (Prov. 3:7–8, 11–12).

Ezra stands before the assembled Israelites and issues the verdict: *You have trespassed and married foreign women, and so increased the guilt of Israel. Now then make confession to the LORD the God of your fathers, and do his will; separate yourselves from the peoples of the land and from the foreign wives.* What Ezra calls *the guilt of Israel* refers back to the days before the exile, when Israel jeopardized the covenants and their future fulfillment (the blessing that will be for "all the families of the earth") by practicing forbidden intermarriage, which threatened both the descent of their nation from Abraham and their commitment to worshiping the Lord alone. In both respects, intermarriage alienated the people of Israel from their God, causing idolatry to flourish in Israel. By continuing the practice after the return from exile and the rebuilding of the temple—that is, after some of the elements of holy land had been restored—the Israelites undercut their covenantal commitment to be a holy people, marked by obedience to the Lord. It is this holiness of the people, lacking which no divine indwelling is possible in the land, that Ezra seeks to restore and foster.

Implementing the Plan

Despite not seeming particularly zealous, the returned exiles agree to Ezra's plan. Furthermore, it is they, not Ezra, who suggest that it be carried out in a systematic fashion: *Then all the assembly answered with a loud voice, "It is so; we must do as you have said. But the people are many, and it is a time of heavy rain; we cannot stand in the open. Nor is this a work for one day or for two; for we have greatly transgressed in this matter. Let our officials stand for the whole assembly; let all in our cities who have taken foreign wives come at appointed times, and with them the elders and judges of every city, till this fierce wrath of our God over this matter be averted from us."* Clearly any other means of ending the marriages would have been much less effective; by giving local officials, elders, and judges control over the enforcement of the edict, the people ensure that maximum compliance will be effected. This proposal for the enforcement of the edict met with the opposition of only four persons, listed by Ezra: *Only Jonathan the son of Asahel and Jahzeiah the son of Tikvah opposed this, and Meshullam and Shabbethai the Levite supported them.* Ezra completely wins the day. The Israelites are willing to undergo the extraordinary pain of separating from wives and children in order to be a people that obeys the Torah and that stands before God as the descendents, in flesh and in covenant, of Abraham, Isaac, and Jacob.

Ezra oversees the implementation of the plan. He *selected men, heads of fathers' houses, according to their fathers' houses.* The task of identifying *all the men who had married foreign women* took three months. Priestly families, Levites, and leading families of Israel are implicated: even the family of *Jeshua the son of Jozadak*, the high priest who with Zerubbabel led the party of returned exiles who rebuilt the temple, has intermarried with non-Israelites. As their penalty, *they pledged themselves to put away their wives, and their guilt offering was a ram of the flock for their guilt*. After listing the offenders at some length (110 cases in all), the book of Ezra concludes: *All these had married foreign women, and they put them away with their children*.

Is this too much to bear? Is this not the "yoke of iron" (Deut. 28:48) of the law's covenantal curse, which gives way to the easy "yoke" (Matt. 11:29) of Jesus? Or are things so simple? Jesus warns: "If any one comes to me and does not hate his own father and mother and wife and children and brothers and sisters, yes, and even his own life, he cannot be my disciple" (Luke 14:26). Jesus is "gentle and lowly of heart" and in him we find "rest for [our] souls" (Matt. 11:29), but the holiness to which he calls us is equally demanding or more so: "He who does not take his cross and follow me is not worthy of me. He who finds his life will lose it, and he who loses his life for my sake will find it" (10:38–39).

Must we not ask with the disciples: "'Then who can be saved?' But he said, 'What is impossible with men is possible with God.' And Peter said, 'Lo, we have left our homes and followed you.' And he said to them, 'Truly, I say to you, there is no man who has left house or wife or brothers or parents or children, for the sake of the kingdom of God, who will not receive manifold more in this time, and in the age to come eternal life'" (Luke 18:26–30).

CONCLUSION TO THE BOOK OF EZRA

I have highlighted the two achievements that stand out among the events recorded in the book of Ezra. First, the people of Israel have returned to the promised land and have rebuilt the temple (holy land). Second, the people of Israel have again taken steps to live in accordance with the Torah (holy people). I sought to place these two achievements within the covenantal context that explains why Ezra so treasures Israel's temple and Torah. Now that we have reached the end of the book of Ezra, however, we may ask again: Are the two achievements that provide the rationale for the book of Ezra in fact much to boast about?

From one perspective, the answer seems resoundingly no. A few rather ragtag bands of Israelites return to Jerusalem and its environs. Energized by King Cyrus and by the prophets Haggai and Zechariah, these ragtag bands, after long delay, manage to rebuild the temple. Even so, the rebuilt temple is barely even a shadow of Solomon's great temple. While the temple sacrifices and festivals resume, the returned exiles appear to make little effort in general to practice holiness in accord with the Torah. Despite the Lord's warnings against intermarriage with the peoples of the land, the returned exiles actively intermarry so as to secure a political and economic foothold. For his part, Ezra the Scribe induces a certain obedience to the Torah, but even this obedience seems a halfhearted and sad affair. There is no indication that all these efforts with regard to either the temple and the Torah will be enduring, and the Davidic line seems to be petering out. With such a reduced temple and such a weak people, who by the end appear to lack any reasonable grounds to imagine that a Davidic king will ever reign again in Jerusalem, can there really be any hope that the promised restoration of Israel is going to come through the path taken by the leaders in the book of Ezra? Does it not seem that these leaders' continuous struggles are hopeless, at best a noble exercise in religious nostalgia and at worst an exemplar of nationalistic fanaticism in religious garb? From this perspective, clearly, it is hardly possible to read the book of Ezra with much enthusiasm. The only possible reading would be to focus strictly upon the radical stripping away of Israel's dignity by foreign nations, as a prefiguration of Christ's passion.

I have chosen to read Ezra from another perspective, one that has room for the kenotic reading but is not limited to it. This perspective affirms that the two achievements recorded in the book of Ezra have enormous value, for two reasons. First, the prayerful and toilsome labor to return to the holy land and to restore the holy people is of enormous value because it allows the people of Israel, after the catastrophe of Babylonian exile, to imagine once again (in accord with the prophecies of Jeremiah) God's ever-greater indwelling in the land and the people's ever-greater formation in the law of their God. Such grace-filled hope lies at the heart of the Torah and is never forgotten, even in the darkest moments and against the greatest odds, by the prophets and holy men and women of Israel. The efforts of particular Israelites, at great sacrifice to themselves, to live up to the vocation of Israel are in themselves magnificent.

Second, the coming of the Davidic Messiah to Zion to fulfill Israel's Torah and temple, so "that the word of the Lord by the mouth of Jeremiah might be accomplished," depends upon the very labors that the book of Ezra recalls for us. How could Jesus have enacted the restoration of Israel if he had been in Babylon, or if there had been no temple and no Torah in relation to which he could make manifest his mission of fulfillment? The path to Jesus goes directly through the extraordinarily difficult labor that the book of Ezra sets forth. Far from being a period of sterile emptiness in which the work of salvation history stalled, this labor against all odds is what sets the stage for the return of YHWH to Zion in Christ Jesus.

As we have seen, the leaders in the book of Ezra do not imagine that they are going to bring off the restoration by themselves. Instead they seek to prepare the land and people, by retrieving Israel's temple and Torah, for the eschatological restoration of Israel that only God can accomplish. The situation described by Jeremiah remains all too true in Ezra: "Run to and fro through the streets of Jerusalem, look and take note! Search her squares to see if you can find a man, one who does justice and seeks truth; that I may pardon her" (Jer. 5:1). This man can and will be none other than Christ Jesus. Far from denying this, the book of Ezra makes it ever clearer, and in this regard the book of Ezra requires from its readers a spiritual ascesis after the high points of the Mosaic and Davidic covenants. Yet, the reader also learns anew the importance of Torah and temple. Salvation history does not stop building upward, toward a greater and greater divine presence. The covenant with Abraham promises land and descendents who will be a blessing to all nations; the covenant with Moses inaugurates the entrance into the promised land (now a locus of divine presence through the ark of the covenant) and gives Abraham's descendents the pattern of holiness through the law of Sinai; the covenant with David points toward the extraordinary indwelling of God's name in the temple at the heart of the land and establishes the role of the king in Israel whose task is to lead the people into the holiness of the law. God and God's holiness come closer and closer to Israel, even while at the same time (due to the increasing awareness of the people's sin) receding farther and farther away.

Both of these elements are present in the book of Ezra. After the ravages of the exile, one sees Israel's sin and weakness with painful clarity. But by their unceasing striving to allow God to accomplish in his own time the consummation of his ever-increasing closeness to Israel according to the messianic modes that the prophets have already sketched (still unimaginable in Ezra), the Israelites of the book of Ezra manifest their weakness as the weakness of one whose name "shall no more be called Jacob, but Israel, for you have striven with God and with men, and have prevailed" (Gen. 32:28). Their mysteriously triumphant striving cannot be separated, as the book of Ezra shows, from their limping (32:31), even if both striving and limping are increasingly embodied only in a remnant and indeed (ultimately) can be embodied only truly and fully in one man, Christ Jesus.

The right reading of the book of Ezra thus requires awareness of the Israelites' achievements and of their weakness. Their weakness is only too evident and hardly needs comment. While their achievements seem small and fleeting, they in fact constitute extraordinary fidelity to God's gifts to Israel and thus also a supreme preparation for the coming of Christ Jesus. After reading about the achievements recorded in the book of Ezra, we can thus say with Jeremiah: "Thy words were found, and I ate them, and thy words became to me a joy and the delight of my heart; for I am called by thy name, O LORD, God of hosts" (Jer. 15:16)! Yet, recognizing the painful kenosis that Ezra records, we can also say with Jeremiah his very next words: "I did not sit in the company of merry-makers, nor did I rejoice; I sat alone, because thy hand was upon me, for thou hadst filled me with indignation. Why is my pain unceasing, my wound incurable, refusing to be healed?" (15:17–18).

God's closeness to Israel in Torah and temple, as expressed by the marvelous striving of the book of Ezra, finds consummation in Christ Jesus, whose perfect justice/love (fulfillment of the Torah) and perfect sacrificial worship (fulfillment of the temple) reveals both God's unimaginably intimate indwelling and the kenotic power of Israel's cruciform limping as opposed to the worldly power of the nations, whether Babylon, Persia, or Rome.

✠ THE BOOK OF NEHEMIAH ✠

Introduction to the Book of Nehemiah

The outline of the book of Nehemiah mirrors that of the book of Ezra. Both books begin with preparations for a return to the land. The first six chapters of both books are devoted to rebuilding what the Babylonians destroyed and detail the numerous persecutions endured by those involved with the work of rebuilding. The second half of both books are dominated by Ezra the Scribe, a priest in the Aaronic line. In both books, Ezra the Scribe focuses on restoring the people's obedience to the commandments of the Torah and in particular to the separation of the people of Israel from the surrounding peoples.

Applying the covenantal framework that Michael Dauphinais and I sketch in *Holy People, Holy Land* (2005), Neh. 1–6 has to do primarily with holy land while Neh. 7–13 has to do primarily with holy people. The aspects of the Mosaic and Davidic covenants that pertain to the holiness of the land, as a locus of divine indwelling, are the ark of the covenant and the temple in Jerusalem. The aspects of the Mosaic and Davidic covenants that pertain to the holiness of the people are the law and the king (whose task it is to establish justice by fulfilling the law in the land). Moses writes: "And when he [the king] sits on the throne of his kingdom, he shall write for himself in a book a copy of this law, from that which is in charge of the Levitical priests, and it shall be with him, and he shall read in it all the days of his life, that he may learn to fear the LORD his God, by keeping all the words of this law and these statutes, and doing them" (Deut. 17:18–19).

Just as with the book of Ezra, therefore, my commentary on the book of Nehemiah will devote significant attention to drawing out the covenantal patterns of holy land and holy people, which come together in Christ Jesus as the incarnate Son of God—"'Emmanuel' (which means, God with us)" (Matt. 1:23)—who fulfills "all righteousness" (3:15). That these covenantal patterns are present in Nehemiah gives particular weight to Nehemiah's descriptions of the work of rebuilding the walls and renewing Torah obedience. The labors of the Israelites who undertook this project are as central to salvation history as are the earlier renewals of the covenant recorded in scripture. For this reason I have not hesitated in this commentary (as in the commentary on Ezra) to include a good bit of summary of the narrative, which might otherwise seem less necessary for a theological commentary.

Since the books of Ezra and Nehemiah share so much in terms of both content and structure, the commentary on Nehemiah necessarily covers similar ground as that of the commentary on Ezra. How, then, do they differ? The book of Ezra focuses on rebuilding the temple and reconstituting obedience to the Torah. By contrast, the first section of the book of Nehemiah focuses on rebuilding the walls of Jerusalem, and the entire book offers much more detail about the lives of the returned exiles in the land. Theologically, this allows for a difference in interpretative emphasis. By contextualizing Israel's Torah and temple within the earlier books of scripture that display the Mosaic and Davidic covenants—particularly Jeremiah—my commentary on Ezra develops more clearly the theology of Israel, whereas my commentary on Nehemiah develops more clearly the theology of the church. This is because Nehemiah's detailed discussions of the stone-by-stone and gate-by-gate reconstruction of the wall of Jerusalem allow for a more figural exploration of the visible church, just as Nehemiah's more detailed discussions of the life of the community allow for perhaps a richer reflection on what it means to live, in Christ, as the people of God. Yet, as we will see, the commentary on Nehemiah also requires a good deal of looking backward to the earlier covenants (and thus sketching a theology of Israel), just as the commentary on Ezra contained a number of references to Christ and his church.

Two issues merit brief discussion before beginning the commentary. In commenting on Nehemiah, as on Ezra, I frequently reflect on Israel's Torah (and Christ Jesus as its fulfillment), and I also argue that neither the book of Nehemiah nor the book of Ezra envisions the full restoration of Israel as possible without, among other elements, a Davidic king. My approaches to Israel's law and kingship are especially important because they belong to the heart of my understanding of the constitutive elements of holy people, a central structural theme in both commentaries. Yet my approaches to Israel's law and kingship require some explanation, both because of contemporary theological debates regarding supersessionism and because the books of Ezra and Nehemiah devote much more attention to Torah and temple than to the topic of kingship, which is rarely broached. This is the place, therefore, to summarize briefly my views regarding the theology of law and of Davidic kingship.

Theology of Law

Since the Torah has such centrality in Neh. 7–13, what theology of Torah guides my interpretation of these chapters? I do not think that the coming of Christ Jesus negates, destroys, or abrogates, in the usual senses of these terms, the commandments of the Torah. What St. Paul calls "the law of the Spirit" (Rom. 8:2) or "the law of Christ" (Gal. 6:2) does not supersede the Torah. However, this claim requires significant explanation because the concept of supersessionism includes modern presuppositions that rule out the theology of Torah that the New Testament teaches (for further discussion see Perrier forthcoming).

Supersessionism as understood today means that one reality follows upon another in the linear continuum of time. When one reality comes after another reality on this temporal continuum, supersessionism allows for only two options: either the later reality does not affect the earlier reality, or the later reality displaces and negates the earlier reality. It will be clear that the view of history here is strictly spatiotemporal, horizontal rather than vertical, rooted in power relationships between entities that compete with each other for time and space (for further discussion see Levering forthcoming). Thus when Paul affirms, "For Christ is the end of the law, that every one who has faith may be justified" (Rom. 10:4), supersessionism as understood today allows only one option for the interpretation of this text: Christ negates the Torah, Christ gives it no further space in the linear continuum of time. The theology of the letter to the Hebrews is then read through this linear lens: "For when there is a change in the priesthood, there is necessarily a change in the law as well. . . . On the one hand, a former commandment is set aside because of its weakness and uselessness (for the law made nothing perfect); on the other hand, a better hope is introduced through which we draw near to God" (Heb. 7:12, 18–19). Christ negates the Torah, on this reading, because after all "it is impossible that the blood of bulls and goats should take away sins" (10:4), and therefore Christ "abolishes" (10:9) such practices.

Given this linear spatiotemporal understanding of Christ's saving work, other New Testament passages become unintelligible. Consider the contortions required to make sense of Matt. 5:17–18, where Christ says: "Think not that I have come to abolish the law and the prophets; I have come not to abolish them but to fulfil them. For truly, I say to you, till heaven and earth pass away, not an iota, not a dot, will pass from the law until all is accomplished." Likewise the theologically rich words of Jesus on the cross as reported by John—"it is finished [fulfilled, consummated]" (John 19:30)—are emptied of any meaning besides the tautology that Jesus's suffering on the cross and his temporal ministry as a whole are now over. The sense of the Torah's fulfillment and consummation that belongs to both Matt. 5:17–18 and John 19:30 (as well as to Rom. 10:4) is, if it is recognized at all, merely contrasted and juxtaposed with other New

Testament passages, so that Matthew becomes the "Jewish" gospel in tension with Paul, or Romans is set in tension with Hebrews, and so forth.

In order to understand fulfillment, therefore, what is needed is a different path than the two options that supersessionism provides. Fulfillment differs from both spatiotemporal negation and spatiotemporal parallel tracks because fulfillment is rooted in a different account of time: when a later reality fulfills an earlier reality, the later reality truly participates in (i.e., is already to some degree hiddenly present in) the earlier reality. This participation breaks the iron bars of a strictly linear spatiotemporal continuum. Not only this, but the earlier reality is taken up and its fullest meaning is expressed in the later reality that fulfills. The earlier reality, while changed, is not negated; rather it comes into its own, as its teleological fullness is revealed. Past, present, and future are not bound to a strictly linear spatiotemporal continuum in which various entities are competing for space. Rather the various entities are internally related to each other by participating in each other. These relationships of participation, whose fullness is known only to God, mean that divine wisdom, not a temporal power struggle, internally defines the realities.

The Torah provides a pattern of holiness whose central tenets are revealed in the Decalogue. These central tenets are then given specification for the particular time and place of Israel by further precepts regarding the relationship of the Israelites to God (precepts regarding worship) and neighbor (precepts regarding economic, legal, social, and political life). Because of sin, neither Israel nor anyone else, without the grace of the Holy Spirit, is able to fulfill the Torah and be holy. Paul says: "All men, both Jews and Greeks, are under the power of sin, as it is written: 'None is righteous, no, not one'" (Rom. 3:9–10, citing Ps. 14:3). Lacking a holy people, no one can fully dwell with God (the true meaning of holy land).

By his supreme charity, Christ on the cross fulfills all these precepts, both the central moral tenets and the goals of Israel's worship and communal life. Christ establishes justice for us, and we find our holiness in Christ when his Holy Spirit unites us to his body through faith and the sacraments of faith. United to Christ ("in Christ"), we fulfill all justice with him and become likened to him by love: "By this we may be sure that we know him, if we keep his commandments. . . . He who loves his brother abides in the light" (1 John 2:3, 10). St. Paul puts it this way: "But now the righteousness of God has been manifested apart from the law, although the law and the prophets bear witness to it, the righteousness of God through faith in Jesus Christ for all who believe. For there is no distinction; since all have sinned and fall short of the glory of God, they are justified by his grace as a gift" (Rom. 3:21–24). This grace comes to us "through the redemption which is in Christ Jesus, whom God put forward as an expiation by his blood, to be received by faith" (3:24–25).

Thus we fulfill the precepts of the Torah in Christ not by offering the animal sacrifices at the temple but by participating in Christ's transcendent fulfillment in his flesh of those sacrificial precepts, that is, when we share in Christ's cross by faith and the sacraments of faith. Paul observes: "Do you not know that all of us who have been baptized into Christ Jesus were baptized into his death?" (6:3). In this relationship of fulfillment, the Torah is taken up by Christ and consummated, not negated: "Do we then overthrow the law by this faith? By no means! On the contrary, we uphold the law" (3:31). "I thank God whom I serve with a clear conscience, as did my fathers" (2 Tim. 1:3).

A final point: "the law of Christ" itself will be taken up into a greater reality, the heavenly Jerusalem, in which it (like the Torah) already participates. There is no rupture between the pilgrim church on earth and the church in heaven, just as there is no rupture between the Torah and Christ. But there is a strong element of discontinuity within the participatory continuity, since heavenly glory will infinitely surpass our present sharing in Christ through faith and the sacraments of faith. "For now we see in a mirror dimly, but then face to face. Now I know in part; then I shall understand fully, even as I have been fully understood" (1 Cor. 13:12). "Beloved, we are God's children now; it does not yet appear what we shall be, but we know that when he appears we shall be like him, for we shall see him as he is" (1 John 3:2).

Theology of Kingship

In Nehemiah (and Ezra) has the Davidic kingship been forgotten? Hans Urs von Balthasar explains Ezra and Nehemiah as "the beginning of Judaism" (1991, 376; cf. 387). Since Judaism is marked by the lack of a Davidic king, it might appear that the books of Nehemiah and Ezra are concerned solely with the return to the land, with the rebuilding of the temple and of the wall of Jerusalem, and with obedience to the Torah. Are Ezra and Nehemiah setting aside Israel's theology of kingship and deliberately instantiating a Judaism that can function quite well without a Davidic king?

I think not. First, as we have already seen, the prophets Haggai and Zechariah play a significant role in the narrative of the book of Ezra and in the rebuilding of the temple. These prophets have a profound interest in the Davidic kingship. The book of Ezra relates: "Now the Prophets, Haggai and Zechariah the son of Iddo, prophesied to the Jews who were in Judah and Jerusalem, in the name of the God of Israel who was over them. Then Zerubbabel the son of Shealtiel and Jeshua the son of Jozadak arose and began to rebuild the house of God which is in Jerusalem; and with them were the prophets of God, helping them" (Ezra 5:1–2). We have seen that Haggai prophesies in the name of the Lord the following about Zerubbabel, who is in the line of David and from whom Jesus descends: "Speak to Zerubbabel, governor of Judah, saying, I am about to shake the heavens and the earth, and to overthrow the throne of kingdoms. . . . On that day, says the LORD of hosts, I will take you, O Zerubbabel my servant, the son of Shealtiel, says the LORD, and make you like a signet ring; for I have chosen you, says the LORD of hosts" (Hag. 2:21–23). Likewise Zechariah suggests that Zerubbabel will, at the coming time of restoration, attain to the eminence of David. The Lord says through Zechariah: "What are you, O great mountain? Before Zerubbabel you shall become a plain; and he shall bring forward the top stone amid shouts of 'Grace, grace to it!'" (Zech. 4:7). Admittedly Zechariah also suggests that Jeshua the priest shall become king in Israel: "Take from them silver and gold, and make a crown, and set it upon the head of Joshua, the son of Jehozadak, the high priest. . . . It is he who shall build the temple of the LORD, and shall bear royal honor, and shall sit and rule upon his throne" (6:11, 13).[1]

Second, in the books of Ezra and Nehemiah the enemies of the people of Israel often accuse them of subversively seeking to restore the Davidic kingship, and the returned exiles do indeed rejoice in the former power of the Davidic kings and desire a Davidic restoration. For example, in the book of Ezra, Rehum and Shimshai write a letter to King Artaxerxes that accuses the returned exiles of seditious activity. Artaxerxes replies that "search has been made, and it has been found that this city from of old has risen against kings, and that rebellion and sedition have been made in it. And mighty kings have been over Jerusalem, who ruled over the whole province Beyond the River, to whom tribute, custom, and toll were paid" (Ezra 4:19–20). On this basis King Artaxerxes commands that work on the rebuilding of Jerusalem and the temple be stopped, and it does not resume again until the reign of King Darius. These "mighty kings" form the backdrop to the book of Ezra; they are by no means forgotten. On the contrary, Artaxerxes is correct that the rebuilding projects strive toward the eschatological restoration when a Davidic king will once more reign in Jerusalem.

The book of Nehemiah makes this element even more explicit. As we will see, Nehemiah's great enemies, Sanballat, Tobiah, and Geshem, accuse him precisely of instigating a rebellion: "They derided us and despised us and said, 'What is this thing that you are doing? Are you rebelling against the king?'" (Neh. 2:19). Nehemiah by no means denies that such a rebellion is his ultimate goal. He simply answers: "The God of heaven will make us prosper, and we his servants will arise and build; but you have no portion or right or memorial in Jerusalem" (2:20). Sanballat, Tobiah, and Geshem are not thereby assuaged. After Nehemiah has finished the wall of Jerusalem so that no breach remained, they try to entrap him by inviting him to a meeting outside the walls. When he refuses to come, "Sanballat for the fifth time sent his servant to me" (6:5). This time Sanballat's servant carries "an open letter in his hand.

---

1. Vanhoye comments that "exegetes believe that in the earlier version of the text the 'crown' was intended for Zerubbabel and that the text was later altered in view of a change in the historical situation," namely, the lack of a successor to the Davidic line (1986, 41).

In it was written, 'It is reported among the nations, and Geshem also says it, that you and the Jews intend to rebel; that is why you are building the wall; and you wish to become their king, according to this report. And you have also set up prophets to proclaim concerning you in Jerusalem, "There is a king in Judah"''' (6:5–7). Sanballat argues that since this report will reach the ears of King Artaxerxes, Nehemiah and Sanballat should meet to discuss the matter. In response, Nehemiah dismisses the matter as utterly groundless: "No such things as you say have been done, for you are inventing them out of your own mind" (6:8). Undoubtedly, Nehemiah had not done the supremely impolitic things that Sanballat reports as popular rumors. But neither can such rumors be dismissed as telling us nothing about the goals of the rebuilding. Nehemiah may likely not have wanted to be king, but the return of a Davidic king is by no means yet humanly impossible, as it would be if Nehemiah and Ezra were already operating within the bounds of later Judaism.

The importance in which the book of Nehemiah holds the return of the Davidic king for the restoration of Israel appears also in the book of Nehemiah's presentation of Ezra the Scribe's speech in Neh. 9. Confessing to the Lord the sins of Israel, Ezra admits that the exile was a just punishment: "Our kings, our princes, our priests, and our fathers have not kept thy law or heeded thy commandments and thy warnings which thou didst give them. They did not serve thee in their kingdom, and in thy great goodness which thou gavest them, and in the large and rich land which thou didst set before them" (9:34–35). Ezra the Scribe looks back upon the kingdom as a great gift of God, a "large and rich land." Having granted the justice of God's punishment, however, Ezra begs that the current situation, in which Israel is at the mercy of a foreign king, be reversed: "Behold, we are slaves this day; in the land that thou gavest to our fathers to enjoy its fruit and its good gifts, behold, we are slaves. And its rich yield goes to the kings whom thou hast set over us because of our sins; they have power also over our bodies and over our cattle at their pleasure, and we are in great distress" (9:36–37). Ezra the Scribe therefore leads the people in renewing their covenantal obligations, clearly with the hope of a restoration that includes a Davidic king ruling in Jerusalem.

PART I

NEHEMIAH 1–6: THE HOLY LAND

Nehemiah 1–6 has primarily to do with holy land, as understood in light of the covenants with Abraham, Moses, and David. The center of the land, the locus of divine indwelling, is Jerusalem, the City of David at whose heart is the temple. The holy land points forward to fulfillment in the body of Christ, both as the incarnate Son and as his body the church. In this consummation the covenantal land is not spiritualized away, so as to become ethereal, inward, and nonbodily. Rather it becomes ever more bodily and visible, in the flesh of Christ and in his members the "living stones" (1 Pet. 2:5) arranged around the "rock" of Peter who bears witness to Christ (Matt. 16:16, 18).

In Neh. 1 Nehemiah hears of the plight of Jerusalem, how its wall and gates remain broken down. Nehemiah 2 describes Nehemiah's rebuilding mission, and Neh. 3 describes the actual repairs to the gates and wall. Nehemiah 4 continues with the work, yet now in the presence of open enemies of the rebuilding. Nehemiah 5 reveals that many of the returned exiles were being forced to sell their land due to famine, so that the land was being owned increasingly by a wealthy few who were oppressing the others. Nehemiah 6 begins with the completion of Jerusalem's wall, a great event in salvation history that is quickly followed by significant threats to Nehemiah's life.

NEHEMIAH 1

Concerning Jerusalem

Flourishing While God's People Suffer

In 445 BC, when the book of Nehemiah commences, Nehemiah is *cupbearer to the king*, that is, to King Artaxerxes of Persia. As a courtier, he has an important position in the Persian Empire.[1] However, in his conversation with *Hanani, one of my brethren*, Nehemiah has to face the contrast that his own comfort and prestige make with the serious difficulties that the people of God, Nehemiah's own people, are presently enduring. *The Jews that survived, who had escaped exile*, are in Judah, but they are poor and weak. They have survived and escaped, while Nehemiah has risen to the comfortable position of cupbearer. Nehemiah is flourishing at the court of Artaxerxes, whereas in Judah and Jerusalem *the survivors there in the province who escaped exile are in great trouble and shame; the wall of Jerusalem is broken down, and its gates are destroyed by fire.*

Nehemiah is hardly the first member of the people of Israel to be placed in such a situation, in which his own good fortune under a foreign king contrasts with the desperate plight of the people of God. Joseph, through his God-given ability to interpret dreams, rose almost to the top of the Egyptian political hierarchy by age thirty: "And Pharaoh said to Joseph, 'Behold, I have set you over

---

1. Blenkinsopp comments on Nehemiah's position: "The wine steward (or cupbearer or butler) had an important and influential office and could therefore serve ideally as a means of access to the king. Classical authors (e.g., Herodotus 3.34; Xenophon, *Cyropaedia* 1.3, 8–9, 11) attest to the high status attaching to this office. The sage Ahiqar, also a cupbearer, is described as second in rank to Esarhaddon at the Assyrian court (Tobit 1:22). . . . The position was one of great trust since, *inter alia*, the cupbearer had to taste the wine to forestall any attempt at poisoning, a favorite means of disposing of the opposition at the Persian court" (1988, 212–13).

all the land of Egypt.' Then Pharaoh took his signet ring from his hand and put it on Joseph's hand, and arrayed him in garments of fine linen, and put a gold chain about his neck; and he made him to ride in his second chariot; and they cried before him, 'Bow the knee!' Thus he set him over all the land of Egypt" (Gen. 41:41–43). Although Pharaoh promises Joseph that "only as regards the throne will I be greater than you" (41:40) and although Joseph marries an Egyptian woman from a priestly family and takes an Egyptian name, Joseph's heart is still with Jacob/Israel his father and his eleven brothers, despite what his elder brothers have done to him. When his brothers are forced to come beg grain from Pharaoh in Egypt, Joseph first hides his identity but later tells them all that is in his heart: "I am your brother, Joseph, whom you sold into Egypt. And now do not be distressed, or angry with yourselves, because you sold me here; for God sent me before you to preserve life" (45:4–5)—in particular to preserve the lives of his family, from which all Israel descends.

Likewise Moses, a member of the tribe of Levi born during a time of persecution of the Hebrew slaves in Egypt, was left by his mother in a basket at the riverbank, only to be discovered by one of Pharaoh's daughters, who recognizes him as "one of the Hebrews' children" (Exod. 2:6) and places him with his mother as a wet nurse. When he is old enough, his mother "brought him to Pharaoh's daughter, and he became her son; and she named him Moses" (2:10). Raised as a son of Pharaoh's daughter, and therefore in a princely manner, Moses nevertheless remains attuned to the sufferings of his people. His labors on behalf of his people begin when he has reached adulthood: "One day, when Moses had grown up, he went out to his people and looked on their burdens; and he saw an Egyptian beating a Hebrew, one of his people. He looked this way and that, and seeing no one he killed the Egyptian and hid him in the sand" (2:11–12). For this action, he gains no credit among either his people (2:13–14) or Pharaoh, who "sought to kill Moses" (2:15), forcing him to flee to Midian.

A further example is Esther, who becomes Ahasueras's queen during a dark time for the Israelites in Babylon (Esth. 2:17). The leading man of the kingdom, Haman, "was filled with fury" (3:5) when Mordecai, Queen Esther's guardian, refuses out of obedience to the Torah to do obeisance to Haman. Haman plots a genocidal campaign against the people of Israel and receives King Ahasueras's approval of the plan. Haman tells King Ahasuerus: "There is a certain people scattered abroad and dispersed among the peoples in all the provinces of your kingdom; their laws are different from those of every other people, and they do not keep the king's laws, so that it is not for the king's profit to tolerate them. If it please the king, let it be decreed that they be destroyed" (3:8–9). At this moment of crisis, Esther uses her power with Ahasuerus to intercede for her people, and the Israelites are saved and Haman punished.

Like Joseph, Nehemiah is an important servant of the king and possesses influence that can be used on behalf of the people of Israel. Like Moses, Nehemiah is moved to action, radically changing the course of his career, by seeing the pitiful state of the people of Israel. Both Joseph and Moses have administrative skills, and it is such abilities that especially characterize Nehemiah. Finally like Esther, Nehemiah employs his influence with the Persian king for the service of his people.

In all of these examples, one sees Jesus's attitude toward rulers: "Render therefore to Caesar the things that are Caesar's, and to God the things that are God's" (Matt. 22:21). Jesus does not condemn the secular power, but instead he makes clear that there is a higher authority, God. Justice for the people of God, and the flourishing of the people of God, belongs rightly to the concerns of those Israelites who occupy positions of influence with rulers.

Nehemiah's Prayer

Nehemiah responds to Hanani's words with solemn mourning, observed likewise in the book of Ezra: *When I heard these words I sat down and wept, and mourned for days; and I continued fasting and praying before the God of heaven.* In praying to God, he emphasizes three elements: God's covenant with Israel, the sins by which Israel has violated the covenant, and God's promise that if Israel were to repent the covenantal curse would be lifted. This simple covenantal piety, seeking the end of exile and the restoration of Israel, guides Nehemiah's actions from henceforth.

In his prayer Nehemiah confesses not only that Israel as a whole has sinned against the covenant, but also that he himself, as a member of the people of Israel, has broken the covenant with God. He asks God: *Let thy ear be attentive, and thy eyes open, to hear the prayer of thy servant which I now pray before thee day and night for the people of Israel thy servants, confessing the sins of the people of Israel, which we have sinned against thee. Yea, I and my father's house have sinned.* Thus his covenantal piety, grounded in the relationship of the whole people to God, recognizes a deeply personal relationship to God, even though the personal relationship to God is understood within the communal relationship to God. "If one member suffers, all suffer together; if one member is honored, all rejoice together" (1 Cor. 12:26).

How does Nehemiah understand "sin"? His covenantal piety is grounded in the Torah; to sin against God is to fail to obey God's law, which is not merely a set of rules but a covenantal relationship that marks out a people separated to the worship of God. Since the covenantal relationship is not with a local god but rather is with the Lord *God of heaven, the great and terrible God*, Nehemiah knows that this God can be trusted to keep *covenant and steadfast love with those who love him and keep his commandments.*

Israel was to have been this community of *those who love him.* However, Nehemiah confesses: *We have acted very corruptly against thee, and have not kept the commandments, the statutes, and the ordinances which thou didst command thy servant Moses.* Even so, because God is faithful, Israel's failure to observe the precepts of holiness does not annul the covenant. Nehemiah reminds God of his promise to Israel (see Deut. 30) that *if you return to me and keep my commandments and do them, though your dispersed be under the farthest skies, I will gather them thence and bring them to the place which I have chosen, to make my name dwell there.* If the people are holy, God will dwell with them in the land, and will rebuild their walls. Despite their sins, the people of Israel are still *thy servants and thy people, whom thou hast redeemed by thy great power and by thy strong hand.* By rebuilding their walls, God will restore their covenantal separation from the idolatry of the surrounding peoples. These rebuilt walls will be more than a physical barrier. "Come to him, to that living stone, rejected by men but in God's sight chosen and precious; and like living stones be yourselves built into a spiritual house, to be a holy priesthood, to offer spiritual sacrifices acceptable to God through Jesus Christ" (1 Pet. 2:4–5).

The desire for intimate union between Israel and God thus inspires Nehemiah's administrative efforts to strengthen the position of the returned exiles in Judah and Jerusalem and in particular to rebuild the walls of Jerusalem. For Nehemiah, too much is at stake for Israel's return to the land to be allowed to fail. Nehemiah prays that God will bless his plan: *O LORD, let thy ear be attentive to the prayer of thy servant, and to the prayer of thy servants who delight to fear thy name; and give success to thy servant today, and grant him mercy in the sight of this man.* As we will see, God's mercy will indeed manifest itself for the glory of his name, so that ultimately all nations will be brought into his mercy. "But you are a chosen race, a royal priesthood, a holy nation, God's own people, that you may declare the wonderful deeds of him who called you out of darkness into his marvelous light. Once you were no people but now you are God's people; once you had not received mercy but now you have received mercy" (1 Pet. 2:9–10). Israel's separation from the nations will ultimately mean that all nations, in Christ, are enabled to enter into the church's visible "walls" of holiness.

The one whom Nehemiah calls *this man* is King Artaxerxes. Nehemiah's mission depends, like Ezra's, upon Artaxerxes' support. Just as Ezra depended upon God moving Artaxerxes' heart, so Nehemiah prays for *mercy in the sight of this man.*

NEHEMIAH 2

Rebuilding—First Steps

Nehemiah's Request

Nehemiah's position as cupbearer entails handing Artaxerxes his wine, an auspicious moment for making requests of the king. Some narrative summary is appropriate here so as to understand the authority that Nehemiah obtains from King Artaxerxes.

Three months after his meeting with Hanani, Nehemiah prepares to make his request by appearing before the king with a noticeably sad expression on his face. The king asks about the cause of this sadness, and Nehemiah, *very much afraid*, takes up his vocation by making his request: *Let the king live for ever! Why should not my face be sad, when the city, the place of my fathers' sepulchres, lies waste, and its gates have been destroyed by fire?* Artaxerxes understands that Nehemiah is requesting to be sent to repair Jerusalem. After a friendly discussion, he grants Nehemiah temporary leave from his position as cupbearer in order to make the repairs.

Nehemiah then asks for and receives a letter from Artaxerxes that does two things: it extends the king's protection upon Nehemiah for his journey, and it commands that sufficient *timber* be given to Nehemiah to *make beams for the gates of the fortress of the temple, and for the wall of the city, and for the house which I shall occupy.* That Nehemiah intends to build himself a house indicates the importance of the position that he has obtained, and that he openly speaks of *the gates of the fortress* and *the wall of the city* shows the trust that Artaxerxes has for him.

Governor of Judah

Traveling to Jerusalem as governor of Judah, Nehemiah at once encounters enemies: *Sanballat the Horonite*, governor of Samaria, and *Tobiah the servant, the Ammonite*.[1] These two recognized in Nehemiah a threat to their authority: *It displeased them greatly that some one had come to seek the welfare of the children of Israel.* "Who will have pity on you, O Jerusalem, or who will bemoan you? Who will turn aside to ask about your welfare?" (Jer. 15:5). "For I will restore health to you, and your wounds I will heal, says the LORD, because they have called you an outcast: 'It is Zion, for whom no one cares!'" (30:17).

Like Ezra, Nehemiah does nothing before he has been in Jerusalem *three days*.[2] After this period, *I arose in the night, I and a few men with me; and I told no one what my God had put into my heart to do for Jerusalem.* He undertakes a secret reconnaissance of Jerusalem's walls. For this mission he leaves Jerusalem *by the Valley Gate*. This choice of gate recalls King Uzziah of Judah, who devoted his reign to increasing the military strength and fortifications of Judah and Jerusalem. He "built towers in Jerusalem at the Corner Gate and at the Valley Gate and at the Angle, and fortified them" (2 Chr. 26:9). Yet this same king, although he "reigned fifty-two years in Jerusalem" and "did what was right in the eyes of the LORD" (26:3–4), sought to usurp for himself the priestly duties in the temple. His arrogance proved his destruction: "When he became angry with the priests leprosy broke out on his forehead, in the presence of the priests in the house of the LORD, by the altar of incense" (26:19). Nehemiah will devote himself to fortifying Jerusalem, but he will carefully respect the distinction between his duties and priestly duties; unlike Ezra, Nehemiah is not a priest. After visiting the *Jackal's Well*, the *Dung Gate*, the *Fountain Gate*, and the *King's Pool*—and inspecting the walls of Jerusalem along the way—Nehemiah reenters Jerusalem *by the Valley Gate*.

1. On Sanballat and Tobiah see Blenkinsopp 1988, 216–19. Blenkinsopp proposes that Sanballat (whose name means "the god Sin has given life" in Babylonian) comes from a family of returned exiles from "one of the Beth-horons settled by Ephraimites in the Shephelah northwest of Jerusalem" (1988, 216), and he notes that Sanballat's family "maintained its control over Samaria for at least a century, during which time its connections with the high priestly family in Jerusalem remained close" (1988, 217). Blenkinsopp finds it likely that Tobiah "was in fact governor of the Ammonite region, whatever its precise status under the Persians, as Sanballat was of Samaria and Geshem (Gashmu) of the Kedarite region" (1988, 218). He adds: "About two centuries later the aristocratic Tobiad family, which was closely related to the Jerusalem priesthood, established itself as a quasi-autonomous power in the Ammonite region, where they presumably already had connections among the Jewish settlers there (cf. Jer. 40:11, 14; 41:10, 15; 49:2). Something of the history of this family can be reconstructed from Josephus (*Ant.* 12.160–236), the Zeno papyri from the mid-third century, and the excavations at 'Araq el-Emir (cf. also 1 Macc. 5:10–13; 2 Macc. 12:17). It would be quite natural to conclude that the Ammonite foe of Nehemiah was the ancestor of these Tobiads" (1988, 218–19).

2. Blenkinsopp points out that "'three days' is simply a conventional way of designating a brief passage of time" (1988, 221).

Only then does he consult with *the Jews, the priests, the nobles, the officials, and the rest that were to do the work*. Not surprisingly given Artaxerxes' support, his proposal for rebuilding the walls gains their support. But he faces serious opposition from *Sanballat the Horonite and Tobiah the servant*, joined now by *Geshem the Arab*, king of Kedar to the south. They accuse him of *rebelling against the king*, Artaxerxes. It is no wonder then that he took so much trouble earlier to keep his plans secret. "Discretion will watch over you; understanding will guard you; delivering you from the way of evil, from men of perverted speech, who forsake the paths of uprightness to walk in the ways of darkness" (Prov. 2:11–13).

Jerusalem and the Heavenly City

In response to his opponents, Nehemiah asserts his authority over Jerusalem: *The God of heaven will make us prosper, and we his servants will arise and build; but you have no portion or right or memorial in Jerusalem*. The Lord said through Jeremiah: "I have loved you with an everlasting love; therefore I have continued my faithfulness to you. Again I will build you, and you shall be built, O virgin Israel!" (Jer. 31:3–4). The ultimate fulfillment of this rebuilding of the walls transcends the earthly Jerusalem, but this does not make the physical rebuilding any less important. *The God of heaven will make us prosper, and we his servants will arise and build*. These earthly efforts prepare for the Messiah and belong to God's work of rebuilding "virgin Israel."

In order to appreciate the scope of Nehemiah's promise that *we his servants will arise and build*, we must remember the city's beginning and end. David built Jerusalem as a royal city from which to govern the twelve tribes. Jerusalem stands on elevated terrain near the boundary that divides the southern and northern tribes. David had to conquer it from the Jebusites, who had not been fully conquered by Saul or by any previous Israelite conquest: "And the king and his men went to Jerusalem against the Jebusites, the inhabitants of the land, who said to David, 'You will not come in here but the blind and the lame will ward you off'—thinking, 'David cannot come in here.' Nevertheless David took the stronghold of Zion, that is, the city of David" (2 Sam. 5:6–7; cf. Judg. 1:21). After conquering the city, David added significantly to its dimensions, as did Solomon the builder of the temple: "David built the city round about from the Millo inward" (2 Sam. 5:9).

The significance of Jerusalem is secured not solely by the construction of the temple at the city's heart, but more fundamentally by God's covenantal promise to David that "I will appoint a place for my people Israel, and will plant them, that they may dwell in their own place, and be disturbed no more; and violent men shall afflict them no more" (7:10). Just as Ps. 119 praises the everlasting Torah, so Ps. 122 praises Jerusalem: "I was glad when they said to me,

'Let us go to the house of the LORD!' Our feet have been standing within your gates, O Jerusalem! Jerusalem, built as a city which is bound firmly together, to which the tribes go up, the tribes of the LORD, as was decreed for Israel, to give thanks to the name of the LORD" (122:1–4). Psalm 122 goes on to praise the Davidic "thrones for judgment" (122:5) and to offer a fervent prayer: "Pray for the peace of Jerusalem! 'May they prosper who love you! Peace be within your walls, and security within your towers!'" (122:6–7).

Thus the final conquest of Jerusalem in 587 by the Babylonians under Nebuchadnezzar is almost unimaginable in the spiritual desolation that it enacts. Nebuchadnezzar's captain, Nebuzaradan, "came to Jerusalem. And he burned the house of the LORD, and the king's house and all the houses of Jerusalem; every great house he burned down. And all the army of the Chaldeans, who were with the captain of the guard, broke down the walls around Jerusalem" (2 Kgs. 25:8–10).

Is this the end of the city? No. Isaiah prophesies the great restoration of Israel and Jerusalem on the day of the Lord's judgment of the nations: "On that day the LORD will punish the host of heaven, in heaven, and the kings of the earth, on the earth. . . . Then the moon will be confounded, and the sun ashamed; for the LORD of hosts will reign on Mount Zion and in Jerusalem and before his elders he will manifest his glory" (Isa. 24:21, 23). The Lord, Isaiah says, "will come down to fight upon Mount Zion and upon its hill. Like birds hovering, so the LORD of hosts will protect Jerusalem; he will protect and deliver it, he will spare and rescue it" (31:4–5). Through Isaiah the Lord promises to protect Jerusalem from the Assyrian invaders, and even if Jerusalem is scourged "the surviving remnant of the house of Judah shall again take root downward, and bear fruit upward; for out of Jerusalem shall go forth a remnant, and out of Mount Zion a band of survivors" (37:31–32). The destruction of Jerusalem will not be final, because the Lord, Creator and Redeemer, "says of Jerusalem, 'She shall be inhabited,' and of the cities of Judah, 'They shall be built, and I will raise up their ruins'" (44:26). Jerusalem will dwell in marital intimacy with the Lord: "You shall no more be termed Forsaken, and your land shall no more be termed Desolate; but you shall be called My delight is in her, and your land Married; for the LORD delights in you, and your land shall be married" (62:4).

Jeremiah likewise prophesies the coming destruction of Jerusalem (Jer. 26), and equally he prophesies restoration. The Lord says through Jeremiah: "In this place of which you say, 'It is a waste without man or beast,' in the cities of Judah and the streets of Jerusalem that are desolate, without man or inhabitant or beast, there shall be heard again the voice of mirth and the voice of gladness, the voice of the bridegroom and the voice of the bride" (33:10–11). The temple will be rebuilt and the Davidic king restored: "In those days and at that time I will cause a righteous Branch to spring forth for David; and he shall execute justice and righteousness in the land. In those days Judah will be saved and Jerusalem will dwell securely. And this is the name by which it will be called: 'The LORD is our righteousness'" (33:15–16).

Ezekiel depicts an "outpouring of thy [God's] wrath upon Jerusalem" (Ezek. 9:8). The Lord commands Ezekiel to preach the destruction of Jerusalem, the temple, and the land of Israel (Ezek. 21). Yet Ezekiel also prophesies restoration: "Thus says the Lord GOD: On the day that I cleanse you from all your iniquities, I will cause the cities to be inhabited, and the waste places shall be rebuilt. . . . And they will say, 'This land that was desolate has become like the garden of Eden'" (36:33, 35). Not only will Jerusalem be restored in population, but also "my servant David shall be king over them; and they shall all have one shepherd" (37:24), and from a new temple will flow miraculous water that produces fruit trees that nourish and heal the nations (Ezek. 47).

This day of cleansing from sin, in which the holy Davidic king will inaugurate his everlasting reign and build the temple from which flows the water of life, comes about in Christ Jesus: he is the "end" of the city. The prophetess Anna, eighty-four years old (seven times twelve), meets the baby Jesus as his parents present him at the temple for circumcision: "And coming up at that very hour she gave thanks to God, and spoke of him to all who were looking for the redemption of Jerusalem" (Luke 2:38). Thus the book of Revelation describes the heavenly Jerusalem, the perfect marriage of God and humankind in Christ: "'Come, I will show you the Bride, the wife of the Lamb.' And in the Spirit he carried me away to a great, high mountain, and showed me the holy city Jerusalem coming down out of heaven from God, having the glory of God. . . . It had a great, high wall, with twelve gates, and at the gates twelve angels, and on the gates the names of the twelve tribes of the sons of Israel were inscribed" (Rev. 21:9–12). The tribes of Israel are united to the apostles of the Messiah in the wall of the heavenly Jerusalem that God has built: "And the wall of the city had twelve foundations, and on them the twelve names of the twelve apostles of the Lamb" (21:14).

When Nehemiah says that God will *prosper* those who *arise and build*, surely he could not have had in view a heavenly Jerusalem. But he does have in view the eschatological restoration of Jerusalem—"the holy city, new Jerusalem," which is "a bride adorned for her husband" (21:2)—and it is this that comes about through Christ Jesus's entrance into the walls of the Jerusalem that Nehemiah has rebuilt. By "journeying toward Jerusalem" (Luke 13:22) and his pasch, Jesus enacts the promised restoration and establishes the walls of "the Jerusalem above" who is "our mother" (Gal. 4:26). Those who have awaited God's forgiveness and sought to do his will become by this restoration "a kingdom and priests to our God" (Rev. 5:10). Only these have a *portion or right or memorial in Jerusalem.* "Nothing unclean shall enter it, nor any one who practices abomination or falsehood, but only those who are written in the Lamb's book of life" (21:27).

NEHEMIAH 3

Rebuilding Continued

The Gates of Jerusalem

Nehemiah does not take sole credit for the rebuilding; on the contrary he distributes the credit generously, beginning with the high priest, the grandson of Jeshua the high priest who was the companion of Zerubbabel. *Then Eliashib the high priest rose up with his brethren the priests and they built the Sheep Gate. They consecrated it and set its doors; they consecrated it as far as the Tower of the Hundred, as far as the Tower of Hananel.* "The word of the LORD by the mouth of Jeremiah" (Ezra 1:1) resonates here: "Behold, the days are coming, says the LORD, when the city shall be rebuilt for the LORD from the tower of Hananel to the Corner Gate. . . . It shall not be uprooted or overthrown any more for ever" (Jer. 31:38, 40).

The high priest and his brethren build and consecrate *the Sheep Gate*. How might we contemplate the Sheep Gate? "Israel is a hunted sheep driven away by lions. First the king of Assyria devoured him, and now at last Nebuchadnezzar king of Babylon has gnawed his bones. Therefore, thus says the LORD of hosts, the God of Israel: Behold, I am bringing punishment on the king of Babylon and his land, as I punished the king of Assyria" (Jer. 50:17–18). After this punishment has occurred, Jeremiah's prophecy continues, the sheep that is Israel shall be restored to its "pasture" (50:19), and "iniquity shall be sought in Israel, and there shall be none; and sin in Judah, and none shall be found; for I will pardon those whom I leave as a remnant" (50:20). Like the Tower of Hananel, the restoration of the Sheep Gate fits within Jeremiah's vision of the forgiveness of sins and a holy people dwelling with their God.

The account of Eliashib the high priest is followed by a detailed list of all those who worked on the repairing of the gates and walls, with the names of the gates. To be brave in Israel is now to rebuild; the list that Nehemiah provides recalls earlier lists of Israel's "mighty men" (2 Sam. 23:8) with their deeds of valor against Israel's enemies. But the heroes now include priests, goldsmiths, perfumers, district rulers, temple servants, gatekeepers, and merchants. This is the people of God in all fullness, seeking holiness by sacrificing their resources and endangering their lives so as to dwell with God in Jerusalem.

They repair Jerusalem, the City of David, with its once and future king in view: *And Shallum the son of Colhozeh, ruler of the district of Mizpah, repaired the Fountain Gate; he rebuilt it and covered it and set its doors, its bolts, and its bars; and he built the wall of the Pool of Shelah of the king's garden, as far as the stairs that go down from the City of David.*[1] These stairs have, for Bede, a mystical sense that develops Nehemiah's understanding of Jerusalem as a place of ascent to God: "For David made the steps by which we should ascend to his city when divine mercy taught us the order of the virtues by which we may seek heavenly things and when it granted us the gift of seeking these same virtues" (2006, 171). Nehemiah's building of walls and stairs here symbolizes the upbuilding of the church's walls through the virtues of its "living stones" (1 Pet. 2:5).

In this interpretation the spiritual meaning of Jerusalem does not displace or negate its physical meaning. Jerusalem, so carefully rebuilt and repaired by Nehemiah and by those who helped him, is the physical center of the Messiah's work for the salvation of the entire world: "He went on his way through towns and villages, teaching, and journeying toward Jerusalem" (Luke 13:22). Jesus tells some skeptical Pharisees during his messianic entrance into Jerusalem, when they criticize him for allowing himself to be hailed by the people as the Davidic king returning to Zion to restore Israel: "I tell you, if these were silent, the very stones would cry out" (19:40). Jerusalem's physical meaning is taken up into the very flesh of Jesus: "Jesus answered them, 'Destroy this temple, and in three days I will raise it up.' The Jews then said, 'It has taken forty-six years to build this temple, and will you raise it up in three days?' But he spoke of the temple of his body" (John 2:19–21).

Nehemiah tells us that *the Tekoites repaired; but their nobles did not put their necks to the work of their* Lord. Although the internal opposition at this stage does not appear very large, it is an ominous sign. Nehemiah will face significant internal opposition from the wealthy to his work of renewal. Even so, the Tekoites shortly afterward are mentioned as having *repaired another section opposite the great projecting tower as far as the wall of Ophel.* Bede gives a mystical interpretation of this tower: "When all righteous people, from the height of contemplation, to which even in this life they raise their mind, looking down

---

1. Fensham tells us that "Mizpah was situated approximately 8 miles north of Jerusalem" (1982, 176).

on temporal things in order to desire celestial ones, in the next life really do ascend to observe the splendour of the Lord's incarnation, when even the glory of divine eternity is revealed" (2006, 177).

The Flock of the Messiah

The list of repairs ends where it began, at the Sheep Gate: *And between the upper chamber of the corner and the Sheep Gate the goldsmiths and the merchants repaired.* The enclosure of the City of David has been completed. Now the gates of Jerusalem may greet the Messiah. "Lift up your heads, O gates! and be lifted up, O ancient doors! that the King of glory may come in. Who is the King of glory? The LORD, strong and mighty, the LORD, mighty in battle!" (Ps. 24:7–8). This mighty Lord, the king of glory, is also "the good shepherd" (John 10:11) and "the door of the sheep" (10:7). The Lord is the Sheep Gate. "I am the door; if any one enters by me, he will be saved, and will go in and out and find pasture. The thief comes only to steal and kill and destroy; I came that they may have life, and have it abundantly. I am the good shepherd. The good shepherd lays down his life for the sheep" (10:9–11).

Bede remarks that the rebuilders of Jerusalem and all those who have worked upon the building of the church share the same goal, namely, union with God through holiness. He therefore offers a strongly ecclesiological reading of Neh. 3: "Those who build the gates and the towers, by which means either the citizens may enter or the enemies be kept out, are none other than the prophets, apostles and evangelists" (2006, 178). The prophets, apostles, and evangelists build through their teaching about faith and charity, which are the gates and buildings of the new Jerusalem, the church. Their teaching prescribes, says Bede, "the form and order of faith and righteous action whereby we should enter the unity of the Holy Church . . . and through whose words we learn how we may refute and repel the adversaries of truth" (2006, 178). Other builders and restorers—pastors and teachers—share, from generation to generation, in the labor of building up the visible "walls" of the church, set apart for holiness. Bede states: "And just as Nehemiah, by enumerating consecutively all the builders of the city, makes them forever memorable, so too the Lord, the Consoler of our poverty, records in heaven the names of all who build his Church among the elect" (2006, 178). The names of the rebuilders, carefully listed by Nehemiah, provide a foretaste of the Book of Life for those who are able to "hear what the Spirit says to the churches" (Rev. 3:13). "He who conquers, I will make him a pillar in the temple of my God; never shall he go out of it, and I will write on him the name of my God, and the name of the city of my God, the new Jerusalem which comes down from my God out of heaven" (3:12).

NEHEMIAH 4

Opposition

Sanballat, governor of Samaria, in a fury asks five questions *in the presence of his brethren and of the army of Samaria*. The army's presence underscores the menacing character of the threat posed by Sanballat to Nehemiah's efforts.[1] Sanballat's five questions together form a theological tapestry that points to the accomplishment of "the word of the LORD by the mouth of Jeremiah" (Ezra 1:1).

What Are These Feeble Jews Doing?

The root of the Hebrew word translated "feeble" is *'ml*, which elsewhere in scripture denotes the withering of a plant and a people without hope (for discussion see Fensham 1982, 180). "The earth mourns and withers, the world languishes ['*ml*] and withers; the heavens languish ['*ml*] together with the earth. The earth lies polluted under its inhabitants; for they have transgressed the laws, violated the statutes, broken the everlasting covenant. . . . The wine mourns, the vine languishes ['*ml*], all the merry-hearted sigh" (Isa. 24:4–5, 7). "Therefore the land mourns, and all who dwell in it languish ['*ml*]" (Hos. 4:3). Yet the Jews under Nehemiah are anything but hopeless or languishing, although before Nehemiah arrived they had indeed fallen into such a plight.

---

1. Fensham comments: "Some think that *ḥayil* does not refer to an army, because Samaria was not a military colony. It is possible that the term *ḥayil* has a wider connotation and denotes the lords . . . who were in command of Samaria, but this does not exclude the military" (1982, 180).

Pharaoh's original response when confronted by Moses and Aaron was similar to Sanballat's response to the efforts of Nehemiah: *What are these feeble Jews doing?* Pharaoh says scornfully: "Moses and Aaron, why do you take the people away from their work? Get to your burdens" (Exod. 5:4)—that is, continue to act as slaves should act. Sanballat sees these *feeble Jews* in the same light: since they are not militarily strong, they can be dismissed. The *feeble Jews* are under bondage to foreign rulers: "I have heard the groaning of the people of Israel whom the Egyptians hold in bondage and I have remembered my covenant" (6:5).

As so often, the Lord acts through the feeble. The prophet and judge Samuel is but a boy when he must tell Eli, old and powerful, that God has forsaken Eli and Eli's sons: "Then Eli perceived that the LORD was calling the boy. Therefore Eli said to Samuel, 'Go, lie down; and if he calls you, you shall say, "Speak, LORD, for thy servant hears"'" (1 Sam. 3:8–9). When the aged Samuel goes to anoint the next king of Israel and admires Jesse's eldest son, God admonishes Samuel: "Do not look on his appearance or on the height of his stature, because I have rejected him; for the LORD sees not as man sees; man looks on the outward appearance, but the LORD looks on the heart" (16:7). David is chosen and anointed, although only a boy. Likewise David's brother and King Saul criticize David for coming into a camp of soldiers while still "but a youth" (17:33), but it is David who kills the Philistine warrior Goliath. The Lord gives Gideon, with only three hundred men, the victory over thousands of Midianite soldiers, "lest Israel vaunt themselves against me [the LORD], saying, 'My own hand has delivered me'" (Judg. 7:2).

Elijah, the prophet of the Lord, finds himself utterly alone: "I, even I only, am left a prophet of the LORD; but Baal's prophets are four hundred and fifty men" (1 Kgs. 18:22). Elijah conquers by God's power, and with the fickle people now on his side, he has the prophets of Baal seized and killed; but this triumph lasts only a very short time. Almost immediately after his combat with the prophets of Baal, Elijah receives a threat on his life from Queen Jezebel. "Then he was afraid, and he arose and went for his life, and came to Beer-sheba, which belongs to Judah, and left his servant there. But he himself went a day's journey into the wilderness, and came and sat down under a broom tree; and he asked that he might die, saying, 'It is enough; now, O LORD, take away my life; for I am no better than my fathers'" (19:3–4).

Could it be that Israel, Elijah, and his fathers, will fail? *What are those feeble Jews doing?* Through Isaiah the Lord reveals that he will triumph through his feeble Servant, although men like Sanballat may still not believe: "Who has believed what we have heard? And to whom has the arm of the LORD been revealed?" (Isa. 53:1). The Servant appears to be nothing either to admire or to fear: "For he grew up before him like a young plant, and like a root out of dry ground; he had no form or comeliness that we should look at him, and no beauty that we should desire him. He was despised and rejected by men; a man of sorrows, and acquainted with grief; and as one from whom men hide their faces he was despised, and we esteemed him not" (53:2–3). Yet, precisely in his feeble weakness, he wins the victory over sin by his sufferings: "Surely he has borne our griefs and carried our sorrows; yet we esteemed him stricken, smitten by God, and afflicted. But he was wounded for our transgressions, he was bruised for our iniquities; upon him was the chastisement that made us whole, and with his stripes we are healed" (53:4–5). Although he seemed feeble, he was in fact the only strong one. All others had abandoned the Lord, and therefore only the feeble one could make satisfaction for sin and restore justice between humankind and God: "All we like sheep have gone astray; we have turned every one to his own way; and the LORD has laid on him the iniquity of us all" (53:6). The powerful of the world mocked and dismissed his suffering and considered him as merely a sinner like themselves: "And they made his grave with the wicked and with a rich man in his death, although he had done no violence, and there was no deceit in his mouth" (53:9). But God will reveal the ultimate triumph of the feeble one: "When he makes himself an offering for sin, he shall see his offspring, he shall prolong his days; the will of the LORD shall prosper in his hand; he shall see the fruit of the travail of his soul and be satisfied; by his knowledge shall the righteous one, my servant, make many to be accounted righteous; and he shall bear their iniquities" (53:10–11).

This is ultimately the answer to Sanballat, who ridiculed the Jews and does not know either what God has done in the past or what God will do in the future through God's *feeble Jews*. St. Paul says: "When I came to you, brethren, I did not come proclaiming to you the testimony of God in lofty words or wisdom. For I decided to know nothing among you except Jesus Christ and him crucified. And I was with you in weakness and in much fear and trembling" (1 Cor. 2:1–3). A faith based upon worldly power is no faith at all; faith must rest solely on the strength-in-weakness of "Jesus Christ and him crucified." Only thereby do we attain to the God who is love, rather than to the false gods of idolatrous pride. Paul can thus observe that "God chose what is foolish in the world to shame the wise, God chose what is weak in the world to shame the strong, God chose what is low and despised in the world, even things that are not, to bring to nothing things that are, so that no human being might boast in the presence of God" (1:27–29). True wisdom, strength, and life are found in the self-giving love of "Christ Jesus, whom God made our wisdom, our righteousness and sanctification and redemption" (1:30).

Will They Restore Things?

Sanballat sees that the Israelites, politically speaking, are impossibly weak, with only Artaxerxes' support giving them any hope at all. He doubts therefore that they can restore the walls of Jerusalem. But because Sanballat sees everything in terms of worldly politics—like Pilate asking Jesus: "Are you the King of the Jews?" (John 18:33) and "What is truth?" (18:38)—Sanballat does not observe that he is asking all the right questions.

Indeed Sanballat would have laughed to scorn such prophecies as Zechariah's: "Thus says the LORD of hosts: I am jealous for Zion with great jealousy, and I am jealous for her with great wrath. Thus says the LORD: I will return to Zion, and will dwell in the midst of Jerusalem, and Jerusalem shall be called the faithful city, and the mountain of the LORD of hosts, the holy mountain" (Zech. 8:2–3). How could the divine wrath reclaiming Jerusalem for God have seemed possible to Sanballat during the age of the Persian Empire? While he might have imagined that unless Artaxerxes were vigilant, the returned Israelites might eventually regain a small portion of their political strength, he could not have feared a full restoration. Not even the later successes of Judas Maccabeus endure for long, despite efforts to fortify "Mount Zion with high walls and strong towers round about, to keep the Gentiles from coming and trampling them down as they had done before" (1 Maccabees 4:60).

What does restoration require? Certainly God must cause Israel "to be inhabited as in your former times" and God must do "more good to you than ever before" (Ezek. 36:11). But restoration also requires other elements prophesied by Ezekiel. Central to restoration is a Davidic king: "I will save my flock, they shall no longer be a prey; and I will judge between sheep and sheep. And I will set up over them one shepherd, my servant David, and he shall feed them: he shall feed them and be their shepherd. And I, the LORD, will be their God, and my servant David shall be prince among them" (34:22–24). In fact, Ezekiel prophesies something more: "I myself [the LORD] will be the shepherd of my sheep" (34:15).

The promised restoration thus requires not merely that a Davidic king shepherd the people, but that the Lord himself be the shepherd. "And the angel said to her, 'Do not be afraid, Mary, for you have found favor with God. And behold, you will conceive in your womb and bear a son, and you shall call his name Jesus. He will be great, and will be called the Son of the Most High; and the Lord God will give to him the throne of his father David, and he will reign over the house of Jacob for ever; and of his kingdom there will be no end'" (Luke 1:30–33).

Will They Sacrifice?

Sanballat knows that the Israelites have been sacrificing in the temple since it was rebuilt, decades before Nehemiah's return. This third question may be viewed in the context of the previous two: Will the *feeble Jews* successfully *restore things* by means of an efficacious *sacrifice* that reconciles human beings to God?[2]

2. Fensham translates this as "are they going to offer there?" Regarding "to offer there," he

The tempter persuades Adam and Eve that if they eat of the forbidden fruit "you will not die" but rather "you will be like God" (Gen. 3:4–5). In contrast to Adam and Eve's prideful and foolish attempt to arrogate divine prerogatives to themselves, Jesus's self-sacrifice, offered in the freedom of perfect love, reverses the state of disobedience that distorted, by its lack of justice, the relationship between humankind and God. "For there is no distinction; since all have sinned and fall short of the glory of God, they are justified by his grace as a gift, through the redemption which is in Christ Jesus, whom God put forward as an expiation by his blood, to be received by faith" (Rom. 3:22–25). "For the Son of man also came not to be served but to serve, and to give his life as a ransom for many" (Mark 10:45).

Will They Finish Up in a Day?

There can be no question of the returned exiles finishing the walls *in a day*, as Sanballat knows, it is a project that will require months. And yet again there is prophetic testimony to just such an event. The Lord says through Isaiah: "Hark, an uproar from the city! A voice from the temple! The voice of the Lord, rendering recompense to his enemies! Before she was in labor she gave birth; before her pain came upon her she was delivered of a son. Who has heard such a thing? Who has seen such things? Shall a land be born in one day?" (Isa. 66:6–8). Similarly in Zechariah we learn: "Behold, a day of the Lord is coming" (Zech. 14:1); and on this day "Jerusalem shall remain aloft upon its site from the Gate of Benjamin to the place of the former gate, to the Corner Gate, and from the Tower of Hananel to the king's wine presses. And it shall be inhabited, for there shall be no more curse; Jerusalem shall dwell in security" (14:10–11). A land will be "born in one day"; on that day, the day of the Lord, "Jerusalem shall dwell in security."

What kind of restoration is this? It is a restoration that occurs through the passover of the Son of man: "At last two came forward and said, 'This fellow said, "I am able to destroy the temple of God, and to build it in three days."'" And the high priest stood up and said, 'Have you no answer to make? What is it that these men testify against you?'" (Matt. 26:60–62). Can the temple be rebuilt "in three days"? When Jesus remains silent, the high priest glimpses the truth: "And the high priest said to him, 'I adjure you by the living God, tell us if you are the Christ, the Son of God.' Jesus said to him, 'You have said so. But I tell you, hereafter you will see the Son of man seated at the right hand of Power, and coming on the clouds of heaven'" (26:63–64). Jesus here identifies himself as the fulfillment of the prophecy of Daniel, who proclaims:

comments: "It is not quite certain what is meant by this expression. It might refer to a foundation offering, or to an offering of thanksgiving for the completion of the task" (1982, 180).

"I saw in the night visions, and behold, with the clouds of heaven there came one like a son of man, and he came to the Ancient of Days and was presented before him. And to him was given dominion and glory and kingdom, that all peoples, nations, and languages should serve him; his dominion is an everlasting dominion" (Dan. 7:13–14). The Son of man receives divine prerogatives that only God can possess. Thus "the high priest tore his robes, and said, 'He has uttered blasphemy'" (Matt. 26:65).

There is more to Sanballat's mocking question, therefore, than he realizes. Ultimately what the day of Jesus Christ accomplishes is the fulfillment of the holy land: "And I saw the holy city, the new Jerusalem, coming down out of heaven from God, prepared as a bride adorned for her husband" (Rev. 21:2). Jesus's day accomplishes this because in Jesus "the dwelling of God is with men. He will dwell with them, and they shall be his people, and God himself will be with them; he will wipe away every tear from their eyes, and death shall be no more, neither shall there be mourning nor crying nor pain any more" (21:3–4). The rebuilding of the walls of Jerusalem by Nehemiah and his helpers belongs to Israel's striving toward the accomplishment of a people who dwell with God in holiness. Their efforts participate in the fullness of the day that God in Christ has brought about and is bringing about.

Nehemiah's efforts are no more in vain than are the church's efforts to establish justice on earth. The people of God are called to strive toward God, to participate in God's work, even with the knowledge that it is God, not the people, who will accomplish the work in a way that goes infinitely beyond what human resources could accomplish. St. Paul says: "We shall all be changed, in a moment, in the twinkling of an eye, at the last trumpet. For the trumpet will sound, and the dead will be raised imperishable, and we shall all be changed. For this perishable nature must put on the imperishable, and this mortal nature must put on immortality" (1 Cor. 15:51–53). Paul's conclusion can be applied not solely to Christian lives but also to the efforts of Nehemiah and his fellow workers: "But thanks be to God, who gives us the victory through our Lord Jesus Christ. Therefore, my beloved brethren, be steadfast, immovable, always abounding in the work of the Lord, knowing that in the Lord your labor is not in vain" (15:57–58).

Will They Revive the Stones out of the Heaps of Rubbish, and Burned Ones at That?

They do so, no doubt—what better stones to use than the ones that had been there before, although also new stones, surely, were found. Here again the question has meaning above what Sanballat knows. The Messiah, the embodiment of *these feeble Jews*, performs the *sacrifice* by which God wills to *restore things* and thereby accomplishes *in one day* that for which Israel had striven. How do human beings participate in this reconciliation of humankind to God? By faith: "Now faith is the assurance of things hoped for, the conviction of things not seen" (Heb. 11:1).

Is such faith, a gift of the Holy Spirit, possible only for those who live after Jesus and are able to hear and profess the gospel? No: "For by it [faith] the men of old received divine approval" (11:2). Among these "men of old," the letter to the Hebrews names Abel, Enoch, Noah, Abraham, Isaac, Jacob, Joseph, Moses, the Israelites who crossed the Red Sea, Rahab the harlot, "Gideon, Barak, Samson, Jephthah, . . . David and Samuel and the prophets—who through faith conquered kingdoms, enforced justice, received promises, stopped the mouths of lions, quenched raging fire, escaped the edge of the sword, won strength out of weakness, became mighty in war, put foreign armies to flight" (11:32–34).

But what does this powerful faith have to do with reviving *the stones out of the heaps of rubbish, and burned ones at that*? Faith is the foundation of a life of self-sacrifice that shares, through the interior action of the Holy Spirit, in Christ's sacrificial cross. Hebrews continues, speaking of those who lived before Christ: "Some were tortured, refusing to accept release, that they might rise again to a better life. Others suffered mocking and scourging, and even chains and imprisonment. They were stoned, they were sawn in two, they were killed with the sword; they went about in skins of sheep and goats, destitute, afflicted, ill-treated—of whom the world was not worthy" (11:35–38). Both the people of the covenants with Israel and the people who receive the new covenant in Christ Jesus and the descent of the Holy Spirit at Pentecost partake in the life of faith, hope, and charity that binds together God's holy people who, as God's dwelling, are the fulfillment of God's holy land. Paul teaches the Corinthians: "You are God's field, God's building" (1 Cor. 3:9).

The "foundation" of this building is Jesus Christ (3:11), who accomplishes the fulfillment of Torah and temple, God's perfect indwelling. He is "the [very] stone which the builders rejected" that has "become the head of the corner" (Ps. 118:22; Matt. 21:42; 1 Pet. 2:7). The apostle Peter teaches: "Come to him, to that living stone, rejected by men but in God's sight chosen and precious; and like living stones be yourselves built into a spiritual house, to be a holy priesthood, to offer spiritual sacrifices acceptable to God through Jesus Christ" (1 Pet. 2:4–5). What does it mean to be "like living stones"? Peter speaks about "trials": "In this [salvation by faith in the risen Christ] you rejoice, though now for a little while you may have to suffer various trials, so that the genuineness of your faith, more precious than gold which though perishable is tested by fire, may redound to praise and glory and honor at the revelation of Jesus Christ" (1:6–7). These "living stones," who are "tested by fire," have received faith, hope, and charity through the Messiah's triumph. Peter says: "But you are a chosen race, a royal priesthood, a holy nation, God's own people, that you may declare the wonderful deeds of him who called you out of darkness into his marvelous light. Once you were no people but now you are God's people; once you had not received mercy but now you have received mercy" (2:9–10).

These are *the stones out of the heaps of rubbish, and burned ones at that*, redeemed and tested by the fire of sacrificial trials, that God has constituted as his holy people in whom he dwells. Regarding those who possess faith and charity, Jesus says that the Holy Spirit "dwells with you, and will be in you" (John 14:17). He adds: "If a man loves me, he will keep my word, and my Father will love him, and we will come to him and make our home with him" (14:23).

The Fox and the Wall

Taking up Sanballat's tone of mockery, *Tobiah the Ammonite* also mocks the rebuilding efforts of Nehemiah and his followers: *Yes, what are they building—if a fox goes up on it he will break down their stone wall!* The mockery pertains to the rebuilt portions of Jerusalem's wall, but again one can suggest further meanings. Jerusalem is the embodiment of the people of God; to speak of the weakness of Jerusalem is to speak also of the weakness of God's people. Those united by faith and charity constitute "the temple of the living God" (2 Cor. 6:16), the church. Can Tobiah's mockery apply to the church? Is the church weak? Can any *fox* destroy its unity?

On the one hand, no *fox*, or opponent of Christ, can destroy the *stone wall* that is the church. When Peter confesses that Jesus is the Christ, Jesus tells him that "you are Peter, and on this rock I will build my church, and the powers of death shall not prevail against it. I will give you the keys of the kingdom of heaven, and whatever you bind on earth shall be bound in heaven, and whatever you loose on earth shall be loosed in heaven" (Matt. 16:18–19). No *fox* can knock the church down.

On the other hand, the church does not possess a strength that will be visible to the worldly minded. The *stone wall* often appears weak to the world. Paul reminds the Corinthians: "When I came to you, brethren, I did not come proclaiming to you the testimony of God in lofty words or wisdom. For I decided to know nothing among you except Jesus Christ and him crucified. And I was with you in weakness and in much fear and trembling" (1 Cor. 2:1–3). Those who have faith see in the "weakness" and "fear and trembling" of the visible church the "wisdom" of "Jesus Christ and him crucified," but this wisdom is invisible to the *fox* who does not know the Lord. Only in faith does the power of the "ministry of reconciliation" appear (2 Cor. 5:18–19).

How does Paul strengthen the *stone wall* against the depredations of the *fox* who rejects Christ? As an "ambassador for Christ" (5:20), Paul is not merely a member of the Christian community; he possesses authority that comes from Christ. This is confirmed when the other apostles, within the unity of the church, recognize his authority: "When they perceived the grace that was given to me, James and Cephas [Peter] and John, who were reputed to be pillars, gave to me and Barnabas the right hand of fellowship" (Gal. 2:9). These pillars govern the visible church. Paul tells the Corinthians: "I write this while I am away from you, in order that when I come I may not have to be severe in my use of the authority which the Lord has given me for building up and not for tearing down" (2 Cor. 13:10). The Lord gives Paul the authority "for building up" the church so that *if a fox goes up on it he will* most certainly not *break down their stone wall,* "which is the church of the living God, the pillar and bulwark of the truth" (1 Tim. 3:15).

In communion with the "pillars" of "the church of the living God," Paul undertakes his "ministry of reconciliation" that builds up the church. He reminds Timothy: "Do not neglect the gift you have, which was given you by prophetic utterance when the elders laid their hands on you" (4:14). The ministry of reconciliation involves a sacramental sharing of the healing and transforming power of Christ's paschal mystery. "And he took bread, and when he had given thanks he broke it and gave it to them, saying, 'This is my body which is given for you. Do this in remembrance of me.' And likewise the cup after supper, saying, 'This cup which is poured out for you is the new covenant in my blood'" (Luke 22:19–20). "And Jesus came and said to them, 'All authority in heaven and on earth has been given to me. Go therefore and make disciples of all nations, baptizing them in the name of the Father and of the Son and of the Holy Spirit, teaching them to observe all things that I have commanded you; and lo, I am with you always, to the close of the age'" (Matt. 28:18–20).

Nehemiah knows that Jerusalem is not merely a city among other cities, but rather is destined for a glorious fulfillment. "Then the moon will be confounded, and the sun ashamed; for the LORD of hosts will reign on Mount Zion and in Jerusalem and before his elders he will manifest his glory" (Isa. 24:23). But Nehemiah does not know how God wills to bring to fulfillment the work in which Nehemiah shares. "Behold, I am doing a new thing; now it springs forth, do you not perceive it?" (43:19).

Prayer and Work

Nehemiah prays for the punishment of the persecutors of the returned exiles, because these persecutors do not recognize the work of the Lord: *Hear, O our God, for we are despised; turn back their taunt upon their own heads, and give them up to be plundered in a land where they are captives. Do not cover their guilt, and let not their sin be blotted out from thy sight; for they have provoked thee to anger before the builders.*[3] When Moses asks the Lord, "I pray thee, show me

3. Fensham observes that "some hold the opinion that 'insult' from the root *k's* should mean 'provoke anger' and that God is the object. The translation is then 'for they have provoked

thy glory" (Exod. 33:18), "the LORD passed before him, and proclaimed, 'The LORD, the LORD, a God merciful and gracious, slow to anger, and abounding in steadfast love and faithfulness, keeping steadfast love for thousands, forgiving iniquity and transgression and sin, but who will by no means clear the guilty'" (33:6–7). The unrepentant who *have provoked thee to anger* will indeed be *captives.* God will manifest his glory in Jerusalem on his day of triumph, when the unrepentant "host of heaven" and "kings of the earth" are "shut up in a prison, and after many days they will be punished" (Isa. 24:21–22).

This day of triumph must have seemed far away for Nehemiah, facing the threatening taunts of Sanballat and Tobiah. Far from being able to respond to Sanballat and Tobiah from a position of worldly strength, Nehemiah can only continue with his task of restoring the wall. The holy people—those chosen by God to be so—participate in this upbuilding of the holy land: *So we built the wall; and all the wall was joined together to half its height. For the people had a mind to work.*[4] The Israelites' apparent weakness is not what Sanballat thinks it is, for God is building up and adorning his bride by turning their hearts to himself. "If she is a wall, we will build upon her a battlement of silver; but if she is a door, we will enclose her with boards of cedar" (Song 8:9).

Yet how can Nehemiah's day of triumph ever come, if at the messianic fulfillment walls are broken down? Jesus's disciples, impressed by the magnificence of the temple (renovated by Herod only shortly before), receive this response: "Do you see these great buildings? There will not be left here one stone upon another, that will not be thrown down" (Mark 13:2). Not only will the walls of the rebuilt temple fall down, but so also the "wall" that separates Israel from the nations round about. "Remember that you were at that time separated from

thee to anger before the builders'" (1982, 182). In Fensham's view, however, a more literal translation is "because they have insulted the builders, please do not forgive their iniquities and sins." He emphasizes nonetheless: "The iniquities and sins were committed by sneering at the work God had commanded. The prayer was thus not vindictive because the Jews were insulted, but because God's work was ridiculed. Thus the prayer was religiously and not nationalistically motivated." Throntveit reflects a similar discomfort with the prayer: "Understandably, the church has been troubled by these prayers. Marcion was appalled by these cries for vengeance and used them, among other texts, to justify his elimination of the Old Testament (and most of the New!) from the canon. More subtle is the practice of contemporary church bodies that omit the imprecatory psalms from their hymnals. My own Lutheran tradition curiously omits the more strident examples from the pew edition while retaining them in the minister's edition. At the root of this uneasiness lies the clear witness of the New Testament, especially Jesus' challenge in the Sermon on the Mount, to love our enemies and pray for those who persecute us (Matt. 5:44; cf. 5:43–48; 18:21–22). Practicing what he preached, Jesus prayed for the forgiveness of those who nailed him to the cross (Luke 23:34). This critique becomes particularly acute in Nehemiah's case in that, not only did he not forgive his enemies, he prayed that they might not be forgiven by God. Without denying the truth of Christ's corrective or its authority for us, however, it must be emphasized that we cannot fairly apply that standard to Nehemiah" (1992, 81).

4. Fensham notes that the literal translation is "and the heart of the people was to do the work" (1982, 182).

Christ, alienated from the commonwealth of Israel, and strangers to the covenants of promise, having no hope and without God in the world. But now in Christ Jesus you who once were far off have been brought near in the blood of Christ. For he is our peace, who has made us both one, and has broken down the dividing wall of hostility" (Eph. 2:12–14). The messianic fulfillment would itself seem to be more a breaking than a rebuilding, since Christ "gave himself for our sins to deliver us from the present evil age" (Gal. 1:4).

Christ's resurrection reveals that the last word goes to upbuilding. "If Christ has not been raised, your faith is futile and you are still in your sins. Then those also who have fallen asleep in Christ have perished. If for this life only we have hope in Christ, we are of all men most to be pitied. But in fact Christ has been raised from the dead, the first fruits of those who have fallen asleep" (1 Cor. 15:17–20). Sustained by the risen Lord and his Spirit, the church's walls will never be torn down. "And I tell you, you are Peter, and on this rock I will build my church, and the powers of death shall not prevail against it" (Matt. 16:18). "For we know that if the earthly tent we live in is destroyed, we have a building from God, a house not made with hands, eternal in the heavens" (2 Cor. 5:1).

Guarding the Wall

Sanballat and his followers, however, see nothing but the early signs of a small geopolitical threat, which they hope to crush before it grows any stronger. *But when Sanballat and Tobiah and the Arabs and the Ammonites and the Ashdodites heard that the repairing of the walls of Jerusalem was going forward and that the breaches were beginning to be closed, they were very angry; and they all plotted together to come and fight against Jerusalem and to cause confusion in it. And we prayed to our God, and set a guard as a protection against them day and night.* For Nehemiah "God is our refuge and strength, a very present help in trouble" (Ps. 46:1); but at the same time, prudence requires establishing *a guard as a protection.*[5] The strength of the returned exiles is waning, and Nehemiah hears rumors of a coming attack. After increasing the military force guarding the wall, Nehemiah tells the leading men of Jerusalem: *Do not be afraid of them. Remember the Lord, who is great and terrible, and fight for your brethren, your sons, your daughters, your wives, and your homes.* Again we see the combination of faith in the Lord and virtuous prudence—the hallmark of Nehemiah's leadership.

The presence of defensive military force averts an attack and enables the people of Israel to resume building the wall. Nehemiah divides his helpers into

---

5. For discussion of these two aspects (trust in the Lord and prudence), see Throntveit 1992, 82–83, who sees Neh. 4 as falling within Israel's "holy war traditions."

two groups: *From that day on, half of my servants worked on construction, and half held the spears, shields, bows, and coats of mail; and the leaders stood behind all the house of Judah, who were building the wall.*[6] Each of Nehemiah's helpers in building the wall also did service as a soldier, so that the defense of Jerusalem was carried out in a unified manner, both by fortification and by soldiery: *Those who carried burdens were laden in such a way that each with one hand labored on the work and with the other held his weapon. And each of the builders had his sword girded at his side while he built.*

In the mystical sense Bede observes that "the builders gird their loins with a sword when those who take pains to persevere in good works, and who take pains to govern those in charge by means of an ordered regimen (that is, to place the living stones in the edifice of the holy city in suitable arrangement), endeavour to restrain in themselves the laxness of wanton behaviour with the sharpness of God's word" (2006, 182). This mystical interpretation raises a further question about life in Christ: is it congruent with perseverance "in good works" and with "an ordered regimen" of life to resort to violence? Even if Nehemiah approves of *each of the builders ha[ving] his sword girded at his side while he built*—and Nehemiah obviously does approve—can we agree, in light of the messianic fulfillment, that building up the city of God does not conflict with bearing weapons for military use?

In other words, does God permit self-defense by violent means? It would seem not, because Christ teaches: "Blessed are the meek, for they shall inherit the earth" (Matt. 5:5); and: "You have heard that it was said, 'An eye for an eye and a tooth for a tooth.' But I say to you, Do not resist one who is evil. But if any one strikes you on the right cheek, turn to him the other also; and if any one would sue you and take your coat, let him have your cloak as well; and if any one forces you to go one mile, go with him two miles" (5:38–41). Similarly, how can one love one's enemy, as Christ commands (5:44), while killing one's enemy? When Jesus was betrayed by Judas, Peter responded by cutting off the ear of one of Judas's party; but Jesus said in rebuke, "No more of this!" (Luke 22:51), and healed the ear. Jesus explains to Peter: "Put your sword into its sheath; shall I not drink the cup which the Father has given me?" (John 18:11). In the same vein Jesus tells Pilate: "My kingship is not of this world; if my kingship were of this world, my servants would fight, that I might not be handed over to the Jews; but my kingship is not from the world" (18:36).

On the other hand, Jesus praises the centurion for his faith without asking him to lay down his weapons (Matt. 8:10). Neither does Cornelius, a centurion whose family Peter baptizes and who inaugurates the mission to the Gentiles, receive a command from Peter or from the Holy Spirit to lay down his weapons (Acts 10). The apostle Paul says, in evident opposition to Christians who

6. Fensham suggests that Nehemiah is here referring to a handpicked group (1982, 187–88).

reject per se the authority of temporal rulers: "For rulers are not a terror to good conduct, but to bad. Would you have no fear of him who is in authority? Then do what is good, and you will receive his approval, for he is God's servant for your good. But if you do wrong, be afraid, for he does not bear the sword in vain; he is the servant of God to execute his wrath on the wrongdoer. Therefore one must be subject, not only to avoid God's wrath but also for the sake of conscience" (Rom. 13:3–5).

In short, while Jesus warns in starkest terms about exacting revenge upon one's enemies out of hatred, he does not forbid—or so the church has understood him—armed defense under certain conditions. When one's neighbor degenerates into disordered violence, loving one's neighbor at times requires preventing—even by force—one's neighbor from wreaking devastation on others.

As governor of Judah under King Artaxerxes, Nehemiah controls the military force that he has established for the defense of Jerusalem: *The man who sounded the trumpet was beside me.* The trumpet is there in case a need arises to call the laborers to the defense of Jerusalem. Having put in place these precautions, Nehemiah also reminds the people: *Our God will fight for us.* "Be strong and of good courage; be not frightened, neither be dismayed; for the LORD your God is with you wherever you go" (Josh. 1:9).

Nehemiah sets a guard over Jerusalem during the night and requires that all the people of Israel sleep within the walls of Jerusalem to make defense easier. While fortifying the city, they are at all times prepared for battle: *So neither I nor my brethren nor my servants nor the men of the guard who followed me, none of us took off our clothes; each kept his weapon in his hand.* Such military vigilance requires spiritual vigilance in order to be just. St. Paul says: "Finally, be strong in the Lord and in the strength of his might. Put on the whole armor of God, that you may be able to stand against the wiles of the devil. For we are not contending against flesh and blood, but against the principalities, against the powers, against the world rulers of this present darkness, against the spiritual hosts of wickedness in the heavenly places" (Eph. 6:10–12). What is this "whole armor of God"? Paul explains: "Stand therefore, having girded your loins with truth, and having put on the breastplate of righteousness, and having shod your feet with the equipment of the gospel of peace; besides all these, taking the shield of faith, with which you can quench all the flaming darts of the evil one. And take the helmet of salvation, and the sword of the Spirit, which is the word of God" (6:14–17).

Having put on this armor of God, one keeps it on through vigilance in prayer: "Pray at all times in the Spirit, with all prayer and supplication" (6:18). Jesus relates the parable of the wise and foolish virgins to urge us to such vigilance. Going to meet the bridegroom, the foolish virgins brought their lamps without extra oil, but the wise virgins brought both lamps and oil. The oil is prayer, by which we are constantly prepared for "the marriage feast" (Matt. 25:10). Without this "oil," when the bridegroom comes, we may find ourselves unable to respond, as Jesus says: "Watch therefore, for you know neither the day nor the hour" (25:13). Lest this sound too daunting, Jesus tells his frightened disciples on the eve of his crucifixion: "I have said this to you, that in me you may have peace. In the world you have tribulation; but be of good cheer, I have overcome the world" (John 16:33).

NEHEMIAH 5

The Fruits of the Land

Usury and Slavery

The difficulty of growing crops while living in Jerusalem and working on the wall leads to a famine among the Israelites. The narrative itself contains strong theological implications.

Some of the returned exiles are wealthy. Others, however, have been compelled by the famine to borrow money at interest, and they have mortgaged and lost their lands. They even have begun to sell their children into slavery. *For there were those who said, "With our sons and our daughters, we are many; let us get grain, that we may eat and keep alive." There were also those who said, "We are mortgaging our fields, our vineyards, and our houses to get grain because of the famine." And there were those who said, "We have borrowed money for the king's tax upon our fields and our vineyards. Now our flesh is as the flesh of our brethren, our children are as their children; yet we are forcing our sons and our daughters to be slaves, and some of our daughters have already been enslaved; but it is not in our power to help it, for other men have our fields and our vineyards."* Worst of all, it is the wealthy among their fellow Jews who are taking their money and their lands and enslaving them.[1] In short, despite Nehemiah's effort to unite them in the political and covenantal mission of rebuilding the holy land, the people are not holy but instead oppress each other, with the resulting *great outcry of the people and of their wives against their Jewish brethren.*

1. Fensham explains that the sons were enslaved only until the debt had been paid off, whereas the daughters could sometimes be taken as a second wife of the creditor (1982, 192). See also Blenkinsopp 1988, 256–59, who notes that "debt-slavery was practiced and permitted throughout the history of Israel (e.g., 2 Kings 4:1–2)" (1988, 257).

The commands of the Lord in the Torah address profiteering: "You shall not lend upon interest to your brother, interest on money, interest on victuals, interest on anything that is lent for interest" (Deut. 23:19). "And if your brother becomes poor, and cannot maintain himself with you, you shall maintain him; as a stranger and a sojourner he shall live with you. Take no interest from him or increase, but fear your God; that your brother may live beside you. You shall not lend him your money at interest, nor give him your food for profit" (Lev. 25:35–37). Likewise, the Lord warns that the people of Israel "are my servants, whom I brought forth out of the land of Egypt; they shall not be sold as slaves" (25:42). Even "if your brother becomes poor beside you, and sells himself to you, you shall not make him serve as a slave: he shall be with you as a hired servant and as a sojourner" (25:39–40). Some wealthy members of the Jewish community, in the very midst of the apparently unified labor to fortify Jerusalem and thereby rebuild the holy land, violate these commandments. What is the use of a rebuilt Jerusalem without a holy people to dwell with God?

Nehemiah is even more disturbed because the problem lies with the leaders, *the nobles and the officials*, who should be counted upon to serve the people. "Thus says the Lord GOD: Ho, shepherds of Israel who have been feeding yourselves! Should not shepherds feed the sheep? You eat the fat, you clothe yourselves with the wool, you slaughter the fatlings; but you do not feed the sheep. The weak you have not strengthened, the sick you have not healed, the crippled you have not bound up, the strayed you have not brought back, the lost you have not sought" (Ezek. 34:2–4). Nehemiah absolves himself and his family from this crime against their own people; during his twelve years as governor, he says, *neither I nor my family ate the food allowance of the governor*. On the contrary, on a daily basis *there were at my table a hundred and fifty men, Jews and officials, besides those who came to us from the nations which were about us*, and provision for all these each day *was one ox and six choice sheep*, in addition to chicken and wine. From far getting rich from his position, Nehemiah must have lost money. He also did not tax the people or acquire land or hold back his own servants from the common work on the wall. *I did not do so, because of the fear of God*.

Establishing Justice

Nehemiah's *fear of God* exemplifies Jesus's command: "You know that the rulers of the Gentiles lord it over them, and their great men exercise authority over them. It shall not be so among you; but whoever would be great among you must be your servant, and whoever would be first among you must be your slave; even as the Son of man came not to be served but to serve, and to give his life as a ransom for many" (Matt. 20:25–28). No ruler in Israel is anything more than a "brother" (Deut. 17:15), a fellow descendant of Abraham. Holiness for the ruler, as for his subjects, requires "that he may learn to fear the LORD his God, by keeping all the words of this law and these statutes, and doing them; that his heart may not be lifted up above his brethren, and that he may not turn aside from the commandment, either to the right hand or to the left" (17:19–20). The task of the true ruler in Israel is to establish justice. "Hear, you heads of Jacob and rulers of the house of Israel! Is it not for you to know justice?" (Mic. 3:1).

As governor, Nehemiah therefore does his best to establish justice among his people: *I took counsel with myself, and I brought charges against the nobles and the officials.* The charges of injustice are twofold: profiteering (*you are exacting interest, each from his brother*) and selling fellow Jews into slavery (*we, as far as we are able, have bought back our Jewish brethren who have been sold to the nations; but you even sell your brethren that they may be sold to us*).[2] Nehemiah does not bring these charges privately but rather at *a great assembly.* The nobles and the officials are indeed "at the point of utter ruin in the assembled congregation" (Prov. 5:14). Although they do not exactly repent, they agree to restore what they had gained by profiteering. *They were silent, and could not find a word to say.* "Be silent, all flesh, before the LORD; for he has roused himself from his holy dwelling" (Zech. 2:13).

Nehemiah shames them by appealing to the fear of God and by announcing that he himself will set the example in refusing to profit from the poverty of the people. When the nobles and the officials remain silent, Nehemiah says: *The thing that you are doing is not good. Ought you not to walk in the fear of our God to prevent the taunts of the nations our enemies? Moreover I and my brethren and my servants are lending them money and grain. Let us leave off this interest.*[3] *Return to them this very day their fields, their vineyards, their olive orchards, and their houses, and the hundredth of money, grain, wine, and oil which you have been exacting of them.* Nehemiah's exhortation resonates with Micah's insistence upon justice: "He has showed you, O man, what is good; and what does the LORD require of you but to do justice, and to love kindness, and to walk humbly with your God?" (Mic. 6:8).

2. Blenkinsopp remarks: "It seems that the accused were not only seizing the persons of fellow Judeans but selling them to foreigners, thus swelling the numbers of those who would have to be bought back and, at the same time, provoking the derision of Gentile neighbors (v. 9). The accusation is in itself quite credible. Phoenicians, Greeks, and Arabs, all of whom had commercial interests in the province, were involved in the lucrative slave trade (cf. Ezek. 27:13; Joel 4[3]:3, 4–8; Amos 1:9), and it would be unremarkable if the assimilationist Judean aristocracy also had a hand in it" (1988, 259).

3. Fensham interprets Neh. 5:10 quite differently from the Revised Standard Version. He takes it to mean that Nehemiah is confessing that he too had loaned money to his fellow Jews at interest and that he now repents and desires to absolve the loans. Fensham's translation is nonetheless close to the Revised Standard Version: "I, my companions, and my servants have also lent them money and grain. Let us absolve this loan!" (1982, 193). By contrast, Blenkinsopp argues that the meaning is that Nehemiah has been able to loan money and goods "without the abuses which they had come together to abolish" (1988, 260).

The nobles and the officials follow Nehemiah's direction: *Then they said, "We will restore these and require nothing from them. We will do as you say."* Justice is reestablished in the land, so that the people are once again united. The earliest Christian community follows a similar practice: "And all who believed were together and had all things in common; and they sold their possessions and goods and distributed them to all, as any had need. And day by day, attending the temple together and breaking bread in their homes, they partook of food with glad and generous hearts, praising God and having favor with all the people" (Acts 2:44–47).

A Promise to the Lord

Nehemiah ensures that this promise is made not only to him as governor but also to the Lord: *And I called the priests, and took an oath of them to do as they had promised.*[4] The *great assembly* is both a restoration of justice and a covenantal renewal of the people's relationship to the Lord. Nehemiah calls down a covenantal curse upon anyone who violates the Torah's commandments against profiteering: *I also shook out my lap and said, "So may God shake out every man from his house and from his labor who does not perform this promise. So may he be shaken out and emptied." And all the assembly said "Amen" and praised the LORD.*[5] Not only is Nehemiah rebuilding the fortifications of Jerusalem (where God has promised to dwell with his people), but he is also rebuilding the covenantal piety that makes for a holy people, united by justice, fit for God's indwelling. Bede comments: "For whoever either refuses to show mercy on poor people or is not ashamed to demand from them, as if lawfully, what they do not have to give, this person is shaken from his house (namely, is cast and shaken out from the fellowship of the Holy Church in which he believed he would remain forever) and deprived of his labours, doubtless, that is, of the fruit of good works" (2006, 185–86). The unjust person who refuses to repent cannot remain in the communion of love, in the church. "Do you not know that the unrighteous will not inherit the kingdom of God? Do not be deceived; neither the immoral, nor idolaters, nor adulterers, nor sexual perverts, nor thieves, nor

4. This sentence has caused confusion. Fensham comments: "Who are the *them*? According to the immediate context it could only be the priests. The verb has the first person as subject (Nehemiah) and the object is the third person plural (the priests?). In such a case the priests were the guilty; they were the landowners who oppressed the people. Other scholars are of the opinion that the priests were summoned to let the oath be taken by the guilty leaders. They might have been witnesses of the oath. In the light of the broader context (cf. v. 7) it seems as if the important citizens and leaders were charged" (1982, 195–96).

5. Blenkinsopp states that "the shaking out the fold of the robe, which served as a kind of pocket, is functionally parallel to the threat of banning or excommunication in Ezra's assembly to deal with foreign marriages (Ezra 10:8)" (1988, 260).

the greedy, nor drunkards, nor revilers, nor robbers will inherit the kingdom of God" (1 Cor. 6:9–10).

Are all doers of these things *shaken out and emptied* from the church? "Is there no balm in Gilead? Is there no physician there? Why then has the health of the daughter of my people not been restored?" (Jer. 8:22). Christ Jesus restores this "health": "Now after John was arrested, Jesus came into Galilee, preaching the gospel of God, and saying, 'The time is fulfilled, and the kingdom of God is at hand; repent, and believe in the gospel'" (Mark 1:14–15). The great assembly that says amen consists of those who repent and believe. Paul says: "And such were some of you. But you were washed, you were sanctified, you were justified in the name of the Lord Jesus Christ and in the Spirit of our God" (1 Cor. 6:11). "After this I looked, and behold, a great multitude which no man could number, from every nation, from all tribes and peoples and tongues, standing before the throne and before the Lamb, clothed in white robes, with palm branches in their hands" (Rev. 7:9). This great assembly is led in the heavenly worship by the twenty-four elders, the angels, and the "four living creatures," all of whom cry out "Amen!" (7:12).

Nehemiah is pleased to report that *the people did as they had promised*. He also prays that God will remember him and bless him for his efforts to rebuild God's people and land: *Remember for my good, O my God, all that I have done for this people*. Is Nehemiah here expressing concern about what will happen to him after his death? "I have seen the business that God has given to the sons of men to be busy with. He has made everything beautiful in its time; also he has put eternity into man's mind, yet so that he cannot find out what God has done from the beginning to the end" (Eccl. 3:10–11). To be remembered *for my good* by God holds out the hope of a future life, a personal good, something more than eternal nonexistence. "For I know that my Redeemer lives, and at last he will stand upon the earth; and after my skin has been thus destroyed, then from my flesh I shall see God" (Job 19:25–26). "He is righteous, he shall surely live, says the Lord God" (Ezek. 18:9).

NEHEMIAH 6

Triumph and Danger

Triumph and Danger

In October 445 BC, when Nehemiah had been governor only a few months, the wall of Jerusalem *was finished*. Nehemiah observes that this accomplishment frightened the enemies of the returned exiles because the enemies *perceived that this work had been accomplished with the help of our God*. "And this city shall be to me [the LORD] a name of joy, a praise and a glory before all the nations of the earth who shall hear of all the good that I do for them; they shall fear and tremble because of all the good and all the prosperity I provide for it" (Jer. 33:9).

This moment of apparent triumph for Nehemiah, however, is also the moment in which his life and leadership come under serious attack. "If I must boast, I will boast of the things that show my weakness" (2 Cor. 11:30). "But many that are first will be last, and the last first" (Mark 10:31). Other examples of great achievements being followed by profound trial abound in scripture. For example, David's highest point is followed by a stream of troubles. The pinnacle of David's life comes when, having united the twelve tribes by defeating the son of Saul, he rejoices in the covenant with God that has been communicated to him by the prophet Nathan: "Then King David went in and sat before the LORD, and said, who am I, O Lord GOD, and what is my house, that thou hast brought me thus far?" (2 Sam. 7:18). Not only has David achieved his most cherished goal, the kingship of a unified Israel, but also God has promised that "your house and your kingdom shall be made sure for ever before me; your throne shall be established for ever" (7:16). In his joy, David prays: "And now, O Lord GOD, thou art God, and thy words are true, and thou hast promised

161

this good thing to thy servant; now therefore may it please thee to bless the house of thy servant, that it may continue for ever before thee; for thou, O Lord God, hast spoken, and with thy blessing shall the house of thy servant be blessed for ever" (7:28–29).

One can imagine the good things that David has in mind when he prays "bless the house of thy servant." God does bless the house of David with an eternal kingship, but not in a way that David could have expected. For although David goes on to defeat the Philistines, Moabites, Syrians, and others, so that he "won a name for himself" (8:13)—and although David becomes so secure that he can be reconciled with what remains of the house of Saul (2 Sam. 9)—nonetheless David soon descends into the utmost misery.

David first commits adultery with the wife of one of his faithful soldiers, Uriah the Hittite. Abandoning justice, David murderously orders that Uriah be abandoned to the enemy in battle. Meanwhile, within his family, his son Amnon rapes his daughter Tamar. His son Absalom kills Amnon and organizes a rebellion that drives David from Jerusalem and nearly overthrows his rule. The land undergoes a famine for three years. Indeed, the strongest image from the later years of David's reign is that of David weeping over his parricidal son: "And the king was deeply moved, and went up to the chamber over the gate, and wept; and as he went, he said, 'O my son Absalom, my son, my son Absalom! Would I had died instead of you, O Absalom, my son, my son!'" (18:33). Is this the blessing that David hoped for from the covenantal promise? David and his house will be blessed, as God promises, but the blessing will come through sufferings.

For his part, Nehemiah's highest point comes when he accomplishes the rebuilding of Jerusalem's wall. At this very time, however, his life comes under threat and a nest of enemies among his own people appears. Nehemiah's trials begin when his enemy *Sanballat* sends him four letters asking for a meeting *in one of the villages in the plain of Ono*. Nehemiah knows better than to leave Jerusalem: *They intended to do me harm*. So four times he refuses the invitation, but a fifth letter from Sanballat is blunter: *It is reported among the nations, and Geshem also says it, that you and the Jews intend to rebel; that is why you are building the wall; and you wish to become their king, according to this report*. As Nehemiah knows, were he to be seen as a rebel against Artaxerxes, the consequences would be dire. His enemies are also using Nehemiah's piety against him. In this regard Sanballat's letter informs Nehemiah that some believe that Nehemiah has *also set up prophets to proclaim concerning you in Jerusalem, "There is a king in Judah."* Sanballat warns in conclusion that *it will be reported to the king according to these words*. Artaxerxes, in short, will soon hear, or has already heard, that Nehemiah is a rebel who hopes to reestablish the kingship in Jerusalem. And surely Nehemiah's efforts to rebuild the land and the people could not have lacked this ultimate goal, even if Nehemiah himself is innocent of hopes to become king.

Having communicated this dire warning, Sanballat again invites Nehemiah to meet, in what seems to be a friendly fashion: *So now come, and let us take counsel together.* Recognizing that Sanballat himself is the source of the rumors, however, Nehemiah refuses to be bullied: *Then I sent to him, saying, "No such things as you say have been done, for you are inventing them out of your own mind." For they all wanted to frighten us, thinking, "Their hands will drop from the work, and it will not be done."* As is his wont, he combines this prudential response to Sanballat with a prayer: *But now, O God, strengthen thou my hands.*[1] At that time Nehemiah still had not *set up the doors in the gates,* obviously a crucial part of any fortification.

Enemies inside the Gates

Sanballat, however, is not the biggest problem that Nehemiah encounters after finishing the wall. Nehemiah's biggest problem is "danger from false brethren" (2 Cor. 11:26), from the leading families of Jerusalem. *Tobiah's* connections with these families, no doubt including some whose crimes against the Torah Nehemiah had exposed in a publicly humiliating manner and who had as a result lost much money, now give Nehemiah serious trouble. Nehemiah tells us that *in those days the nobles of Judah sent many letters to Tobiah, and Tobiah's letters came to them.* Although a faithful friend of Sanballat, Tobiah belongs by his own marriage, and through his son's marriage, to prominent families of returned exiles, and therefore his connections in Jerusalem go deep: *For many in Judah were bound by oath to him, because he was the son-in-law of Shecaniah the son of Arah: and his son Jehohanan had taken the daughter of Meshullam the son of Berechiah as his wife.*

Thus the nobles in Jerusalem, with whom Nehemiah as governor must deal on a daily basis, support and communicate with an archenemy of the rebuilding and pass on Nehemiah's words to him: *Also they spoke of his good deeds in my presence, and reported my words to him.* Nehemiah may have succeeded in unifying the people of God with respect to obeying the laws of the Torah on profiteering and slave-dealing, but at the very moment of his greatest success it becomes clear that he has not succeeded in accomplishing a deeper political unity, since he has to deal with families of returned exiles that were prominent long before his own return to the land. The families of the nobles retain their old allegiances, including support for, or at least desire to negotiate with, the enemies of the rebuilding of the wall. In their loyalty to Shecaniah's son-in-law they forget that their true family is the covenantal people of God. "'Who are my mother and my brothers?' And looking around on those who sat about

1. The Revised Standard Version inserts "O God." See Fensham 1982, 203.

him, he said, 'Here are my mother and my brothers! Whoever does the will of God is my brother, and sister, and mother'" (Mark 3:33–35).

Using his connections among the leading families, *Tobiah sent letters to make me afraid*. The nobles forget that "no one can serve two masters; for either he will hate the one and love the other, or he will be devoted to the one and despise the other. You cannot serve God and mammon" (Matt. 6:24). Like Paul, Nehemiah thus suffers both "danger from my own people" and "danger from Gentiles," "danger in the city" and "danger in the wilderness" (2 Cor. 11:26). "Do not be conformed to this world but be transformed by the renewal of your mind, that you may prove what is the will of God, what is good and acceptable and perfect" (Rom. 12:2).

A False Prophet

Tobiah and Sanballat also draw upon their ability to manipulate Jerusalem's prophets. Nehemiah visits the prophet *Shemaiah the son of Delaiah, son of Mehetabel* at Shemaiah's house in Jerusalem, evidently because he believes that Shemaiah has a prophecy regarding him. Shemaiah proposes another place of meeting: *Let us meet together in the house of God, within the temple, and let us close the doors of the temple; for they are coming to kill you, at night they are coming to kill you.* Since Nehemiah is not a priest—and also since, as a servant of the Persian king, he may have been a eunuch and thus excluded from the temple for this reason as well (see Lev. 21:17–24)[2]—such an action would be for Nehemiah a sin against God. Nehemiah therefore recognizes that Shemaiah cannot truly be speaking the word of God. Nehemiah's response to Shemaiah once again expresses his combination of piety and prudence: *Should such a man as I flee? And what man such as I could go into the temple and live?*[3] *I will not go in. And I understood, and saw that God had not sent him, but he had pronounced the prophecy against me because Tobiah and Sanballat had hired him. For this purpose he was hired, that I should be afraid and act in this way and sin, and so they could give me an evil name, in order to taunt me.*

Unlike the false prophet Shemaiah, who places money above truth in speaking God's word, Nehemiah resists the temptation to place the preservation of his own earthly life above his fear of God. The Lord said to Jeremiah: "The prophets are prophesying lies in my name; I did not send them, nor did I command them or speak to them. They are prophesying to you a lying vision, worthless divination, and the deceit of their own minds" (Jer. 14:14). What will happen

2. For further discussion of the suggestion that Nehemiah was a eunuch, see Fensham 1982, 157, 204. Blenkinsopp reviews this question and determines that "none of the arguments advanced [for Nehemiah being a eunuch] is very persuasive. Some royal wine stewards were eunuchs but others were not" (1988, 213).
3. This could also be "to stay alive" (Fensham 1982, 205).

to such false prophets? The Lord says that they will reap the very destruction that their false prophecy denied would occur: "By sword and famine those prophets shall be consumed. And the people to whom they prophesy shall be cast out in the streets of Jerusalem, victims of famine and word, with none to bury them—them, their wives, their sons, and their daughters. For I will pour out their wickedness upon them" (14:15–16).

Shemaiah belongs to the long history of false prophets, whose words corrupt both the holiness of Israel and the hopes of Israel to dwell with God in the land. By contrast, Nehemiah shows that "if you cry out for insight and raise your voice for understanding, if you seek it like silver and search for it as for hidden treasures; then you will understand the fear of the LORD and find the knowledge of God" (Prov. 2:3–5). Nehemiah's obedience to the temple laws enables him to discern false prophecy. It also preserves him, as he recognizes, from political destruction.

The Lord "stores up sound wisdom for the upright; he is a shield to those who walk in integrity, guarding the paths of justice and preserving the way of his saints" (2:7–8). John says: "Beloved, do not believe every spirit, but test the spirits to see whether they are of God; for many false prophets have gone out into the world" (1 John 4:1). Nehemiah "tests the spirits" by the standard of the commandments of the Torah. "All scripture is inspired by God and profitable for teaching, for reproof, for correction, and for training in righteousness, that the man of God may be complete, equipped for every good work" (2 Tim. 3:16–17). As Nehemiah's example shows, scripture instructs the one who loves God.

A Man of Trials

Why does the Lord allow Nehemiah to be tempted in this way as part of Nehemiah's mission of rebuilding the walls of Jerusalem and thereby preparing for the restoration of Israel? For his part, Nehemiah does not question his trials, but instead simply calls down a covenantal curse upon the rulers and false prophets who tried to ruin him and thereby thwart the rebuilding of Jerusalem: *Remember Tobiah and Sanballat, O my God, according to these things that they did, and also the prophetess Noadiah and the rest of the prophets who wanted to make me afraid.* Yet, why these trials? Even if God enables Nehemiah to withstand them, why does God permit them?

God said to Jeremiah, a man of great trials: "Behold, I make you this day a fortified city, an iron pillar, and bronze walls, against the whole land, against the kings of Judah, its princes, its priests, and the people of the land. They will fight against you; but they shall not prevail against you, for I am with you, says the LORD, to deliver you" (Jer. 1:18–19). Surely Jeremiah could not have anticipated what the Lord meant by "they will fight against you." His life is filled with terrible sufferings. "Pashhur beat Jeremiah the prophet, and put him in the stocks that were in the upper Benjamin Gate of the house of the LORD" (20:2). "So they took Jeremiah and cast him into the cistern of Malchiah, the king's son, which was in the court of the guard, letting Jeremiah down by ropes. And there was no water in the cistern, but only mire, and Jeremiah sank in the mire" (38:6). Is this the fate of one whom the Lord has made "a fortified city"?

Even more so Job, whom the Lord exhibits as a model of fidelity: "And the LORD said to Satan, 'Have you considered my servant Job, that there is none like him on the earth, a blameless and upright man, who fears God and turns away from evil? He still holds fast his integrity, although you moved me against him, to destroy him without cause'" (Job 2:3). Satan tells God that, if Job's own health is threatened, Job will give way to despair: "'Skin for skin! All that a man has he will give for his life. But put forth thy hand now, and touch his bone and his flesh, and he will curse thee to thy face.' And the LORD said to Satan, 'Behold, he is in your power; only spare his life'" (2:4–6). Under the intense pressure of physical illness, Job curses "the day of his birth" (3:1), and he has to endure his friends who seek to find the roots of his suffering in human sin. Yet Job does not curse the Lord. Neither, however, does the Lord answer Job's "why?" The Lord says instead: "Where were you when I laid the foundation of the earth?" (38:4).

Satan is allowed to tempt Christ by offering him political power, economic power, and power over human health—the three temptations to which human beings most fall prey (Matt. 4:1–11). Christ is exposed to the worst that other human beings can do. As he says: "Foxes have holes, and birds of the air have nests; but the Son of man has nowhere to lay his head" (Luke 9:58). Even his disciples do not stand by him. At Gethsemane, he asks them in his agony to "watch with me" (Matt. 26:38), but three times "he came and found them sleeping" (26:43). Judas betrays him, and "all the disciples forsook him and fled" (26:56). Peter denies him three times. The Romans and the people, along with his own disciples, are complicit in his crucifixion. He is scourged, stripped, and mocked: "And they stripped him and put a scarlet robe upon him, and plaiting a crown of thorns they put it on his head, and put a reed in his right hand. And kneeling before him they mocked him, saying, 'Hail, King of the Jews!' And they spat upon him, and took the reed and struck him on the head" (27:28–30). He is "derided," "mocked," and "reviled" as he hangs upon the cross (27:39–44). To this treatment, Christ Jesus responds: "Father, forgive them; for they know not what they do" (Luke 23:34). Through these trials the new Jerusalem—the fulfillment of the land as the locus of divine indwelling—is built and its walls secured.

On the one hand, Nehemiah's trials, like the sufferings of Jeremiah and Job, evade explanation. Could not God have rebuilt Jerusalem without such trials? On the other hand, Christ's sufferings teach us that love attains its height in the midst of trials. In this light, Nehemiah's trials serve him as an antidote to pride or complacency after finishing the wall. "My son, do not regard lightly the discipline of the Lord, nor lose courage when you are punished by him. For the Lord disciplines him whom he loves, and chastises every son whom he receives" (Heb. 12:5–6, quoting Prov. 3:11–12). Drawing on this proverb, the letter to the Hebrews urges patient endurance of trials: "It is for discipline that you have to endure. God is treating you as sons; for what son is there whom his father does not discipline? If you are left without discipline, in which all have participated, then you are illegitimate children and not sons" (Heb. 12:7–8). This discipline recalls us to trusting in God as children, rather than trusting in our own power.

PART II

NEHEMIAH 7–13: THE HOLY PEOPLE

Ezra the Scribe, a priest descended from Aaron, is the most important figure of Neh. 7–13, which has primarily to do with holy people called to obey the Torah (especially regarding intermarriage). These chapters emphasize that the holy people of God must not "love the world or the things in the world" because "the world passes away, and the lust of it; but he who does the will of God abides for ever" (1 John 2:15, 17). At the same time, these chapters complement the earlier emphasis on holy land through rebuilding the wall of Jerusalem. The indwelling of God in Jerusalem and its temple requires the holy obedience of the people of God, because only "the righteous shall possess the land, and dwell upon it for ever" (Ps. 37:29). The good thief says: "'Do you not fear God, since you are under the same sentence of condemnation? And we indeed justly; for we are receiving the due reward of our deeds; but this man has done nothing wrong.' And he said, 'Jesus, remember me when you come in your kingdom'" (Luke 23:40–42).

A summary of the remaining chapters may be helpful. Nehemiah 7 is a genealogy that repeats Ezra 2 and thereby ties the rebuilding of the walls of Jerusalem to the people who returned from Babylonian exile and rebuilt the temple. Just as Ezra 3 describes the celebration of the feasts of the seventh month by the returned exiles, so Neh. 8 describes the celebration of the feasts of the seventh month by the people under Nehemiah and Ezra the Scribe. At the center of this celebration is Ezra the Scribe's public reading of the Torah before all the people in Jerusalem, when the people learn how to observe the feasts. Nehemiah 9 describes the day of repentance and recounts Ezra the Scribe's solemn confession of the sins that have plagued the people of Israel since the exodus. Ezra the Scribe shows that the exile is not yet over because the people are still subject to foreign rulers. He therefore makes a covenant, which Neh. 10 describes. This covenant obligates the returned exiles to obey the Torah and to provide for the temple service. Nehemiah 11 lists the inhabitants of Jerusalem and the surrounding villages, and Neh. 12 lists the priests and Levites and depicts the solemn dedication of the wall of Jerusalem. Lastly, Neh. 13 briefly tells of the separation of the people from their foreign wives and then explores in detail Nehemiah's sadness upon returning to Jerusalem from a stay in Babylon to find that the temple had been violated and neglected, that the sabbath was not being observed, and that many Israelites had again married foreign wives. Nehemiah once more cleanses the fallen people, and so the book comes to an end.

NEHEMIAH 7

Consolidating the Holy People

Having completed Jerusalem's wall and established the corresponding religious service, Nehemiah takes three steps to strengthen his position and that of Jerusalem in the face of the various serious external and internal threats. These steps all have to do with the consolidation of the holy people in Jerusalem, as befits the rebuilding of the holy land demarcated by the wall of Jerusalem.

First, with internal and external kinds of threats in view, Nehemiah *gave my brother Hanani and Hananiah the governor of the castle charge over Jerusalem, for he was a more faithful and God-fearing man than many.*

How does Nehemiah's preference for his own brother relate to other biblical examples of preference for family members? The greatest leader of Israel, Moses, depends heavily upon his brother Aaron throughout his career, despite Aaron's complicity in building the golden calf and Aaron's criticism of Moses's foreign wives. Aaron receives his position due to his eloquence. Moses complains that "I am not eloquent, either heretofore or since thou hast spoken to thy servant; but I am slow of speech and of tongue'" (Exod. 4:10). The Lord says: "Is there not Aaron, your brother, the Levite? I know that he can speak well. . . . He shall speak for you to the people; and he shall be a mouth for you, and you shall be to him as God" (4:14, 16).

King David does not elevate his brothers to high position, but he does elevate the three sons of his sister Zeruiah—Joab, Abishai, and Asahel. In many ways, he comes to regret this preference for his family, because his sister's children are ungovernable. Saul's general, Abner, kills Asahel in battle; for that deed "Joab and Abishai his brother slew Abner" (2 Sam. 3:30). David puts it soon after: "I am this day weak, though anointed king; these men the sons of Zeruiah are too hard for me" (3:39).

The brothers Judas Maccabeus, Jonathan, and Simon—sons of Mattathias—display admirable concord in restoring the temple and its fortifications and in fighting Israel's enemies. "The man Judas and his brothers were greatly honored in all Israel and among all the Gentiles, wherever their name was heard" (1 Maccabees 5:63).

Since Nehemiah's brother Hanani was the one who first alerted Nehemiah to Jerusalem's plight, in light of the above parallels we can understand Nehemiah's action without condemning it as self-serving nepotism.

Second, against the external threat, Nehemiah ordered that the gates of Jerusalem be opened only in the morning and be guarded as heavily as possible. Such a precaution was particularly necessary because *the city was wide and large, but the people within it were few and no houses had been built.*

Third, against the internal threat of disunity, Nehemiah proposes *to assemble the nobles and the officials and the people to be enrolled by genealogy. And I found the book of the genealogy of those who came up at the first.* Among the returned exiles, some well-established families have supported Nehemiah, while others have supported Tobiah. Appealing to a deeper unity, Nehemiah here publishes the census of the original party of returned exiles, which we encountered in Ezra 2. He thereby claims this census as the founding document of *his* mission of return and restoration. *The whole assembly together was forty-two thousand three hundred and sixty* (cf. Ezra 2:64). This number-rich census possesses mystical perfection, due to its combinations of the numbers 3, 6, 7, 10, and 12.

All three of these steps to deeper unity of the people—the appointment of Hanani and Hananiah over Jerusalem, the strengthening of the system of gates, and the republishing of the genealogy—culminate in that year's celebration of the feasts *of the seventh month*: the day of praise, the day of repentance, and the feast of booths.[1] Indeed, symbolically this indicates a new beginning to the holy people's return to the land, since the original group celebrates the feasts of the seventh month immediately upon their return to the land (Ezra 3).

And when the seventh month had come, the children of Israel were in their towns. In order to strengthen Jerusalem, Nehemiah needs more of the leading families to live in Jerusalem; and the seventh month provides an important reminder to all the people about the centrality of Jerusalem for their lives.[2] Nehemiah therefore acts in the seventh month to renew the holy people and begin anew the return and restoration. In this renewal, he is aided by the presence of Ezra the Scribe.

---

1. Pointing out that Leviticus and Numbers require that Yom Kippur, the day of repentance, be celebrated on the tenth rather than the twenty-fourth day of the seventh month, Blenkinsopp suggests that perhaps "at that point in time Yom Kippur was either unknown or at least not firmly established" (1988, 155).

2. Fensham holds that Nehemiah "wanted to draw up a genealogy of the people to see where the different families were living in order to place some of them in Jerusalem" (1982, 211) and that Nehemiah employed the older genealogy "to ascertain which families had returned, and to reorganize the population of the province of Judah" (1982, 214).

NEHEMIAH 8

The Torah, Pattern of Holiness

Ezra and Holiness: The Water Gate

Ezra the Scribe now takes center stage, although Nehemiah is with him.[1] Just as in the book of Ezra, the presence of Ezra the Scribe signals a shift in focus toward Torah obedience, the mark of the holy people.

And Nehemiah, who was governor, and Ezra the priest and scribe, and the Levites who taught the people said to all the people, "This day is holy to the LORD your God; do not mourn or weep." The day of praise was *the first day of the seventh month.* "In the seventh month, on the first day of the month, you shall observe a day of solemn rest, a memorial proclaimed with blast of trumpets, a holy convocation" (Lev. 23:24). The people come together in Jerusalem *before the Water Gate.*[2] The Water Gate is in the wall of Jerusalem, not in the temple precincts where only males were allowed.

When *all the people gathered as one man into the square before the Water Gate,* they are standing by the wall of Jerusalem. Yet the image of the Water Gate can recall Ezekiel's prophetic vision regarding the fulfillment of the temple (Ezek.

---

1. Blenkinsopp holds that Neh. 8 "deals with Ezra alone, since the mention of Nehemiah at 8:9 is an addition from the time when the work of the two had been synchronized (cf. 12:26, 36)" (1988, 284). He points out that the verbs in Neh. 8:9–10 are in the singular.

2. Fensham states: "We may have here a careful description of the liturgical ritual of public worship in postexilic times, namely, the people coming to form a congregation, the request to read the law, opening of the book of the law, the rising of the congregation, the benediction of the congregation, reply of the congregation, kneeling down to hear the word (Gk. *proskyneō*), the sermon(?), reading from the law, oral transmission by translation, and dismissal for a festival" (1982, 215). Historians surmise that at least Neh. 8 and perhaps Neh. 9–10 belonged originally to Ezra's memoirs.

40–48). The people are hungry for eternal food; they seek medicine unto eternal life and a bathing that purifies from sins. Ezekiel prophesies: "Then he brought me back to the door of the temple; and behold, water was issuing from below the threshold of the temple toward the east (for the temple faced east); and the water was flowing down from below the south end of the threshold of the temple, south of the altar" (47:1). In the prophetic vision, this is no mere water; beginning as a small flow, it becomes a vast river, and Ezekiel is told in the vision that "everything will live where the river goes" (47:9). The trees that line the river produce miraculous food and medicinal leaves.

Jesus is this gate from which the water of life issues. He says in the temple on the last day of the feast of booths: "If any one thirst, let him come to me and drink" (John 7:37). Likewise Jesus's conversation with the Samaritan woman confirms the arrival of the temple's fulfillment: "Jesus answered her, 'If you knew the gift of God, and who it is that is saying to you, "Give me a drink," you would have asked him and he would have given you living water'" (4:10).

When the people gather *before the Water Gate*, their unity points to the unity of humankind that the Lord promised through Isaiah: "I [the Lord] am coming to gather all nations and tongues; and they shall come and shall see my glory, and I will set a sign among them" (Isa. 66:18–19). Beginning in Jerusalem, the water of life will water "all the nations" or "all the families of the earth." "For as many of you as were baptized into Christ have put on Christ. There is neither Jew nor Greek, there is neither slave nor free, there is neither male nor female; for you are all one in Christ Jesus. And if you are Christ's, then you are Abraham's offspring, heirs according to promise" (Gal. 3:27–29). By sharing in Christ's passover through baptism, we become "one body" with him: "For by one Spirit we were all baptized into one body—Jews or Greeks, slaves or free—and all were made to drink of one Spirit" (1 Cor. 12:13).

This unity does not, however, end the separation of God's people from the nations. Jesus tells his disciples: "Behold, I send you out as sheep in the midst of wolves; so be wise as serpents and innocent as doves" (Matt. 10:16). Love itself produces the separation, because love threatens to unseat the world's commitment to sin: "Brother will deliver up brother to death, and the father his child, and children will rise against parents and have them put to death; and you will be hated by all for my name's sake" (10:21–22).

The Torah as the Water of Wisdom

Ezra nourishes the people with *the book of the law of Moses which the Lord had given to Israel*. The *law of Moses* offers the pattern of human holiness, which is fulfilled by the incarnate Word, Christ Jesus. *And Ezra the priest brought the law before the assembly, both men and women and all who could hear with understanding, on the first day of the seventh month. And he read from it facing the square before the Water Gate from early morning until midday, in the presence of the men and the women and those who could understand; and the ears of all the people were attentive to the book of the law.*

This law nourishes the soul. "He who holds to the law will obtain wisdom. She [Wisdom] will come to meet him like a mother, and like the wife of his youth she will welcome him. She will feed him with the bread of understanding, and give him the water of wisdom to drink" (Sirach 15:1–3). Wisdom says of herself that she is both God's law for the entire creation and Israel's Torah as established in the temple. Regarding the entire creation, Wisdom says: "I came forth from the mouth of the Most High, and covered the earth like a mist. . . . In every people and nation I have gotten a possession" (24:3, 6). Wisdom receives a command from the Creator to dwell uniquely in Israel: "Then the Creator of all things gave me a commandment, and the one who created me assigned a place for my tent. And he said, 'Make your dwelling in Jacob, and in Israel receive your inheritance'" (24:8). Wisdom takes up her place in the temple: "In the holy tabernacle I ministered before him, and so I was established in Zion. In the beloved city likewise he gave me a resting place, and in Jerusalem was my dominion" (24:10–11).

Wisdom gives herself to us to eat and drink, and she does so through the Torah: to absorb the Torah is to be filled with living wisdom. "Come to me, you who desire me, and eat your fill of my produce. . . . All this is the book of the covenant of the Most High God, the law which Moses commanded us as an inheritance for the congregations of Jacob. It fills men with wisdom, like the Pishon, and like the Tigris at the time of the first fruits" (24:19, 23–25).

Ezra the Scribe gives this "bread of understanding" and "water of wisdom" (15:3) to the returned exiles at the *Water Gate*—food and drink that Jesus, in the prophesied time of fulfillment, gives more perfectly as "Christ the power of God and the wisdom of God" (1 Cor. 1:24), "the Word" (John 1:1), "the image of the invisible God" (Col. 1:15) in whom "the whole fulness of deity dwells bodily" (2:9). Jesus says: "I am the bread of life. Your fathers ate the manna in the wilderness, and they died. This is the bread which comes down from heaven, that a man may eat of it and not die. I am the living bread which came down from heaven; if any one eats of this bread, he will live for ever; and the bread which I shall give for the life of the world is my flesh" (John 6:48–51).

How will Jesus give his own flesh? The Last Supper provides the answer—in the sacramental body and blood: "And he took bread, and when he had given thanks he broke it and gave it to them, saying, 'This is my body which is given for you. Do this in remembrance of me.' And likewise the cup after supper, saying, 'This cup which is poured out for you is the new covenant in my blood'" (Luke 22:19–20). "The cup of blessing which we bless, is it not a participation in the blood of Christ? The bread which we break, is it not a participation in the body of Christ?" (1 Cor. 10:16). Wisdom incarnate gives us the fullness of himself as "bread," so that in him, transformed by the "water of wisdom" of the Holy Spirit, we become holy temples of God. "They beheld God, and ate and drank" (Exod. 24:11).

Worshiping the Lord through His Torah

And Ezra the scribe stood on a wooden pulpit which they had made for the purpose. Nehemiah names those who stand by Ezra, as an indication of the unity of the holy people: *Mattithiah, Shema, Anaiah, Uriah, Hilkiah, and Maaseiah on his right hand; and Pedaiah, Mishael, Malchijah, Hashum, Hashbaddanah, Zechariah, and Meshullam on his left hand.* All these men had been involved in repairing the wall (Neh. 3). When Ezra, from his pulpit, opens the book of the law, *all the people stood.* Before reading, Ezra and the people glorify God: *And Ezra blessed the* LORD, *the great God; and all the people answered, "Amen, Amen," lifting up their hands; and they bowed their heads and worshiped the* LORD *with their faces to the ground.* Ezra not only reads the Torah aloud to the people; he also ensures that its meaning is at the same time taught to the people by Levites who know the law: *Also Jeshua, Bani, Sherebiah, Jamin, Akkub, Shabbethai, Hodiah, Maaseiah, Kelita, Azariah, Jozabad, Hanan, Pelaiah, the Levites, helped the people to understand the law, while the people remained in their places.* Proclamation of the Torah is not separated from commentary upon it.

This is so because the Torah is not for the elite only but for all in Israel: *And they read from the book, from the law of God, clearly; and they gave the sense, so that the people understood the reading.* God's word would fall flat if it were comprehensible only to the learned. "The secret things belong to the LORD our God; but the things that are revealed belong to us and to our children for ever, that we may do all the words of this law" (Deut. 29:29). "For this commandment which I command you this day is not too hard for you, neither is it far off. . . . But the word is very near you; it is in your mouth and in your heart, so that you can do it" (30:11, 14).

The Torah is not self-interpreting: *They gave the sense, so that the people understood the reading.*[3] Like no other, the risen Christ is fully able to give the sense. In the risen Christ's encounter with two men on the road to Emmaus "he said to them, 'O foolish men, and slow of heart to believe all that the prophets have spoken! Was it not necessary that the Christ should suffer these things and enter into his glory?' And beginning with Moses and all the prophets, he interpreted to them in all the scriptures the things concerning himself" (Luke 24:25–27). Only Christ is able to give sense to the entirety of human history. Before his coming, human history and its purposes remained an inscrutable mystery, because the aspirations of human knowing and loving are mocked by

3. Fensham suggests that this may simply mean translating from Hebrew to Aramaic (1982, 217–18).

the onslaught of sin and death. "All is vanity. . . . There is no remembrance of former things, nor will there be any remembrance of later things yet to happen among those who come after" (Eccl. 1:2, 11). But Christ's victory over death through supreme love provides the missing interpretive key to the story of human history.

The Seer of the book of Revelation fears that no one will be able to interpret the world's history of suffering, which he describes as "a scroll written within and on the back, sealed with seven seals" (Rev. 5:1) and held in the hand of God the Father. Does the history of human suffering have a meaning? One of the twenty-four elders tells the Seer: "Weep not; lo, the Lion of the tribe of Judah, the Root of David, has conquered, so that he can open the scroll and its seven seals" (5:5). Prompted by the elder, the Seer recognizes Christ the paschal lamb, the omnipotent and all-knowing Lord who is filled with the Holy Spirit (5:6–7).

As soon as the Lamb takes the scroll, "the four living creatures and the twenty-four elders fell down before the Lamb, each holding a harp, and with golden bowls full of incense, which are the prayers of the saints" (5:8). A "new song" comes from their lips: "Worthy art thou to take the scroll and to open its seals, for thou wast slain and by thy blood didst ransom men for God from every tribe and tongue and people and nation, and hast made them a kingdom and priests to our God, and they shall reign on earth" (5:9–10). Countless angels join in the song, praising Christ crucified as "worthy . . . to receive power and wealth and wisdom and might and honor and glory and blessing!" (5:12). Finally, all creatures join in this praise, led by the twenty-four elders (5:14).

In short, all of creation receives its consummation, its *sense, so that the people understood the reading*, from the power of Christ Jesus's passover as shared through the eucharistic liturgy of the church founded upon the twenty-four elders, the twelve tribes of Israel and the twelve apostles. Human beings "from every tribe and tongue and people and nation" share in the slain Lamb, in accord with "the mystery of his [the Father's] will, according to his purpose which he set forth in Christ as a plan for the fulness of time, to unite all things in him, things in heaven and things on earth" (Eph. 1:9–10). "Therefore God has highly exalted him and bestowed on him the name which is above every name, that at the name of Jesus every knee should bow, in heaven and on earth and under the earth, and every tongue confess that Jesus Christ is Lord, to the glory of God the Father" (Phil. 2:9–11).

Repentance and Praise

All the people wept when they heard the words of the law. They weep because they, like their fathers, have not kept the commandments. "The joy of our hearts has ceased; our dancing has been turned to mourning. The crown has fallen from our head; woe to us, for we have sinned! For this our heart has become sick, for these things our eyes have grown dim, for Mount Zion which lies desolate; jackals prowl over it" (Lam. 5:15–18). The people do not however need to weep on this day; it is a solemn day of rejoicing. *And Nehemiah, who was the governor, and Ezra the priest and scribe, and the Levites who taught the people said to all the people, "This day is holy to the LORD your God; do not mourn or weep."* Ezra instructs them on how to behave in accordance with God's command for this festival: *Go your way, eat the fat and drink sweet wine and send portions to him for whom nothing is prepared; for this day is holy to our LORD; and do not be grieved, for the joy of the LORD is your strength.*

The day of praise anticipates that day when it may fully be said of God: "Thou hast turned for me my mourning into dancing; thou hast loosed my sackcloth and girded me with gladness, that my soul may praise thee and not be silent. O LORD my God, I will give thanks to thee for ever" (Ps. 30:11–12). The people's first lesson in Torah is thus that God has established a day for rejoicing, for ultimately Israel is not created to weep. Not that their weeping is, in itself, inappropriate: "The LORD saw it [human injustice], and it displeased him that there was no justice. He saw that there was no man, and wondered that there was no one to intervene" (Isa. 59:15–16). But lack of human justice, terrible though it is, will be healed and redeemed by the Lord. "And he will come to Zion as Redeemer, to those in Jacob who turn from transgression, says the LORD" (59:20). The combination of mourning for sins and rejoicing over God's mercy exhibits our complete dependence upon God. "Then what becomes of our boasting? It is excluded" (Rom. 3:27).

And all the people went their way to eat and drink and to send portions and to make great rejoicing, because they had understood the words that were declared to them. It is appropriate that the first festival of the seventh month commands rejoicing, because without knowing joyfully the greatness and gifts of the living God, one cannot appreciate either the costliness of sin or the wondrous gift of salvation.[4] "Commit your way to the LORD; trust in him, and he will act" (Ps. 37:5).

Celebrating the Feast of Booths

On the second day the heads of fathers' houses of all the people, with the priests and the Levites, came together to Ezra the scribe in order to study the words of the law. Inspired by Ezra's solemn reading the day before, the leaders of the people renew their pursuit of holiness so that they might be fit to dwell with God in

---

4. Throntveit points out: "The 'joy of the LORD' (v. 10), freshly renewed through the teaching of Ezra and the Levites, will strengthen the people for the soul-searching that lies ahead in chapters 9 and 10" (1992, 97).

the land. The study of Torah—"the sword of the Spirit, which is the word of God" (Eph. 6:17)—belongs at the heart of holiness. "If thy law had not been my delight, I should have perished in my affliction. I will never forget thy precepts; for by them thou hast given me life. I am thine, save me; for I have sought thy precepts" (Ps. 119:92–94).

Their study of the Torah focuses upon how to practice the feast of booths. By learning to celebrate this feast that reenacts the exodus, they are formed as a people journeying toward dwelling with God in the land: *And they found it written in the law that the* LORD *had commanded by Moses that the people of Israel should dwell in booths during the feast of the seventh month, and that they should publish and proclaim in all their towns and in Jerusalem, "Go out to the hills and bring branches of olive, wild olive, myrtle, palm, and other leafy trees to make booths, as it is written."* After making the booths, the people celebrate the feast of booths *seven days; and on the eighth day there was a solemn assembly, according to the ordinances.*

The seven days signify God's work of creation, the eighth day their need for new creation. Bede says that "that Solomon built the temple in seven years but finished and dedicated it in the eighth signifies that during all the time of this world, which is encompassed in seven days, the Lord is building a Church by gathering the faithful to its heavenly edifice" (2006, 6–7). This mystical interpretation emphasizes that the aim of the feast of booths is the "new Jerusalem," which is God's holy bride. "For behold, I create new heavens and a new earth; and the former things shall not be remembered or come into mind. But be glad and rejoice for ever in that which I create; for behold, I create Jerusalem a rejoicing, and her people a joy" (Isa. 65:17–18).

The booths dot Jerusalem; the people dwell in the booths *each on his roof, and in their courts and in the courts of the house of God, and in the square at the Water Gate and in the square at the Gate of Ephraim.* For the first time since the days of the Davidic kings, Jerusalem—and not only the temple—stands as a place where the people of Israel dwell with their God. They reenact their pilgrimage to the land, now with a double meaning: recollecting the exodus from Egyptian slavery and remembering also their recent return to the land from Babylonian exile. This return to the land is recalled as a new exodus: *All the assembly of those who had returned from the captivity made booths and dwelt in the booths.* This is the first time since Joshua that the people have celebrated the feast of booths in this way: *For from the days of Jeshua the son of Nun to that day the people of Israel had not done so.*[5] They celebrate the feast of booths

---

5. As we have seen, Ezra's party of returning exiles celebrated the feast of booths upon arriving in Jerusalem. Blenkinsopp comments: "The statement that it had not been done *in this manner* since the time of Joshua must be taken programmatically rather than literally, as in the other instances where this kind of formula is used in C [the Chronicler] (2 Chron. 30:26; 35:18). It implies a correspondence between Ezra's aliyah and the exodus from Egypt, and between return to the homeland of the deportees and Joshua's occupation of the land. The reader is therefore

in hope that the goal of the original exodus will come about: "And the LORD said to Moses, 'Say to all the congregation of the people of Israel, You shall be holy; for I the LORD your God am holy'" (Lev. 19:1–2).

Such holiness comes true in Christ Jesus, who provides an eternal "booth" at journey's end. In this respect St. Paul reminds us: "Here indeed we groan, and long to put on our heavenly dwelling, so that by putting it on we may not be found naked. For while we are still in this tent, we sigh with anxiety; not that we would be unclothed, but that we would be further clothed, so that what is mortal may be swallowed up by life. He who has prepared us for this very thing is God" (2 Cor. 5:2–5). This "heavenly dwelling" is the fullness of "the body of Christ," the church: "Now you are the body of Christ and individually members of it" (1 Cor. 12:27).

Reading the Torah to the People of God

Ezra's effort to overcome the exile follows the path of covenant renewal undertaken by King Josiah—even though Ezra is a priest, not a Davidic king. King Josiah's public reading of the Torah was a desperate attempt to avert the exile before it happened: "And the king went up to the house of the LORD, and with him all the men of Judah and all the inhabitants of Jerusalem, and the priests and the prophets, all the people, both small and great; and he read in their hearing all the words of the book of the covenant which had been found in the house of the LORD" (2 Kgs. 23:2). Like Josiah, Ezra publicly proclaims the Torah to the people and gains the people's agreement that they will obey what they hear in the Torah. Similarly, just as under Josiah the people of Israel kept the feast of passover for the first time since Joshua—"for no such passover had been kept since the days of the judges who judged Israel, or during all the days of the kings of Israel or of the kings of Judah" (23:22)—so also under Ezra the first celebration of the feast of booths since Joshua's time occurs. The people still require a Davidic king for their restoration, but until God raises up such a king, the covenantal quest to dwell with God can continue under Ezra the Scribe/priest.

During the seven days of the feast of booths, Ezra never stops reading the Torah to the people: *Day by day, from the first day to the last day, he read from the book of the law of God.* That the reading of the Torah continues for seven days places the people's return to the land within the divine pattern of creation. The seven-day reading likewise suggests, with the psalmist, that the Torah is a microcosm of creation: "For ever, O LORD, thy word is firmly fixed in the heavens" (Ps. 119:89).

---

invited to think of Joshua's assembly at Shechem in the course of which statutes and ordinances were made and written and the people rededicated itself to the service of YHVH (Josh. 24)" (1988, 292).

As the consummation of the people's return to the holy land, the seven-day reading also calls to mind Joshua's first conquest in the promised land, the conquest of Jericho. The conquest of Jericho expresses a moment of new creation, in which the people, like Adam and Eve, are enabled to dwell in holiness with God in the land. The seventh day completes the miraculous conquest: "On the seventh day they rose early at the dawn of day, and marched around the city in the same manner seven times: it was only on that day that they marched around the city seven times. And at the seventh time, when the [seven] priests had blown the trumpets, Joshua said to the people, 'Shout; for the LORD has given you the city'" (Josh. 6:15–16).

If the seven days signal a new creation, the eighth day begins the history of Israel anew, freed from the weight of past sins. The eighth day after birth, according to the Torah, is the day on which "the flesh of his foreskin shall be circumcised" (Lev. 12:3). Circumcision is the mark of the Abrahamic covenant: "And God said to Abraham, 'As for you, you shall keep my covenant, you and your descendants after you throughout their generations. This is my covenant, which you shall keep, between me and you and your descendants after you: Every male among you shall be circumcised" (Gen. 17:9–10). Like the seven days, the eighth day also has a connection with the conquest of Jericho. Before the conquest of Jericho, the Lord commands Joshua: "Make flint knives, and circumcise the people of Israel" (Josh. 5:2), since during the exodus circumcision had not been performed. The conquest (and reconquest) of the land is thus more spiritual than military.

Moses prophesies that after the exile brought about by the covenantal curse, God will "gather you again from all the peoples where the LORD your God has scattered you" (Deut. 30:3) and "will circumcise your heart and the heart of your offspring, so that you will love the LORD your God with all your heart and with all your soul, that you may live" (30:6). "Real circumcision is a matter of the heart, spiritual and not literal" (Rom. 2:29).

Could it be that the day of "circumcision" of the heart so that the people may dwell with God has arrived? The task of the returned exiles is to strive to make it so, even while knowing that only God can actually accomplish it. "So when they had come together, they asked him, 'Lord, will you at this time restore the kingdom to Israel?' He said to them, 'It is not for you to know times or seasons which the Father has fixed by his own authority. But you shall receive power when the Holy Spirit has come upon you'" (Acts 1:6–8).

NEHEMIAH 9

Holiness and Repentance

Day of Repentance: Hope in the Midst of Affliction

Ezra leads the community of returned exiles in a day of mourning and repentance for *their sins and the iniquities of their fathers*. In order to be created anew, the people of Israel must repent for past sins. The Lord spared Judah under King Josiah due to Josiah's sincere repentance. "Thus says the LORD, the God of Israel: Regarding the words which you have heard, because your heart was penitent, and you humbled yourself before the LORD, when you heard how I spoke against this place, and against its inhabitants, that they should become a desolation and a curse, and you have rent your clothes and wept before me, I also have heard you" (2 Kgs. 22:18–19). While the Lord ultimately does not hold back the covenantal curse, he makes sure that the curse does not come about in Josiah's time. Thus Ezra intends for the returned exiles to manifest sincere repentance in hopes that God will hear them and graciously fulfill his promise of restoration.

The day of repentance possesses three elements. First, *the Israelites separated themselves from all foreigners*. At the heart of Israel's sins is the desire to act and worship in the same way that other nations act and worship: they "feared other gods and walked in the customs of the nations whom the LORD drove out before the people of Israel, and in the customs which the kings of Israel had introduced" (2 Kgs. 17:7–8; cf. 17:19–20). Second, *they stood up in their place and read from the book of the law of the LORD their God for a fourth of the day.* "My soul cleaves to the dust; revive me according to thy word! When I told of my ways, thou didst answer me; teach me thy statutes! Make me understand the way of thy precepts, and I will meditate on thy wondrous works. My soul melts away for sorrow; strengthen me according to thy word! Put false ways far from me; and graciously teach me thy law!" (Ps. 119:25–29). Without knowing God's law, they cannot put it into action. Third, *they made confession and worshiped the* Lord *their God.*

This third element is twofold: worship and confession of sins. The Levites lead the people in the worship of the Lord: *Upon the stairs of the Levites stood Jeshua, Bani, Kadmiel, Shebaniah, Bunni, Sherebiah, Bani, and Chenani; and they cried with a loud voice to the* Lord *their God. Then the Levites, Jeshua, Kadmiel, Bani, Hashabneiah, Sherebiah, Hodiah, Shebaniah, and Pethahiah said, "Stand up and bless the* Lord *your God from everlasting to everlasting. Blessed be thy glorious name which is exalted above all blessing and praise."*

Blessed Be Thy Glorious Name

Why *blessed be thy glorious name?* Why is the divine name singled out for blessing in worship? As a people, Israel receives its own name from its striving to know the name of the Lord. The definitive experience of Jacob, the father of the twelve tribes, can once more serve as a reminder. Just as Jacob is about to return to the promised land, he leads his family across the River Jabbok, and "Jacob was left alone; and a man wrestled with him until the breaking of the day" (Gen. 32:24). This "man," whom Jacob later identifies as God, says to Jacob: "'Let me go, for the day is breaking.' But Jacob said, 'I will not let you go, unless you bless me.' And he said to him, 'What is your name?' And he said, 'Jacob.' Then he said, 'Your name shall no more be called Jacob, but Israel, for you have striven with God and with men, and have prevailed'" (32:26–28). Jacob then reveals the object of his striving, namely, knowledge of God. "Then Jacob asked him, 'Tell me, I pray, your name.' But he said, 'Why is it that you ask my name?' And there he blessed him. So Jacob called the name of the place Peniel, saying, 'For I have seen God face to face, and yet my life is preserved'" (32:29–30). Jacob is blessed and receives the name "Israel" because he strives to know God's name.

Similarly the great revelation to Moses, the revelation that stands at the center of God's separation of Israel from the surrounding nations, is the revelation of God's name. "Then Moses said to God, 'If I come to the people of Israel and say to them, "The God of your fathers has sent me to you," and they ask me, "What is his name?" what shall I say to them?' God said to Moses, 'I am who I am.' And he said, 'Say this to the people of Israel, 'I am has sent me to you'" (Exod. 3:13–14). Moses also receives a second name for God, one that had previously been revealed: "God also said to Moses, 'Say this to the people of Israel, "The Lord, the God of your fathers, the God of Abraham, the God of Isaac, and the God of Jacob, has sent me to you": this is my name for ever'" (3:15).

To know the glorious name of God is more than to know a mere concept; it is to experience and share in the personal reality of the living God. It is a cause for rejoicing. "O give thanks to the LORD, call on his name, make known his deeds among the peoples! Sing to him, sing praises to him, tell of all his wonderful works! Glory in his holy name; let the hearts of those who seek the LORD rejoice!" (Ps. 105:1–3). Similarly Jesus, the Son of the Father, shares in the Father's divine name, as do, in an adoptive way, those who have faith in Jesus. "Holy Father, keep them in thy name, which thou hast given me, that they may be one, even as we are one. While I was with them, I kept them in thy name, which thou hast given me" (John 17:11–12).

In the worship of *the* LORD *your God* led by the Levites, the people learn two universal truths about the God who has elected Israel. First, God is *from everlasting to everlasting*. "'I am the Alpha and the Omega,' says the Lord God, who is and who was and who is to come, the Almighty" (Rev. 1:8). He is the only God. "Know therefore this day, and lay it to your heart, that the LORD is God in heaven above and on the earth beneath; there is no other" (Deut. 4:39). God is eternal and transcendent, but not aloof. "For thus says the high and lofty One who inhabits eternity, whose name is Holy: 'I dwell in the high and holy place, and also with him who is of a contrite and humble spirit'" (Isa. 57:15). Only as transcending and creating time and space can he bestow his gifts upon time and space. "Do not be deceived, my beloved brethren. Every good endowment and every perfect gift is from above, coming down from the Father of lights with whom there is no variation or shadow due to change" (Jas. 1:16–17). God, *from everlasting to everlasting*, is the giver of all gifts.

Second, God's *glorious name . . . is exalted above all blessing and praise*. Our human words, no matter how exalted, express perfections that we experience only as the finite perfections of creatures. Thus our words of praise cannot be univocally applied to God, who is infinite. God does not belong to any scale of perfection, because he infinitely exceeds that which he creates. It is in this sense that Jesus upholds the prerogatives of God: "And a ruler asked him, 'Good Teacher, what shall I do to inherit eternal life?' And Jesus said to him, 'Why do you call me good? No one is good but God alone'" (Luke 18:18–19). Similarly the Lord teaches through Isaiah: "For my thoughts are not your thoughts, neither are your ways my ways, says the LORD. For as the heavens are higher than the earth, so are my ways higher than your ways and my thoughts than your thoughts" (Isa. 55:8–9).

On the other hand, creatures are related to the Creator as effect to cause. Therefore human words about God are not meaningless. When John writes that "God is love" (1 John 4:16), the word "love," which expresses a perfection in creatures, exists in a supereminent way in the Creator, from whom creatures receive the perfection of love. Scripture makes clear that finite love receives its meaning from infinite, creative love. "In this is love, not that we loved God but that he loved us and sent his Son to be the expiation for our sins. Beloved, if God so loved us, we also ought to love one another. No man has ever seen God; if we love one another, God abides in us and his love is perfected in us" (4:10–12).

Confession of Sins in Covenantal Context

After the Levites lead the worship, Ezra leads the people's *confession*.[1] The confession of sins involves two elements: praising the God against whom the people have sinned and enumerating the people's sins. Some attention to the narrative thread of the confession is thus necessary in order to grasp its theological import.

Ezra begins by praising the Lord as the one God, the Creator: *Thou art the LORD, thou alone; thou hast made heaven, the heaven of heavens, with all their host, the earth and all that is on it, the seas and all that is in them; and thou preservest all of them; and the host of heaven worships thee.* "For I know that the LORD is great, and that our Lord is above all gods. Whatever the LORD pleases he does, in heaven and on earth, in the seas and all deeps" (Ps. 135:5–6). This one Creator God who governs all things has made covenant with Israel, and so Ezra next recites the two covenants that are most central to the formation of the holy people who dwell in the promised land.

First he sets forth the covenant with Abraham and God's fulfillment of his promise in this covenant: *Thou art the LORD, the God who didst choose Abram and bring him forth out of Ur of the Chaldeans and give him the name Abraham; and thou didst find his heart faithful before thee, and didst make with him the covenant to give to his descendants the land of the Canaanite, the Hittite, the Amorite, the Perizzite, the Jebusite, and the Girgashite; and thou hast fulfilled thy promise, for thou art righteous.* "He is mindful of his covenant for ever, of the word that he commanded, for a thousand generations, the covenant which he made with Abraham, his sworn promise to Isaac, which he confirmed to Jacob as a statute, to Israel as an everlasting covenant, saying, 'To you I will give the land of Canaan as your portion for an inheritance'" (Ps. 105:8–11).

Second he describes the covenant with Moses. God gives the descendents of Abraham a law that manifests to them the requirements of holiness, and God leads them into the promised land so as to dwell with God. In this regard Ezra emphasizes God's powerful deeds and intimate presence among the people, the coming of heaven to earth. His powerful deeds accomplish the exodus: *And thou didst see the affliction of our fathers in Egypt and hear their cry at the Red Sea, and didst perform signs and wonders against Pharaoh and all his servants and*

---

1. Fensham notes regarding Ezra's lengthy prayer: "If we have here the redactional work of the Chronicler, it is interesting that it is one of his favorite methods to insert a prayer for purposes of exhortation" (1982, 227). He also compares Ezra's prayer to Ps. 78, 105, 106, 135, 136, which offer histories of Israel.

all the people of his land, for thou knewest that they acted insolently against our father; and thou didst get thee a name, as it is to this day. And thou didst divide the sea before them, so that they went through the midst of the sea on dry land; and thou didst cast their pursuers into the depths. "He led them in safety, so that they were not afraid; but the seas overwhelmed their enemies" (Ps. 78:53). Once the people have left Egyptian slavery behind them, God makes himself known intimately by giving his holy law. *Thou didst come down upon Mount Sinai, and speak with them from heaven and give them right ordinances and true laws, good statutes and commandments, and thou didst make known to them thy holy sabbath and command them commandments and statutes and a law by Moses thy servant. Thou didst give them bread from heaven.* "For what great nation is there that has a god so near to it as the LORD our God is to us, whenever we call upon him? And what great nation is there, that has statutes and ordinances so righteous as all this law which I set before you this day?" (Deut. 4:7–8).

Ezra then turns to the litany of the sins of God's chosen people. He begins with their desire, during the exodus, to abandon God and return to the relative comfort of Egypt: *They stiffened their neck and appointed a leader to return to their bondage in Egypt*, and *they . . . made for themselves a molten calf*. "They made a calf in Horeb and worshiped a molten image. They exchanged the glory of God for the image of an ox that eats grass. They forgot God, their Savior, who had done great things in Egypt" (Ps. 106:19–21).

Ezra juxtaposes these sins with God's constant patience, mercy, and faithfulness. He notes that *thou art a God ready to forgive, gracious and merciful, slow to anger and abounding in steadfast love, and didst not forsake them* despite their longings after Egyptian comforts. Even after their worship of the *molten calf, the pillar of cloud* and *the pillar of fire* guide their travels. Not only this, but God *gavest thy good Spirit to instruct them*, as well as miraculous manna and water from the rock. Ezra recalls as well Moses's observation that *forty years didst thou sustain them in the wilderness, and they lacked nothing; their clothes did not wear out and their feet did not swell* (see Deut. 8:4). And God leads them into the land, where they *were filled and became fat, and delighted themselves in thy [God's] great goodness.*

Despite Israel's sins during the exodus, then, God remains wonderfully good to Israel. Ezra confesses, however, that Israel continues to sin after the exodus: *Nevertheless they were disobedient and rebelled against thee and cast thy law behind their back and killed thy prophets, who had warned them in order to turn them back to thee, and they committed great blasphemies.* By those words, Ezra sums up the condition of the Israelites during the period of the judges. Still God is merciful and hears Israel's prayers: *According to thy great mercies thou didst give them saviors who saved them from the hand of their enemies.* Yet, as Ezra confesses, Israel falls into sin again and again, despite the deliverances and warnings provided by the Lord. For this reason, Ezra recalls that God justly punished the people by exile to Assyria and Babylon: *Many years thou didst bear with them, and didst warn them by thy Spirit through the prophets; yet they would not give ear. Therefore thou didst give them into the hand of the peoples of the lands.* "Many times he delivered them, but they were rebellious in their purposes, and were brought low through their iniquity" (Ps. 106:43). Ezra does not end there, but once more observes that God does not abandon the people: *Thou [God] hast dealt faithfully and we have acted wickedly.*

Ezra concludes the confession of sins with a stern evaluation of the people's current condition. Whereas it might seem that he would celebrate the rebuilding of the temple, the rebuilding of the walls of Jerusalem, and the resumption of the liturgical feasts in accordance with the law, instead he says: *Behold, we are slaves this day; in the land that thou gavest to our fathers to enjoy its fruit and its good gifts, behold, we are slaves.* Behind Ezra's words is the lack of the Davidic king; until God restores the Davidic king, the people will not have truly returned from exile. Ezra notes that the land's *rich yield goes to the kings whom thou hast set over us because of our sins; they have power also over our bodies and over our cattle at their pleasure, and we are in great distress.*

Ezra's solemn confession of sins is first and foremost a plea for the Lord to repeat his historical pattern and take mercy once more upon the people, in particular through the gift of a Davidic king. God is constant in his love, and the people will be blessed if they remain constant to their God despite their afflictions. The Lord will help "his servant Israel, in remembrance of his mercy, as he spoke to our fathers, to Abraham and to his posterity for ever" (Luke 1:54–55). Examples of God's consistency include Daniel's companions Shadrach, Meshach, and Abednego, who emerge unscathed from the fiery furnace (Dan. 3:26–27). Daniel himself, despite an apparent sentence of death, "got down upon his knees three times a day and prayed and gave thanks before his God, as he had done previously" (6:10) and is later delivered from the den of lions. Ruth, ancestress of King David, refuses to leave the side of her mother-in-law despite the threat of starvation: "Your people shall be my people, and your God my God; where you die I will die, and there will I be buried" (Ruth 1:16–17). And King Solomon prays at the dedication of the temple: "And hearken thou [God] to the supplication of thy servant and of thy people Israel, when they pray toward this place; yea, hear thou in heaven thy dwelling place; and when thou hearest, forgive" (1 Kgs. 8:30). "And Mary said, 'My soul magnifies the Lord, and my spirit rejoices in God my Savior, for he has regarded the low estate of his handmaiden. For behold, henceforth all generations will call me blessed; for he who is mighty has done great things for me, and holy is his name'" (Luke 1:46–49).

Second, Ezra's confession calls upon the people finally to become a holy people. "As obedient children, do not be conformed to the passions of your former ignorance, but as he who called you is holy, be holy yourselves in all your conduct; since it is written, 'You shall be holy, for I am holy'" (1 Pet.

1:14–16). In Christ such holiness is possible. "He was destined before the foundation of the world but was made manifest at the end of the times for your sake. Through him you have confidence in God, who raised him from the dead and gave him glory, so that your faith and hope are in God" (1:20–21).

Third, Ezra's confession prevents the people from imagining that God, due to his earlier covenants, *owes* Israel the gift of restoration. In Jesus's parable the Pharisee no longer considers himself needy in relation to God, because he has striven to obey God's commands. "But the tax collector, standing far off, would not even lift up his eyes to heaven, but beat his breast, saying, 'God, be merciful to me a sinner!'" (Luke 18:13). Through pride, the Pharisee has become his own source of spiritual consolation; and lacking God, he lacks everything. Jesus comments: "I tell you, this man [the tax collector] went down to his house justified rather than the other [the Pharisee]; for every one who exalts himself will be humbled, but he who humbles himself will be exalted" (18:14). "Clothe yourselves, all of you, with humility toward one another, for 'God opposes the proud, but gives grace to the humble'" (1 Pet. 5:5).

Making Covenant

At this stage Ezra unfolds the last aspect of his plan: he desires to make a covenant with God that obligates the people to full obedience to the Torah, in hopes that their faithfulness will encourage God's merciful restoration of Israel. In Ezra's words: *Because of all this we make a firm covenant and write it, and our princes, our Levites, and our priests set their seal to it.*

In making this covenant, Ezra once more imitates the covenant renewal that King Josiah undertook to stave off exile. Josiah, after reading the Torah to all the people of Judah in Jerusalem, "stood by the pillar and made a covenant before the LORD, to walk after the LORD and to keep his commandments and his testimonies and his statues, with all his heart and all his soul, to perform the words of this covenant that were written in this book [the Torah]; and all the people joined in the covenant" (2 Kgs. 23:3). King Josiah's covenant differs from previous covenants in that the people, not God, initiate it and in that the people alone, not God, make commitments. Likewise, Ezra's covenant is initiated by the people and commits the people, not God, to particular actions. But whereas Josiah's covenant was too late, Ezra hopes that his covenant, now that the covenantal curse has been applied and the people restored to the land, will invite a further act of God's mercy.

King Josiah's subjects violated the covenant that they made with the Lord, and the Lord punished them with exile. "And the men who transgressed my covenant and did not keep the terms of the covenant which they made before me, I will make like the calf which they cut in two and passed between its parts

. . . and I will give them into the hand of their enemies" (Jer. 34:18, 20). Even so, Josiah's covenant at least has the effect that God promises that Josiah's "eyes shall not see all the evil which I will bring upon this place" (2 Kgs. 22:20). By contrast, perhaps Ezra's covenant, if obeyed, will lead God to restore Israel through the rebirth of the Davidic kingship.

NEHEMIAH 10

Renewal of the Covenant

The list of signers of the covenant begins with *Nehemiah* and includes the *priests*, *Levites*, and *chiefs of the people*. These leaders sign as representatives of the whole community, by whom they are joined in the covenantal oath: *The rest of the people, the priests, the Levites, the gatekeepers, the singers, the temple servants, and all who have separated themselves from the peoples of the lands to the law of God, their wives, their sons, their daughters, all who have knowledge and understanding, join with their brethren, their nobles, and enter into a curse and an oath to walk in God's law which was given by Moses the servant of God, and to observe and do all the commandments of the* LORD *our Lord and his ordinances and his statutes.*

The following are the obligations to which they commit themselves by *oath*, obligations that together make up the renewal of the holy people.[1] If they fail in these covenantal obligations, the covenantal *curse* will take effect. Given the goal of eschatological restoration, I connect these covenantal obligations with the Lord's Prayer as taught by Jesus to his disciples:

1. Blenkinsopp comments: "In general, the articles [of the oath/pledge] are more rigorist than corresponding legislation in the Pentateuch; witness the prohibition of intermarriage, the extension of the sabbath commandment, and the more comprehensive law of the seventh year. It is tempting to think of the pledge as a sectarian document, a forerunner of the halakah of Pharisee and Essene which went beyond the demands of the Mosaic law while acknowledging its ultimate authority. While it is certainly later than Nehemiah—how much later we cannot say—it deals with issues of concern during his administration and purports to show how his program was brought to a successful conclusion" (1988, 319).

1. *We will not give our daughters to the peoples of the land or take their daughters for our sons.* || "Our Father who art in heaven, hallowed be thy name" (Matt. 6:9). As we saw in the book of Ezra, because of the worship of multiple gods that arises from intermarriage, Israel—despite having been separated from the nations for the worship of the Lord—has not yet fully manifested to the nations the utterly unique glory of God's name. The first obligation of this new covenant seeks to curtail intermarriage and idolatry and thereby truly honor God's name. The Lord promises through Ezekiel: "I will vindicate the holiness of my great name, which has been profaned among the nations, and which you have profaned among them" (Ezek. 36:23).

2. *If the peoples of the land bring in wares or any grain on the sabbath day to sell, we will not buy from them on the sabbath or on a holy day.* || "Thy kingdom come" (Matt. 6:10). The faithful observance of the sabbath points to the eschatological restoration of Israel, the perfect dwelling of all families of the earth with God: "For as the new heavens and the new earth which I will make shall remain before me, says the LORD; so shall your descendents and your name remain. From new moon to new moon, and from sabbath to sabbath, all flesh shall come to worship before me, says the LORD" (Isa. 66:22–23). This eschatological restoration will return the kingship to Israel. "But if you listen to me, says the LORD, and bring in no burden by the gates of this city on the sabbath day, but keep the sabbath day holy and do no work on it, then there shall enter by the gates of this city kings who sit on the throne of David, riding in chariots and on horses, they and their princes, the men of Judah and the inhabitants of Jerusalem; and this city shall be inhabited for ever" (Jer. 17:24–25).

3. *We will forego the crops of the seventh year and the exaction of every debt.* || "Thy will be done, on earth as it is in heaven" (Matt. 6:10). "Great is thy mercy, O LORD!" (Ps. 119:156). God's will is mercy. Even during King Josiah's reforms, the people of Judah violate their covenantal obligation to keep the Jubilee year (Exod. 23:10–11). Jeremiah describes the command regarding the Jubilee: "Thus says the LORD, the God of Israel: I made a covenant with your fathers when I brought them out of the land of Egypt, out of the house of bondage, saying, 'At the end of six years each of you must set free the fellow Hebrew who has been sold to you and has served you six years; you must set him free from your service'" (Jer. 34:13–14). Until King Josiah the Israelites do not obey this command, but under Josiah the people of Judah "repented and did what was right in my [God's] eyes by proclaiming liberty, each to his neighbor, and you made a covenant before me in the house which is called by my name" (34:15). However the Israelites reenslave those that they liberated: "You turned around and profaned my name when each of you took back his

male and female slaves, who you had set free according to their desire, and you brought them into subjection to be your slaves" (34:16).

4. *We also lay upon ourselves the obligation to charge ourselves yearly with the third part of a shekel for the service of the house of our God: for the showbread, the continual cereal offering, the continual burnt offering, the sabbaths, the new moons, the appointed feasts, the holy things, and the sin offerings to make atonement for Israel, and for all the work of the house of our God.* || "Give us this day our daily bread" (Matt. 6:11). "You shall remember the LORD your God, for it is he who gives you the power to get wealth" (Deut. 8:18). These offerings show that the people recognize that all good things come from God. By these offerings, they affirm "that man does not live by bread alone, but that man lives by everything that proceeds out of the mouth of the LORD" (8:3).

5. *We have likewise cast lots, the priests, the Levites, and the people, for the wood offering, to bring it into the house of our God, according to our fathers' houses, at times appointed, year by year, to burn upon the altar of the LORD our God, as it is written in the law.* || "And forgive us our debts, as we also have forgiven our debtors" (Matt. 6:12). "Isaac said to his father Abraham, . . . 'Behold, the fire and the wood; but where is the lamb for a burnt offering?' Abraham said, 'God will provide himself the lamb for a burnt offering, my son'" (Gen. 22:7–8). St. Peter says: "He himself bore our sins in his body on the tree, that we might die to sin and live to righteousness. By his wounds you have been healed" (1 Pet. 2:24). The *wood offering* points to the ultimate forgiveness of our debts "on the tree."

6. *We obligate ourselves to bring the first fruits of our ground and the first fruits of all fruit of every tree, year by year, to the house of the LORD; and also to bring to the house of our God, to the priests who minister in the house of our God, the first-born of our sons and of our cattle, as it is written in the law, and the firstlings of our herds and of our flocks; and to bring the first of our coarse meal, and our contributions, the fruit of every tree, the wine and the oil, to the priests, to the chambers of the house of our God; and to bring to the Levites the tithes from our ground.* || "And lead us not into temptation" (Matt. 6:13). The northern kingdom offered its tithes at its idolatrous shrines: "Come to Bethel, and transgress; to Gilgal, and multiply transgression; bring your sacrifices every morning, your tithes every three days; offer a sacrifice of thanksgiving of that which is leavened, and proclaim freewill offerings, publish them; for so you love to do, O people of Israel!" (Amos 4:4–5). Holy offering of tithes and firstfruits, by contrast, leads to the accomplishment of the blessing promised to Abraham. The presentation of Jesus in the temple is the supreme example. "And when the time came for their purification according to the law of Moses, they brought him up to Jerusalem to present him to the Lord (as it is written in the law of the

Lord, 'Every male that opens the womb shall be called holy to the Lord') and to offer a sacrifice according to what is said in the law of the Lord" (Luke 2:22–24). The devout Israelite Simeon, "looking for the consolation of Israel" (2:25), was led by the Holy Spirit to expect that "he should not see death before he had seen the Lord's Christ" (2:26). Simeon is therefore present in the temple when the holy family arrive, and he holds the baby Jesus in his arms "and blessed God and said, 'Lord, now lettest thou thy servant depart in peace, according to thy word; for mine eyes have seen thy salvation which thou hast prepared in the presence of all peoples, a light for revelation to the Gentiles, and for glory to thy people Israel'" (2:28–32). The temple offerings and tithes express Israel's commitment to trust in the Lord alone and not to give way to the temptation of idolatry.

7. *It is the Levites who collect the tithes in all our rural towns. And the priest, the son of Aaron, shall be with the Levites when the Levites receive the tithes; and the Levites shall bring up the tithe of the tithes to the house of our God, to the chambers, to the storehouse. For the people of Israel and the sons of Levi shall bring the contribution of grain, wine, and oil to the chambers, where are the vessels of the sanctuary, and the priest that minister, and the gatekeepers and the singers. We will not neglect the house of our God.* || "But deliver us from evil" (Matt. 6:13). "The point is this: he who sows sparingly will also reap sparingly, and he who sows bountifully will also reap bountifully. Each one must do as he has made up his mind, not reluctantly or under compulsion, for God loves a cheerful giver. . . . You will be enriched in every way for great generosity, which through us will produce thanksgiving to God" (2 Cor. 9:6–7, 11). By contrast an evil day awaits those who neglect what is due to God: "Because you did not serve the LORD your God with joyfulness and gladness of heart, by reason of the abundance of all things, therefore you shall serve your enemies whom the LORD will send against you, in hunger and thirst, in nakedness, and in want of all things; and he will put a yoke of iron upon your neck, until he has destroyed you" (Deut. 28:47–48).

Through these covenantal obligations, the people renew their relationship with God by promising to be holy and constant in their worship, and thereby to dwell with God in the land. These covenantal obligations constitute a prayer to the Lord asking for his blessing. "He was praying in a certain place, and when he ceased, one of his disciples said to him, 'Lord, teach us to pray'" (Luke 11:1).

NEHEMIAH 11

Repopulating Jerusalem

The covenantal obligations of the holy people would be useless if Jerusalem remained underpopulated, since the goal of the people is to dwell with God in the holy land, whose center is Jerusalem, the meeting place of the people and their God. Bede comments according to the mystical sense: "The remaining cities of Israel represent the devout lifestyle of the common people of God, whereas the act of settling in Jerusalem specifically represents the conduct of those who, having already overcome the struggle of the vices, draw near to the vision of heavenly peace with an unimpeded mind" (2006, 203–4). Those are drawing near to this vision who, having seen the Lord, "returned to Jerusalem with great joy, and were continually in the temple blessing God" (Luke 24:52).

Jerusalem's significance is indicated by the fact that *the leaders of the people lived in Jerusalem*. But Jerusalem needs not only the leaders, but also the people. Therefore, *the people blessed all the men who willingly offered to live in Jerusalem*. Just as the holy people must tithe to the temple, so also the holy land requires its tithe. *The people cast lots to bring one out of ten to live in Jerusalem the holy city*.

Why this tithe? A triumphant psalm says about Jerusalem: "Great is the Lord and greatly to be praised in the city of our God! His holy mountain, beautiful in elevation, is the joy of all the earth, Mount Zion, in the far north, the city of the great King. Within her citadels God has shown himself a sure defense" (Ps. 48:1–3). This "sure defense" includes military defense against the invasion of foreign kings, but more importantly it refers to God's "steadfast love . . . in the midst of thy temple" (48:9). God's love provides an impregnable fortress: "As thy name, O God, so thy praise reaches to the ends of the earth. Thy right hand is filled with victory; let Mount Zion be glad! Let the daughters of Judah rejoice because of thy judgments!" (48:10–11). Thus the psalmist urges the Israelites: "Walk about Zion, go round about her, number her towers, consider well her ramparts, go through her citadels; that you may tell the next generation that this is God, our God for ever and ever. He will be our guide for ever" (48:12–14). Yet what would Zion be if it had no "next generation"?

Nehemiah strives to ensure that the glory of Zion is not lost. Once again, his mission aims not merely at physically fortifying and strengthening the city. At the heart of his mission is the desire for the restoration of the holy people. Other psalms give evidence to this covenantal understanding of those who devote themselves to Jerusalem, whose center is the temple. "O LORD, I love the habitation of thy house, and the place where thy glory dwells" (Ps. 26:8). "One thing have I asked of the LORD, that will I seek after; that I may dwell in the house of the LORD all the days of my life, to behold the beauty of the LORD, and to inquire in his temple" (27:4).

Who are the people who return to live in Jerusalem? Among them are many families of *priests* and *Levites*,[1] as well as *certain of the sons of Judah and of the sons of Benjamin*, numbering in the thousands. There are also families of *gatekeepers*. The king—Artaxerxes, one assumes—has also given instructions regarding the temple service: *For there was a command from the king concerning them, and a settled provision for the singers, as every day required. And Pethahiah the son of Meshezabel, of the sons of Zerah the son of Judah, was at the king's hand in all matters concerning the people.*[2]

Jerusalem, then, is being revived, as are its surrounding *villages, with their fields*. Could it be that "the word of the LORD by the mouth of Jeremiah" (Ezra 1:1) is coming true? "For thus says the LORD: When seventy years are completed for Babylon, I will visit you, and I will fulfil to you my promise and bring you back to this place. . . . You will seek me and find me; when you seek me with all your heart, I will be found by you, says the LORD, and I will restore your fortunes and gather you from all the nations" (Jer. 29:10, 13–14).

Without Nehemiah's labors on behalf of the people, there could have been no restoration. And yet Nehemiah's upbuilding of the holy people and holy land does not attain the goal of perfect holiness and divine indwelling. That awaits the Messiah, who "knew no sin" (2 Cor. 5:21) and who is "God with us" (Matt. 1:23).

1. Blenkinsopp 1988, 326, counts 1,192 priests and 284 Levites.
2. Fensham supposes that the mention of the king here probably "refers to the Persian king who was interested in the continuation of cultic practices (cf. Ezra 4:8–10; 7:21–24). V. 24 gives the name of the Jewish ambassador at the Persian court. This official was appointed by the king to give him advice in connection with Jewish affairs" (1982, 248).

NEHEMIAH 12

The Holy People

Nehemiah shows that the priests and Levites in his time trace their lineage back to the priests and Levites who came with the first returned exiles and thus have the closest possible connection to preexilic times. He gives relatively lengthy lists of the priestly and Levitical families, up to *the days of Nehemiah the governor and of Ezra the priest the scribe.*[1]

This effort to connect with preexilic times inspires Nehemiah's organization of *the dedication of the wall of Jerusalem.*[2] Recall that King David brings the ark

---

1. On historical difficulties regarding the accuracy of these genealogical lists, see Fensham 1982, 250–54; and Blenkinsopp 1988, 332–41. Blenkinsopp remarks: "The addition of a phrase at the end of the lists synchronizing the high priesthood of Joiakim with Nehemiah and Ezra allows the compiler to conclude with a recall of the great personalities of that decisive epoch of reform and consolidation. The synchronism is correct for Ezra but not for Nehemiah, contemporary of the high priest Eliashib. By the compiler's time, however, the two names were already firmly linked, both were present simultaneously in Jerusalem, and their respective activities had been amalgamated into one continuous work of salvage and restoration. The order in which their names appear does not, therefore, have any bearing on the issue of chronological priority. As at 8:9, the governor has precedence over anyone else in the province and so is named first" (1988, 341).

2. Fensham observes with respect to the historical chronology: "It is clear that 12:27ff. is to be connected to either 11:36 or quite probably 6:15. It is difficult to tell how much time had elapsed between the finishing of the wall and its dedication" (1982, 255). In Blenkinsopp's view: "At this point we return finally to the NM [Nehemiah Memoir] after the long insertion 7:5b–12:26. The remainder of the book draws on the NM with much editorial paraphrase, expansion, and no doubt omissions. The dedication of the wall is the expected finale to the completion of the city's defenses, including the synoicism. It brings Nehemiah's work to an appropriately solemn and satisfactory conclusion, even though several problems still awaited solution. The event is not dated. It would be natural to assume that it took place soon after the completion of the wall and the repopulation of the city, therefore within the first year of his administration (cf. 1:1; 2:1;

---

of the covenant up to Jerusalem with great joy, "leaping and dancing before the
LORD" (2 Sam. 6:16). The restoration of Jerusalem occasions similar joy. The
leaders of the people of Israel *sought the Levites in all their places, to bring them
to Jerusalem to celebrate the dedication with gladness, with thanksgivings and with
singing, with cymbals, harps, and lyres.* Not only the Levites, but also everyone
associated with the temple, are called upon for the festival. The temple singers
lend their services to the celebration: *And the sons of the singers gathered together
from the circuit round Jerusalem and from the villages of the Netophathites; also
from Beth-gilgal and from the region of Geba and Azmaveth; for the singers had
built for themselves villages around Jerusalem.* The greatest role belongs to the
priests and Levites, whose responsibility it is to purify ritually all who would
properly celebrate the restoration of Zion: *And the priest and the Levites purified
themselves; and they purified the people and the gates and the wall.*

Can these people, these gates, this wall recapture what before the exile it
meant to be the people of Israel and the City of David? Is not the presence of
the Lord much reduced?

The Lord may not yet have returned in power—and will indeed first return in weakness—but the rebuilt Jerusalem is the City of David, as the book
of Nehemiah emphasizes through frequent invocation of David's name. The
priests, Levites, singers, and gatekeepers perform their duties *according to the
command of David and his son Solomon.* The temple singers seem to take on
a particularly important role, due to the connection of the psalms with King
David: *For in the days of David and Asaph of old there was a chief of the singers, and there were songs of praise and thanksgiving to God.* During the solemn
procession celebrating the dedication of the wall, *the princes of Judah* and the
leading priests march into Jerusalem accompanied by others *with the musical
instruments of David the man of God.* Bede says: "In this life too the sons of
the priests sound their trumpets for the dedication of God's city because by
preaching they enkindle the hearts of their hearers to remembrance of the
celestial homeland" (2006, 212).

They divide into two companies, led by Ezra and Nehemiah respectively.[3]
Ezra's path into Jerusalem proceeds *by the stairs of the city of David, at the ascent
of the wall, above the house of David, to the Water Gate on the east.* Nehemiah
leads the other company along the wall, and the two companies meet at the
temple. *And they offered great sacrifices that day and rejoiced, for God had made
them rejoice with great joy; the women and children also rejoiced. And the joy of
Jerusalem was heard afar off.* "Praise the LORD! For it is good to sing praises to
our God; for he is gracious, and a song of praise is seemly. The LORD builds

6:15). If so, it has been moved to make way for the Ezra material" (1988, 343).

3. Blenkinsopp states: "There can be little doubt that the inclusion of Ezra the scribe at the
head of the southbound group, corresponding to Nehemiah in the other, is an editorial addition
from the time when the activity of the two men had been amalgamated into one movement of
reform" (1988, 346).

up Jerusalem; he gathers the outcasts of Israel" (Ps. 147:1–2). That *the joy of Jerusalem was heard afar off* links Nehemiah's celebration of the wall with Zerubbabel's celebration of the temple, when "the people shouted with a great shout, and the sound was heard afar" (Ezra 3:13). Similarly Nehemiah connects his leadership with that of Zerubbabel by observing that in his days, as *in the days of Zerubbabel*, the singers and gatekeepers receive public support. Nehemiah notes, too, that *the Levites set apart that which was for the sons of Aaron.* The Aaronic priesthood still functions as it did in the time of Zerubbabel, despite the difficulties that the returned exiles have since faced, and the law is being followed meticulously.

What is *the joy of Jerusalem*, when God *made them rejoice with great joy*? It is, first, that the walls of Jerusalem have been restored. But more importantly, it is that the precious threads between the present people and the present city with the preexilic people and the preexilic city remain intact: the stones of broken Jerusalem, left for dead, are restored once again to their proper places. "'For this my son was dead, and is alive again; he was lost, as is found.' And they began to make merry" (Luke 15:24).

Ezekiel's prophecy thus comes true, if not yet in its deepest meanings of bodily resurrection. The Lord "brought me [Ezekiel] out by the Spirit of the LORD, and set me down in the midst of the valley; it was full of bones" (Ezek. 37:1). God asks Ezekiel: "'Son of man, can these bones live?' And I answered, 'O Lord GOD, thou knowest.' Again he said to me, 'Prophesy to these bones, and say to them, O dry bones, hear the word of the LORD. Thus says the Lord GOD to these bones: Behold, I will cause breath to enter you, and you shall live'" (37:3–5). In Ezekiel's vision, he prophesies to the bones and they come alive. God then explains the vision to him: "Son of man, these bones are the whole house of Israel. Behold, they say, 'Our bones are dried up, and our hope is lost; we are clean cut off'" (37:11). God commands Ezekiel to prophesy the restoration of the people of Israel. Speaking through Ezekiel, God tells Israel: "I will open your graves, and raise you from your graves, O my people; and I will bring you home into the land of Israel. . . . And I will put my Spirit within you, and you shall live, and I will place you in your own land; then you shall know that I, the LORD, have spoken, and I have done it" (37:12, 14).

The holy people have indeed come back to the holy land. "Rejoice in the LORD, O you righteous, and give thanks to his holy name!" (Ps. 97:12). Bede says: "God is that king who makes his citizens joyful by his presence" (2006, 217).

NEHEMIAH 13

Final Efforts at the Renewal of the Holy People

Are Nehemiah's and Ezra's efforts—the solemn rebuilding of the wall, the reading of the law, the renewal of the covenantal obligations, the joyous celebrations, and so forth—in vain? If the people are not yet holy, have their efforts been presumptuous? Nehemiah 13 calls to mind Jesus at Gethsemane, when Jesus returns from prayer to find his disciples sleeping. Nehemiah likewise finds the people of Israel once again "sleeping." Recall too how presumption ruins King David's first attempt to bring the ark of the Lord to Jerusalem: "And when they came to the threshing floor of Nacon, Uzzah put out his hand to the ark of God and took hold of it, for the oxen stumbled. And the anger of the LORD was kindled against Uzzah; and God smote him there because he put forth his hand to the ark" (2 Sam. 6:6–7). Nehemiah discovers three areas of profound corruption, each of which is sufficient to destroy the hoped-for holiness of the people and the land.

The situation that Nehemiah encounters is comprehensible because falling away from the Lord belongs to the scriptural economy. Ultimately, divine mercy in Christ Jesus will raise and restore fallen Israel.

Corruption of the People: Faith

The people of Israel are corrupted. Among them are descendents not of Abraham but of Ammon and Moab—contrary to God's command through Moses: "No Ammonite or Moabite shall enter the assembly of the LORD; even to the tenth generation none belonging to them shall enter the assembly of the LORD for ever" (Deut. 23:3). This forgotten law is remembered when *they read from the book of Moses in the hearing of the people*, and in response *they separated from Israel all those of foreign descent.*[1] Not surprisingly, however, the corruption of the people goes far beyond merely the presence of some descendents of Ammon and Moab. Nehemiah reports: *In those days also I saw the Jews who had married women of Ashdod, Ammon, and Moab; and half of their children spoke the language of Ashdod, and they could not speak the language of Judah, but the language of each people.* Clearly the identity of the people of Israel as the Abrahamic people of God and bearer of the word of God is at serious risk. There can be no "peace" in Israel if its "walls" and "towers" (Ps. 122:7) no longer separate the people of God from false gods.

Nehemiah recognizes that the consequence of the dissolution of the people of Israel into the nations will be idolatry. How can the people be holy and dwell with God in the land if they do not worship the Lord alone? As Nehemiah warns the people: *Did not Solomon king of Israel sin on account of such women? Among the many nations there was no king like him, and he was beloved by his God, and God made him king over all Israel; nevertheless the foreign women made even him to sin.* In contrast to the Israelites' orderly separation described in the book of Ezra, Nehemiah records his own experience of somewhat chaotic conflict in which he employs his authority to the hilt. *And I contended with them and cursed them and beat some of them and pulled out their hair; and I made them take oath in the name of God, saying, "You shall not give your daughters to their sons, or take their daughters for your sons or for yourselves."* If the people of Israel lose their distinctiveness, God would have restored them to the holy land to no purpose, and the people would have once more betrayed God's covenantal mercy. Nehemiah puts it this way: *Shall we then listen to you [the supporters of intermarriage] and do all this great evil and act treacherously against our God by marrying foreign women?* "It is actually reported that there is immorality among you" (1 Cor. 5:1). "You are the salt of the earth; but if salt has lost its taste, how shall its saltness be restored? It is no longer good for anything except to be thrown out and trodden under foot by men" (Matt. 5:13).

Moses's valedictory song (Deut. 31:30) urges Israel to remain faithful to the Lord: "They sacrificed to demons which were no gods, to gods they had never known, to new gods that had come in of late, whom your fathers had never dreaded. You were unmindful of the Rock that begot you, and you forgot the

---

1. Blenkinsopp comments: "This action seems to duplicate that of Ezra described at much greater length in Ezra 9–10. It may even have been intended to duplicate it, part of the strategy of presenting the reforms of the two men *ad modum unius*. There is, however, the significant difference that the requirement of divorcing foreign wives is passed over both here and in the covenant stipulations. The incidents related in the final extract of the NM [Nehemiah Memoir] confirm that this omission was not by oversight. For even though the bad effects of exogamous marriage are stressed (13:23–27), this remedy is not adopted, and the member of the high priestly family who married a Sanballat woman was himself expelled from the community. We would be justified in finding here another confirmation of the predictable failure of this measure of Ezra's" (1988, 352).

God who gave you birth" (32:17–18). The result of such idolatry is alienation from God: "The LORD saw it, and spurned them, because of the provocation of his sons and his daughters. And he said, 'I will hide my face from them, I will see what their end will be, for they are a perverse generation, children in whom is no faithfulness'" (32:19–20). This is what is happening again to God's "children," the people of Israel, who have forgotten their God and begun to assimilate into the false worship of the nations around them. Nehemiah rightly diagnoses it as a lack of faith. "But as for you, man of God, shun all this; aim at righteousness, godliness, faith, love, steadfastness, gentleness. Fight the good fight of the faith; take hold of the eternal life to which you were called when you made the good confession in the presence of many witnesses" (1 Tim. 6:11–12). Bede states: "Today too in the Holy Church people marry foreign women whenever they contaminate their conscience with the delights of sins that properly pertain to the Gentiles" (2006, 225).

Corruption of the Temple: Hope

The corruption of the temple involves disarray among the priests and the Levites. The source of the corruption appears to be *Eliashib the priest*, but he clearly has much support.[2] When Nehemiah leaves Judah and returns to the service of Artaxerxes, Eliashib gives to *Tobiah*, Nehemiah's enemy, *a large chamber [in the temple courts] where they had previously put the cereal offering, the frankincense, the vessels, and the tithes of grain, wine, and oil, which were given by commandment to the Levites, singers, and gatekeepers, and the contributions for the priests.*[3] Tobiah's occupation of a temple storeroom makes one wonder whether he has been siphoning off some of the contributions intended for the support of the temple.

Somewhat like Moses, who returns from Mount Sinai to discover the chief priest implicated in the making of the golden calf, Nehemiah returns from King Artaxerxes to a disastrous situation. Nehemiah has to cleanse the temple: *And after some time I asked leave of the king and came to Jerusalem, and I then*

---

2. Blenkinsopp states that "Eliashib the priest" (13:4) and "Eliashib the high priest" (13:28) are not the same person (1988, 353–54).

3. Nehemiah tells us in 5:14 that he was governor in Jerusalem for "twelve years," ending in 433 BC. Fensham holds therefore that Nehemiah discovers the corruptions on a return trip (1982, 260–61). Blenkinsopp notes that "the last possible date for his return would be the year of the death of Artaxerxes I Long Hand, that is, 423 B.C.E., but it was almost certainly much earlier" (1988, 354). Blenkinsopp adds: "Nehemiah's absence at the court and return to Jerusalem may be seen as a chapter in the political history of the province and the struggle between the governor and the Sanballat-Tobiah-Geshem axis, with the former holding off the encroachments of the latter. In this struggle, which also divided loyalties within the province, the basic political issue seems to have been the establishment of the province's autonomy over against its neighbors" (1988, 355).

discovered the evil that Eliashib had done for Tobiah, preparing for him a chamber in the courts of the house of God. And I was very angry, and I threw all the household furniture of Tobiah out of the chamber. Then I gave orders and they cleansed the chambers; and I brought back thither the vessels of the house of God, with the cereal offering and the frankincense. He also confronts Tobiah and Sanballat, who have made inroads in Jerusalem through intermarriage. *Eliashib the high priest's* grandson is *the son-in-law of Sanballat the Horonite.* When Nehemiah discovers this connection with the archenemy of the rebuilding, Nehemiah *chased him [the grandson] from me.* He expels Eliashib's grandson from the Israelite community on the grounds that he has contaminated the high priestly lineage not merely by intermarriage but by breaking the precept of the Torah. "The priest who is chief among his brethren . . . shall take to wife a virgin of his own people, that he may not profane his children among his people; for I am the LORD who sanctify him" (Lev. 21:10, 14–15).

Nehemiah's position is also similar to that of Jesus, although Nehemiah's cleansing of the temple does not have messianic overtones. "And Jesus entered the temple of God and drove out all who sold and bought in the temple, and he overturned the tables of the money-changers and the seats of those who sold pigeons. He said to them, 'It is written, "My house shall be called a house of prayer"; but you make it a den of robbers'" (Matt. 21:12–13). Bede notes that "we ought to compare this zeal of Nehemiah to that of the Lord Saviour when, finding vendors and buyers in the temple, he made a whip from cords and drove them all outside. Nehemiah, in this as in his other undertakings, aptly conveyed a type of the true Consoler and Cleanser" (2006, 222).

Around the same time, Nehemiah discovers *that the portions of the Levites had not been given to them; so that the Levites and the singers, who did the work, had fled each to his field.* The Lord commands through Moses regarding the tithes owed to the Levites: "To the Levites I have given every tithe in Israel for an inheritance, in return for their service which they serve, their service in the tent of meeting" (Num. 18:21). Whether or not Tobiah is the one who took *the portions of the Levites,* someone did. The result is that during Nehemiah's absence, the functioning of the temple service has collapsed. Nehemiah *remonstrated with the officials and said, "Why is the house of God forsaken?"* Earlier he was forced to bring charges against "the nobles and the officials" (Neh. 5:7) for usury and enslaving fellow Israelites; now he finds himself reprimanding them for abandoning the temple service during his absence, despite the good intentions of the people during the time of the dedication of the wall of Jerusalem.

In order to bring the situation back under control, Nehemiah *gathered them [the officials] together and set them in their stations.* He reorganizes the chain of command. *I appointed as treasurers over the storehouses Shelemiah the priest, Zadok the scribe, and Pedaiah of the Levites, and as their assistant Hanan the son of Zaccur, son of Mattaniah, for they were counted faithful.* Clearly many others were not counted faithful. It is to Nehemiah's credit that he does not despair, although he does invoke a covenantal curse upon Eliashib's family *because they have defiled the priesthood and the covenant of the priesthood and the Levites.* Nehemiah prays that his actions will take positive root and not dissolve again upon his absence: *Remember me, O my God, concerning this, and wipe not out my good deeds that I have done for the house of my God and for his service.*

As Nehemiah recognizes, the danger is that the returned exiles will treat the temple service as if their God does not exist and use the temple instead for political and economic ends. Such misappropriation of God's gifts ultimately flows from a profound lack of hope in the Lord's power to accomplish good ends for those who serve him. The logic of hopelessness is set forth in the Wisdom of Solomon in a striking depiction: "For they reasoned unsoundly, saying to themselves, 'Short and sorrowful is our life, and there is no remedy when a man comes to his end, and no one has been known to return from Hades'" (Wisdom of Solomon 2:1). According to such reasoning, death ends all: "Because we were born by mere chance, and hereafter we shall be as though we had never been; because the breath in our nostrils is smoke, and reason is a spark kindled by the beating of our hearts. When it is extinguished, the body will turn to ashes, and the spirit will dissolve like empty air" (2:2–3). Against the sentimental tripe that a dead person "lives on" in our memories, this despairing viewpoint continues: "Our name will be forgotten in time, and no one will remember our works; our life will pass away like the traces of a cloud, and be scattered like mist that is chased by the rays of the sun and overcome by its heat" (2:4). On this view, death begins an eternity of endless moments; the dead person never, ever will think or love again.

The fruit of this view is hedonism in its various forms. "Come, therefore, let us enjoy the good things that exist, and make use of the creation to the full as in youth. Let us take our fill of costly wine and perfumes, and let no flower of spring pass by us. Let us crown ourselves with rosebuds before they wither" (2:6–8). Yet this hedonism is by no means harmless. Beneath it lurks a profound violence. Not only is anything permitted in the pursuit of personal pleasure, but also those who seek holiness pose an actual affront: "Let us oppress the righteous poor man; let us not spare the widow nor regard the gray hairs of the aged. But let our might be our law of right, for what is weak proves itself to be useless" (2:10–11). The Wisdom of Solomon says of such denial of the existence of a provident God: "Thus they reasoned, but they were led astray, for their wickedness blinded them, and they did not know the secret purposes of God, nor hope for the wages of holiness" (2:21–22).

Nehemiah calls upon the Israelites not to allow such false reasoning to shape their actions. In fact, God's temple is destined for a fulfillment that will preserve those who serve God. A psalm captures Nehemiah's attitude during these days: "These things I remember, as I pour out my soul: how I went with the throng, and led them in procession to the house of God, with glad shouts and songs of thanksgiving, a multitude keeping festival. Why are you cast down, O my soul, and why are you disquieted within me? Hope in God" (Ps. 42:4–5). "As a hart longs for flowing streams, so longs my soul for thee, O God. My soul thirsts for God, for the living God. When shall I come and behold the face of God?" (42:1–2).

Corruption of the Sabbath: Love

The sabbath has also been corrupted: *In those days I saw in Judah men treading wine presses on the sabbath, and bringing in heaps of grain and loading them on asses; and also wine, grapes, figs, and all kinds of burdens, which they brought into Jerusalem on the sabbath day; and I warned them on the day when they sold food.* Throughout Judah and even in Jerusalem, the sabbath is turning into a market day, a day of work. The making of money and the convenience of commerce trump the worship of God.

This of course is no new problem. Moses had trouble persuading the people not to gather manna on the sabbath: "On the seventh day some of the people went out to gather, and they found none. And the LORD said to Moses, 'How long do you refuse to keep my commandments and my laws? See! The LORD has given you the sabbath, therefore on the sixth day he gives you bread for two days; remain every man of you in his place, let no man go out of his place on the seventh day'" (Exod. 16:27–29). It is not solely a problem among the returned exiles; part of the problem comes from Jerusalem containing people of other nationalities. *Men of Tyre also, who lived in the city, brought in fish and all kinds of wares and sold them on the sabbath to the people of Judah, and in Jerusalem.* Little wonder that it becomes a market day, since even those people who observe the sabbath are no doubt enticed by the prospect of the *fish and all kinds of wares.*

Again, however, the root of the problem turns out to be *the nobles of Judah,* with whom Nehemiah has so frequently locked horns. Nehemiah warns them that their transgressing of the sabbath—mirroring as it does the very behavior that brought down upon Israel the covenantal curse—will destroy all that the returned exiles have tried so hard to restore: *Then I remonstrated with the nobles of Judah and said to them, "What is this evil thing which you are doing, profaning the sabbath day? Did not your fathers act in this way, and did not our God bring all this evil on us and on the city? Yet you bring more wrath upon Israel by profaning the sabbath."* The Lord warned through the prophet Jeremiah, before the exile: "If you listen to me, says the LORD, and bring in no burden by the gates of this city on the sabbath day, but keep the sabbath day holy and do no work on it, then there shall enter by the gates of this city kings who sit on the throne of David . . . and this city shall be inhabited for ever" (Jer. 17:24–25). If the Israelites keep the sabbath, the temple will be a thriving center of worship for all the surrounding lands. But if the Israelites profane the sabbath, then God promises to "kindle a fire in its gates, and it shall devour the palaces of Jerusalem and shall not be quenched" (17:27).

Nehemiah institutes three practical remedies. First, he uses his control over the gates of Jerusalem to cut off the business traffic on the evening before the sabbath: *When it began to be dark at the gates of Jerusalem before the sabbath, I commanded that the doors should be shut and gave orders that they should not be opened until after the sabbath. And I set some of my servants over the gates, that no burden might be brought in on the sabbath day.* This shows once more how his concern to rebuild the walls and gates of Jerusalem has at its heart the goal of being able to obey God's law in Jerusalem.

Second, Nehemiah scares away those who attempt to continue business as usual directly outside the gates. *Then the merchants and sellers of all kinds of wares lodged outside Jerusalem once or twice. But I warned them and said to them, "Why do you lodge before the wall? If you do so again I will lay hands on you." From that time on they did not come on the sabbath.* How sad it is to place the quest for money above the quest for union with God! The book of Revelation depicts such tragic focus on money, exposed on the day of judgment as an effort to cling to what is passing away: "The merchants of these wares, who gained wealth from her [Babylon], will stand far off, in fear of her torment, weeping and mourning aloud, 'Alas, alas, for the great city that was clothed in fine linen, in purple and scarlet, bedecked with gold, with jewels, and with pearls! In one hour all this wealth has been laid waste'" (Rev. 18:15–17).

Third, Nehemiah calls upon the Levites to guard the gates for the sake of the Lord. *And I commanded the Levites that they should purify themselves and come and guard the gates, to keep the sabbath day holy.* The Levites take up again their sacred role as defenders of the worship of the Lord, after Moses (himself a Levite) comes down from Mount Sinai and finds the golden calf: "Moses stood in the gate of the camp, and said, 'Who is on the LORD's side? Come to me.' And all the sons of Levi gathered themselves together to him" (Exod. 32:26).

Nehemiah sees that the problem regarding the sabbath has to do with the people's love. Jesus puts it this way: "No one can serve two masters; for either he will hate the one and love the other, or he will be devoted to the one and despise the other. You cannot serve God and mammon" (Matt. 6:24). Do they love mammon above God? By encouraging faithful observance of the sabbath, Nehemiah seeks to ensure that the people are formed in such a way as to place God above mammon. In light of these efforts, Nehemiah prays once again: *Remember this also in my favor, O my God, and spare me according to the greatness of thy steadfast love.*

The Greatest of These Is Love

Nehemiah's final threefold effort toward the restoration of Israel as God's holy people and holy land is a work of love.

First, the corruption of the people means that they are no longer united, even by their language. The unity of Israel is not a mere nationalistic goal, but rather signals their love for God and their commitment to his ongoing covenantal purposes. Nehemiah tries to restore this commitment, rooted in love. "If I speak in the tongues of men and angels, but have not love, I am a noisy gong or a clanging cymbal" (1 Cor. 13:1).

Second, the corruption of the temple by siphoning off monies that should go to the temple suggests that the people do not understand why support for the temple is needed. The temple is not a mere institution, but rather makes possible the communication of God's loving gifts to the people. Nehemiah emphasizes that this divine love is valuable above all else. "If I give away all I have, and if I deliver my body to be burned, but have not love, I gain nothing" (13:3).

Third, the corruption of the sabbath by buying and selling on the sabbath indicates that the distinctive commitment to God that should mark Israel is being watered down and forgotten. The people's trust in God has become less than their commitment to commerce. Nehemiah reminds them that God is the source of every good for humans. "Love never ends" (13:8).

Put another way, faced with the corruption of the people, Nehemiah seeks to strengthen their faith in the Lord, which is being lost by speaking in the tongues of communities who worship other gods. Faced with the corruption of the temple, he seeks to strengthen their hope that the Lord, as the source from whom all gifts flow, will bless their sacrifices. And faced with the corruption of the sabbath, he seeks to strengthen their love for the Lord and the corresponding commitment to live for the Lord rather than for the rhythm of commerce. "Why do you sleep? Rise and pray that you may not enter into temptation" (Luke 22:46).

Nehemiah's Request

"So faith, hope, love abide, these three; but the greatest of these is love" (1 Cor. 13:13). But will Nehemiah endure, or will sin and death cut off him and his works forever from the living God? Nehemiah prays that God will remember his efforts for renewal: *Spare me according to the greatness of thy steadfast love.* As Nehemiah sums up his work: *Thus I cleansed them from everything foreign, and I established the duties of the priests and Levites, each in his work; and I provided for the wood offering, at appointed times, and for the first fruits. Remember me, O my God, for good.*

Thus the crises that Nehemiah faces upon his return to the land prompt him three times, as he writes about them, to pray: *Remember me.* His works and his very person, he knows, will utterly vanish without God's sustaining power. "What is man that thou art mindful of him, and the son of man that thou dost care for him?" (Ps. 8:4). Nehemiah knows, too, that "when the wicked dies, his hope perishes, and the expectation of the godless comes to nought" (Prov. 11:7).

In his thrice-repeated prayer, Nehemiah, the great rebuilder of Jerusalem, expresses his dependence upon God for the results of his labors and for his own future good. A later builder, Peter, becomes the "rock" on whom Christ Jesus "will build my church, and the powers of death shall not prevail against it" (Matt. 16:18). Peter denies Jesus three times. Just as Nehemiah's rebuilding efforts cannot escape the failures caused by human sin, so Peter, on whom the church is built, embodies these failures. The Lord requires that those who build love the Lord, rather than human praise. "When they had finished breakfast, Jesus said to Simon Peter, 'Simon, son of John, do you love me more than these?' He said to him, 'Yes, Lord; you know that I love you.' He said to him, 'Feed my lambs'" (John 21:15). Jesus twice repeats this pattern of question and answer. At the end of this exchange Peter says to Jesus: "'Lord, you know everything; you know that I love you.' Jesus said to him, 'Feed my sheep'" (21:17).

This is what Nehemiah has tried to do, as a faithful builder and shepherd over Israel. Surely Nehemiah may say, with St. Paul, that "by the grace of God I am what I am, and his grace toward me was not in vain. On the contrary, I worked harder than any of them, though it was not I, but the grace of God which is with me" (1 Cor. 15:10).

Will Nehemiah find that "in the day of Christ I may be proud that I did not run in vain or labor in vain" (Phil. 2:16)? Nehemiah's prayer recalls that of the good thief: "Jesus, remember me when you come in your kingdom" (Luke 23:42). Thus Nehemiah's work will be fully accomplished only in "the holy city Jerusalem coming down out of heaven from God, having the glory of God" (Rev. 21:10–11). "Then the King will say to those at his right hand, 'Come, O blessed of my Father, inherit the kingdom prepared for you from the foundation of the world'" (Matt. 25:34).

In this final separation, when the walls of Jerusalem have once and for all been built, love will judge us: "And another book was opened, which is the book of life. And the dead were judged by what was written in the books, by what they had done. . . . And if any one's name was not found written in the book of life, he was thrown into the lake of fire" (Rev. 20:12, 15). "Its [the new Jerusalem's] gates shall never be shut by day—and there shall be no night there; they shall bring into it the glory and the honor of the nations. But nothing unclean shall enter it, nor any one who practices abomination or falsehood" (21:25–27). With the great rebuilder of Jerusalem's walls, let all those who desire to dwell with God in holiness pray: *Remember me, O my God, for good.* "Amen. Come, Lord Jesus!" (22:20).

CONCLUSION TO THE
BOOK OF NEHEMIAH

Through his friend Simplicianus, Augustine learned the story of the Neoplatonic philosopher Marius Victorinus's conversion to Christianity. Augustine describes it this way: "Victorinus read holy scripture, and all the Christian books he investigated with special care. After examining them he said to Simplicianus, not openly but in the privacy of friendship, 'Did you know that I am already a Christian?' Simplicianus replied: 'I shall not believe that or count you among the Christians unless I see you in the Church of Christ.'" To this challenge, Victorinus "laughed and said: 'Then do walls make Christians?'" (1991, 136 §8.2.4).

Nehemiah reminds us that, as Victorinus eventually came to realize, the answer is yes: walls do make Christians. The visible church is built up from generation to generation. Just as Ezra the Scribe proclaims the Torah from within the rebuilt walls of Jerusalem, so centuries later Victorinus professes his faith in the public gathering of the church. Augustine describes this gathering: "As soon as they saw him, they suddenly murmured in exaltation and equally suddenly were silent in concentration to hear him. He proclaimed his unfeigned faith with ringing assurance. All of them wanted to clasp him to their hearts, and the hands with which they embraced him were their love and their joy" (1991, 137 §8.2.5). Israel is not invisible, and neither is the church. Without Nehemiah's work of rebuilding (holy land) and the continual striving to recall the people to Torah obedience (holy people), Christ's accomplishment of "the word of the LORD by the mouth of Jeremiah" (Ezra 1:1) could not have been made symbolically manifest. The visible work goes hand in hand with the invisible work. In the church as the "new Jerusalem," Christ is the cornerstone, Peter is the rock, and the citizens assist in the work of building, sustained by the Holy Spirit: "Work out your own salvation with fear and trembling; for God is at work in you, both to will and to work for his good pleasure" (Phil. 2:12–13).

Does this affirmation regarding the church's visibility, however, make for a triumphalist church? The book of Nehemiah shows us how far from triumphalism the visible Jerusalem is. Rather, an ecclesiology nourished in the book of Nehemiah continually returns to Christ's pasch, to the people of God's dependence upon divine mercy in Christ. After the rebuilding of Jerusalem, just as after Christ's resurrection, the people of God still strive for holiness, so often falling short. "And when they saw him they worshiped him; but some doubted" (Matt. 28:17). This imperfect worship reveals its consequences already at Corinth. St. Paul warns the Corinthians: "I do not commend you, because when you come together it is not for the better but for the worse. For, in the first place, when you assemble as a church, I hear that there are divisions among you; and I partly believe it, for there must be factions among you in order that those who are genuine among you may be recognized" (1 Cor. 11:17–19).

The recognition of the genuine occurs in the Eucharist. St. Paul continues: "When you meet together, it is not the Lord's supper that you eat. For in eating, each one goes ahead with his own meal, and one is hungry and another is drunk. What! Do you not have houses to eat and drink in? Or do you despise the church of God and humiliate those who have nothing? What shall I say to you? Shall I commend you in this? No, I will not" (11:20–22). In words that hearken back to Nehemiah's dismay at the people's corruption of the temple, Paul agonizes about the Corinthians' disregard for charity in the public worship of the church. Lacking charity toward each other, the Corinthians partake in the Eucharist to their own destruction. Paul says: "Whoever, therefore, eats the bread or drinks the cup of the Lord in an unworthy manner will be guilty of profaning the body and blood of the Lord. . . . For any one who eats and drinks without discerning the body eats and drinks judgment upon himself. That is why many of you are weak and ill, and some have died" (11:27, 29–30). The genuine members of the "body of Christ" (12:27) differ by their charity from the "weak and ill" and spiritually dead members. Paul urges all the Corinthians to "strive to excel in building up the church" (14:12).

But if the situation has hardly changed from Nehemiah's and Ezra's day, has Christ's pasch changed nothing and his Spirit been rendered powerless? Certainly not, because Paul also says: "We all, with unveiled face, beholding the glory of the Lord, are being changed into his likeness from one degree of glory to another; for this comes from the Lord who is the Spirit" (2 Cor. 3:18). Paul insists that the promised new creation has come about in Christ: "Therefore, if any one is in Christ, he is a new creation; the old has passed away, behold, the new has come" (5:17). Yet the point remains that we, whose weaknesses remain even "in Christ," cannot be counted upon to build the city of God, the new Jerusalem. The work is God's: "All this is from God, who through Christ reconciled us to himself and gave us the ministry of reconciliation" (5:18).

Paul can thus say of himself and the other apostles that "we are God's fellow workers" and of the Corinthians that "you are God's field, God's building" (1 Cor. 3:9). But are Ezra and Nehemiah "God's fellow workers," or did they lead the people astray, following the path that led eventually to the destructive messianic wars against Rome in the first and second centuries AD? Do they belong among the great fellow workers of salvation history, or does salvation history come to a halt in them? Paul cautions: "For many, of whom I have often told you and now tell you even with tears, live as enemies of the cross of Christ. Their end is destruction, their god is the belly, and they glory in their shame, with minds set on earthly things. But our commonwealth is in heaven, and from it we await a Savior, the Lord Jesus Christ" (Phil. 3:18–20). Did Ezra and Nehemiah fail by seeking a strictly earthly commonwealth? Did they fail to "press on toward the goal for the prize of the upward call of God in Christ Jesus" (3:14)? By no means!

Thus, with Ezra, Nehemiah, Paul, and all the saints, we may conclude in praise: "Now to him who is able to strengthen you according to my gospel and the preaching of Jesus Christ, according to the revelation of the mystery which was kept secret for long ages but is now disclosed and through the prophetic writings is made known to all nations, according to the command of the eternal God, to bring about the obedience of faith—to the only wise God be glory for evermore through Jesus Christ! Amen" (Rom. 16:25–27).

BIBLIOGRAPHY

Augustine. 1991. *Confessions*. Translated by Henry Chadwick. Oxford: Oxford University Press.

Balthasar, Hans Urs von. 1987. *Truth Is Symphonic: Aspects of Christian Pluralism*. Translated by Graham Harrison. San Francisco: Ignatius.

———. 1991. *The Glory of the Lord: A Theological Aesthetics*, vol. 6: *Theology: The Old Covenant*. Translated by Brian McNeil and Erasmo Leiva-Merikakis. Edited by John Riches. San Francisco: Ignatius.

Bede. *On Ezra and Nehemiah*. 2006. Translated by Scott DeGregorio. Translated Texts for Historians 47. Liverpool: Liverpool University Press.

Behr, John. 2007. "From Apostolic Church to Church Catholic, and Back Again." *Pro ecclesia* 16:14–17.

Blenkinsopp, Joseph. 1988. *Ezra-Nehemiah: A Commentary*. Old Testament Library. Philadelphia: Westminster.

Bryan, Steven M. 2002. *Jesus and Israel's Traditions of Judgement and Restoration*. Cambridge: Cambridge University Press.

Collins, John J. 2005. "Is a Postmodern Biblical Theology Possible?" Pp. 131–61 in Collins's *The Bible after Babel: Historical Criticism in a Postmodern Age*. Grand Rapids: Eerdmans.

Daley, Brian E. 2007. "The Acts and Christian Confessions: Finding the Start of a Doctrinal Tradition." *Pro ecclesia* 16:18–25.

Dauphinais, Michael, and Matthew Levering. 2005. *Holy People, Holy Land: A Theological Introduction to the Bible*. Grand Rapids: Brazos.

Davies, Gordon F. 1999. *Ezra and Nehemiah*. Berit Olam. Collegeville, MN: Liturgical Press.

Fensham, F. Charles. 1982. *The Books of Ezra and Nehemiah*. New International Commentary on the Old Testament. Grand Rapids: Eerdmans.

Friedman, Richard Elliot. 1987. *Who Wrote the Bible?* San Francisco: Harper.

Grabbe, Lester L. 1998. *Ezra-Nehemiah*. Old Testament Readings. London: Routledge.

Halivni, David Weiss. 1997. *Revelation Restored: Divine Writ and Critical Responses*. Boulder, CO: Westview.

Halpern, Baruch. 1990. "A Historiographic Commentary on Ezra 1–6: Achronological Narrative and Dual Chronology in Israelite Historiography." Pp. 81–142 in *The Hebrew Bible and Its Interpreters*. Edited by William H. Propp, Baruch Halpern, and David N. Freedman. Winona Lake, IN: Eisenbrauns.

Harink, Douglas. 2003. *Paul among the Postliberals: Pauline Theology beyond Christendom and Modernity*. Grand Rapids: Brazos.

Hays, Richard B. 1999. "Victory over Violence: The Significance of N. T. Wright's Jesus for New Testament Ethics." Pp. 142–58 in *Jesus and the Restoration of Israel: A Critical Assessment of N. T. Wright's Jesus and the Victory of God*. Edited by Carey C. Newman. Downers Grove, IL: InterVarsity.

Levering, Matthew. 2002. *Christ's Fulfillment of Torah and Temple: Salvation according to Thomas Aquinas*. Notre Dame: University of Notre Dame Press.

———. Forthcoming. *Participatory Biblical Exegesis: A Theology of Biblical Interpretation*. Notre Dame: University of Notre Dame Press.

McGonville, J. G. 1986. "Ezra-Nehemiah and the Fulfillment of Prophecy." *Vetus Testamentum* 36:205–24.

Perrier, Emmanuel. Forthcoming. "The Election of Israel Today: Supersessionism, Post-Supersessionism, and Fulfillment." *Nova et vetera*.

Reimer, James. 1999. "Theological Orthodoxy and Jewish Christianity." Pp. 430–48 in *The Wisdom of the Cross: Essays in Honor of John Howard Yoder*. Edited by Stanley Hauerwas et al. Grand Rapids: Eerdmans.

Rowe, C. Kavin, and Richard B. Hays. 2007. "What Is a Theological Commentary?" *Pro ecclesia* 16:26–32.

Schlabach, Gerald. 1999. "Deuteronomic or Constantinian: What Is the Most Basic Problem for Christian Social Ethics?" Pp. 449–71 in *The Wisdom of the Cross: Essays in Honor of John Howard Yoder*. Edited by Stanley Hauerwas et al. Grand Rapids: Eerdmans.

Throntveit, Mark A. 1992. *Ezra-Nehemiah*. Interpretation. Louisville: John Knox.

Vall, Gregory. Forthcoming. "'Man Is the Land': The Sacramentality of the Land of Israel." In *John Paul II and the Jewish People*. Edited by David G. Dalin and Matthew Levering. Lanham, MD: Rowman & Littlefield.

Vanhoye, Albert. 1986. *Old Testament Priests and the New Priest according to the New Testament*. Translated by J. Bernard Orchard. Petersham, MA: St. Bede.

Weaver, Alain Epp. 2001. "Constantianism, Zionism, Diaspora: Towards a Political Theology of Exile and Return." *Mennonite Central Committee Occasional Paper* 28:1–24.

Weinandy, Thomas G. 2005. "The Supremacy of Christ: Aquinas' *Commentary on Hebrews*." Pp. 223–44 in *Aquinas on Scripture: An Introduction to His Biblical Commentaries*. Edited by Thomas G. Weinandy, Daniel A. Keating, John P. Yocum. New York: Clark.

Witherington, Ben, III. 2006. *Matthew*. Macon, GA: Smith & Helwys.

Wyschogrod, Michael. 1983. *The Body of Faith: God in the People Israel*. New York: Harper & Row.

Yoder, John Howard. 1984. *The Priestly Kingdom: Social Ethics as Gospel*. Notre Dame: University of Notre Dame Press.

———. 2003. *The Jewish-Christian Schism Revisited*. Edited by Michael G. Cartwright and Peter Ochs. Grand Rapids: Eerdmans.

SUBJECT INDEX

SCRIPTURE INDEX

Revelation

Romans

Ruth